PARK'S
SUCCESS WITH HERBS

PARK'S SUCCESS
WITH
HERBS

by

Gertrude B. Foster

and

Rosemary F. Louden

with

Photographs by the authors and the
staff photographers of the Geo. W. Park
Seed Co.

GEO. W. PARK SEED CO., INC.
GREENWOOD, SOUTH CAROLINA

Contents

FOREWORD

In the more than one hundred years of our existence, The Geo. W. Park Seed Company's primary goal has always been to bring to you, the gardening public, our friends and customers, the best that the Plant Kingdom has to offer. Included is a large and ever-growing selection of herbs, garnered from all over the world.

As this selection has grown and improved, we have come to realize the importance of a definitive book on the subject—one that would not only describe the herbs and their uses, but also tell something of their fascinating history, and, perhaps more important, how to grow them most successfully. To this end, we approached two charming and knowledgeable herbarists, Gertrude B. Foster and her daughter, Rosemary F. Louden.

Both are recognized, both in America and abroad, as experts in the matter of herbs. Gertrude Foster has had over 40 years of experience growing herbs, cooking with them, and writing about them in numerous books and magazine articles. She has introduced many hard-to-find herb varieties to the American gardening public. Rosemary Louden is much in demand as a designer of herb gardens and lecturer on cooking with herbs. We visited with both of them in Connecticut and again in Greenwood and are convinced that no two authors could be better qualified to write our herb book. It certainly has been delightful to have been associated with them in this undertaking.

We hope that this book, which contains the largest collection of herb seedling photographs in full color ever published, will help you to attain Success with Herbs.

William J. Park, President
Geo. W. Park Seed Co., Inc.
Greenwood, South Carolina

INTRODUCTION

During forty years in which we have grown herbs, first for seed and then for photographing for the original quarterly herb magazine, we have wished we could present the plants in color. The opportunity came to us through William J. Park, president of the largest family-owned seed firm in the country. Their book *Success With Seeds* was the inspiration of our work in writing and photographing herb plants in color for this book. The need for pictures of herbs, in seedling stage and as mature plants has been brought home to us during 33 years of issuing our magazine. It is the successor to Laurel Hill Herb Farm which produced a list of 100 kinds of herb seed during World War II and until 1951. That was started because herb seeds which had been imported were no longer available.

Philip W. Foster and one author grew the plants. He printed by hand the packets for the seeds, the lists and growing instructions in a small booklet called *It Is Easy To Grow Herbs*. The magazine is still produced from our garden, put together by hand and uses black and white photographs taken by the printer, my husband. His post-college training in photography has been the basis of skills in lithography which make the magazine possible.

Co-author and daughter Rosemary F. Louden has herself been "grown" in the herb tradition. She imparts a special view of herbs available only to a person conceived and raised in a life and livelihood of herbs. Her photographs of dishes made from her recipes in the book and gardens she planned and planted, complement her sections on garden planning. I am grateful to her and to my husband who has always planted a large garden of herbs wherever we have lived. Our son, Christopher, while not a part of the family business, has proved the magic of herbs by marrying Jill, the daughter of Britain's foremost authority on herb gardening.

It has been exciting to visit George W. Park Seed Company where the splendid scientific staff gave us encouragement and cooperation. Dr. Jim Alston and his assistant Earlene Freeman provided data on seed germination not only of herbs on Park's list but also the odd ones we could supply. Al Scheider has shown great interest and patience in readying our unprofessional typing for the skilled typesetters. David Brownlee who is staff photographer of Geo. W. Park Seed Company provided seedling pictures of herbs and enlarged the color photographs we supplied where necessary. Those taken by Philip Foster were done as the plants developed in one season. They are as close to full size as possible. David Brownlee provided advice and cooperation as the book progressed. Viola Parrott enabled him to return to his studio on weekends to work with Al Scheider in pulling it all together. The devotion of many people who work together as individuals and a team for the superb organization is something we appreciate and admire.

Mr. Park gave the authors total freedom in choosing the subjects of the book and every other phase of it. He is truly dedicated to the integrity of seeds, the encouragement of growing flowers, herbs and pot-herbs, with the attention to meticulous details of service to gardeners that is awesome. We were priviledged to work on a Park's Success volume. It includes over 100 plants which are classed as herbs because of their fragrance, flavoring or medicinal capacities. We hope that the book will bring the pleasure of growing herbs to many more gardeners. It can become a fascination, a way of looking at historic plants to realize how dependent man is upon them. Women may have been the first herb growers by bringing healing herbs close to domiciles while men were off hunting. The Bible starts in a garden where, Gerard says, Adam was the first herbarist. The book contains only one wholly poisonous plant Castor Bean, for the purpose of showing that even herbs can be dangerous and benign, according to how they are used. It is important to know the plants before using herbs and best of all to grow them.

> Gertrude B. Foster
> Rosemary Foster Louden

Tussie-Mussie or nosegay of herbs

Historically, herbs have been used for various medicinal purposes, and the author discusses such uses. However, neither author nor Park Seed Co., as the publisher of this book makes any recommendation that herbs be used for medicinal purposes.

Herbs and Flowers in a Garden Setting

CHAPTER I

If You Have Herbs

There has never been a time when it was more helpful to grow herbs. Advances in technology and communication have brought plants and foods of the whole world to our attention. However, we face a critical need to conserve all that we have in the way of fuel and energy. Herbs are plants which give more, for the time and space devoted to them, than any other category of growing things. The Biblical injunction, (Genesis 1:29) "I have given you every herb bearing seed . . . to you it shall be for meat," has much deeper meaning than culinary terms. If you have herbs you will look at plants with new respect.

There are many more species of seasoning plants which can be grown in our gardens than the Anise, Coriander, and Mint mentioned in the Bible. Through rapid transportation and movement of peoples, the knowledge of what makes cuisines of different continents special has spread widely. Often it is the herb or spice which transforms a chicken dish into a French or even a Thai delicacy. In this book, we describe and give cultural information for over 100 herbs. Many are easy to grow from seed. Others are propagated by cuttings or divisions. Not all are edible but every one is interesting for its fragrance, history and various uses. We hope you will be led by it to the special enchantment that these dual-purpose plants exert over your taste and appreciation of form and beauty.

Herb or Spice

There is a fundamental difference between an herb and a spice, in the view of this gardener. Both groups of plants are used in cooking, perfume, medicine or commerce. To the person who wishes to grow them, climate has an important limitation. By our definition, *Herbs* are those plants whose roots, stems, leaves, flowers and fruits (seeds or seed pods) are used in some form *and* which grow in the temperate zone. *Spices* are plants whose parts are used similarly but grow in the tropics. Vanilla is an example. It is the 'bean' or seed pod of the Vanilla orchid. Even in the tropics, it has to be cultivated and hand-pollinated for control of the crop. If the jungle insect which visits the orchid flower is not present, there will be no vanilla beans. It is a vine to be grown in a warm greenhouse in the temperate zone so has been left out of the book because of its expensive special needs.

Protective Aromas

Some of the reasons for having herbs in the garden extend beyond the culinary or medicinal use made of them. Their scents actually help other plants. Insect damage is less where a crop is interplanted with herbs of varied fragrances. They confuse the egg-laying moths whose caterpillars hatch to lay waste cabbages and other members of the Brassicas. Summer Savory, Coriander and other annual herbs are protective of vegetables in which they are interplanted. After a number of years of growing in the same location, it is possible that certain aromatic plants will be discovered by garden insects. This is especially true if plants are not in the best of vigor. But most often they are protected by their own essential oils.

Herbs Among The Vegetables

If the only place that has well-drained soil and ample sun, is where your vegetable garden lies, let herbs beautify it. Some, such as Parsley or Bush Basil, make handsome edgings. Others to be sown successively between rows are Dill and Chervil. Summer Savory next to a row of bush beans is right at hand for picking to cook with them. Thinnings of these herbs are piquant in salads, there is no need to wait for maturity time as is required for vegetables. Basil is ready for pressing into a Pesto sauce for pasta before tomatoes are ripening. It seems hard for people to learn that herbs are best when fresh, they don't have to be dried before adding to soup, stew or salad. It would be a shame to let green beans dry on the vine before using them. In the same vein, do not pass up the tender foliage of Dill, which is at its fullest before the plants flower, just for seed heads to put with cucumbers to make Dill pickles. Often people forget to sow Dill seed but plant lots of cucumbers. Then they run around trying to find the herb for the pickle.

Herb Garden Planting

Herbs Growing in a Window Box

A Place For Herbs

There is another instance in the Bible where herbs have a special place. (I Kings 21:29) "Ahab spake unto Naboth saying 'Give me thy vineyard, that I may have it for a garden of herbs, *because it is near unto my house:* and I will give thee for it a better vineyard than it, or, if it seem good to thee, I will give thee the worth of it in money." Today, the worth of a garden of herbs can be counted in a great many ways. Having it near the house, especially the kitchen end, saves steps. Whenever the herb garden is visited, early morning or late afternoon, there is an appetizing ambience. Remember to gather a handful of mixed herbs or sprigs of Sage, Thyme and Wormwood. If you don't have any immediate use in mind, put a bouquet in a vase just to look at or sniff. You will discover that the pebbly surface of garden Sage leaves may act as a wick and allow some water to run off onto the window sill. One of the wonders of plants' own planning! Put some with vegetable scraps to go on the compost, too.

Herbs In The Kitchen

Herbs to use in the kitchen mean romance with your cooking. Their pleasant scents have been extolled by Shakespeare and other poets. The zesty odor of fresh Thyme is the same today as it was in the 9th century to Charlemagne, who ordered a great list of herbs to be planted in household gardens. It takes some of the drudgery out of meal preparation and clean up, to think of the continuity of life that is represented by Basil in a pot on the kitchen windowsill. A wreath of silvery Wormwoods, known as Artemisias, hung upon the kitchen cabinet, carries the mind back to the days when the Romans brought the herb to Great Britain. You can do more than think about herbs if their harvest is in jars, packets in the freezer and gleaming colored vinegars of French Tarragon, Basil, Salad Burnet and Chive flowers on a pantry shelf.

Give Them Proper Care

In the kitchen, people tend to put the herbs near, on or over the stove. That is wasteful of their precious flavors and colors. Even worse is setting herbs in glass jars in bright light. Store the ones used most often in a cool place such as a cabinet on a shelf away from the stove. Keep the main supply, from which you refill the pretty jars with names of herbs on them, in cold storage. Large growers of herbs for commercial use store the dried leaves under refrigeration. The gardener who has a new crop every year need not go to such extremes. It is well to check the supply as the new harvest comes in so that those jars lurking in the back of the cupboard are replenished with new dried herbs. The aroma will keep for more than a year, but the color diminishes. If leaves have been left whole, as Sage and Mint are often packed for use in tea, their contents can be added to potpourri (a mixture of dried herbs, flower petals and spices used for scenting sachets, pillows and room freshening).

Herbs In The Freezer

The packaged frozen vegetables, mixed to represent national gourmet dishes, are much more expensive than single boxes of each ingredient. If you look at the list of what is in them, you will see that you can buy peas, onions, carrots, to make French style vegetables. By adding your own Mint from the freezer, you have a famous dish. The motto, "Cook and Conserve With Herbs", with which we started an herb seed growing business in 1941, is worth considering 40 years later. The herbs, such as Parsley and Chives, in a dish may have more vitamins and minerals than any of the other ingredients. This is especially true with leftovers. Some children are growing up today with no knowledge of recreated dishes. They do learn a lot about over-salted frozen dinners in tiny portions on a tray.

By separating small squares of meat in unidentifiable gravy, peas and wet mashed potatoes, the packager tries to make them look as tasty as the color picture on the box. With herbs at hand, home-made TV dinners may be really delicious. Herbs freeze well, by themselves or with vegetables which they will flavor later. Then the cook can control the sodium content of the meal and can leave out the MSG. Portions may be normal size because you are not paying for the color printing and advertising.

Time And Money Savers

As many women come home to another job in the kitchen after work, it is time-saving to pick up ready-prepared food on the way. If they had time to take out a pocket calculator to figure up what it costs per pound for stale bread, mixed with dried onion or garlic salt or powder and unknown herbs; the stuffing heated up with water and butter, on top of the stove, would prove shocking. The same thing is true of the mealy mixtures supposed to stretch hamburger and other meats. The same high sodium content and rather stale-tasting onion and garlic ghosts are there in unappetising form at a high price. If the recipes for gourmet dishes in smart culinary magazines are analyzed, it is easy to see that much the same effect can be achieved by cooking ahead. Then, the casserole put in the oven for dinner may be ready as quickly as some dishes cooked by microwave. It can also be more attractive. Pasta, rice and potatoes are three important themes upon which to play variations with herbs. There is no trick to avoiding the complicated procedures of the French chef; cook this, set it aside; cook that, keep it warm and finally mingle all together to bake for an hour. (We lived with one once and it was his wife who washed up all those numerous pots and pans.) By planning ahead and *chain cooking,* as the late Rosetta Clarkson's husband called it, you can have your basic starchy ingredients prepared. They will be ready in the refrigerator for flavor and color from fresh vegetables and herbs when you need them the next night.

Spending days in the kitchen is not a gardener's favorite game, except at the high season of harvest of *pot-herbs* or vegetable crops which need freezing or canning. Fresh herbs may be put with peas (Mint), beans (Savory) or tomatoes (Basil) when you are doing any of these. Once you catch the herb enthusiasm, you will have something in preparation for the following day while cooking supper or lunch. Then it is not necessary to live on steak or hamburger to have time to yourself between meals. Put a vase of fresh herbs on the kitchen table to remind yourself of what Chervil, Chives and Sweet Marjoram (the Fines Herbes) do for a French omelette. Have small pliofilm bags of French Tarragon, Parsley and Dill leaves in the hydrator with your lettuce. They will keep as well as it does.

Special Diets

One of the best reasons for herbs in the kitchen is to supply flavor in place of salt in low-sodium or low-fat diets. Lemon juice is suggested as a replacement for salt, on fish, meat and in salads. Unfortunately, lemons have become expensive. There are lemon-flavored herbs which can be grown easily in the garden. Lemon Balm and Lemon Basil are started from seed and harvested all summer. Lemon Geranium and Lemon Verbena are good pot plants. Lemon Thyme is a hardy perennial, in the low ground cover type or more upright green or golden-edged leaf form. There are other lemon herbs for tea and citrus taste in food. Lemon Grass is of tropical origin but will grow in a container indoors. All these help the depression that seizes the cook who must face a set of limitations in a diet. Herbs make it possible to feed the family as usual with tasty foods without the addition of salt. There is a list of herbs which are low in sodium to aid those on a diet. Unfortunately, almost every canned soup and prepared meat is loaded with monosodium glutamate, which is an enhancer of natural sodium in foods as well as their flavors. It sometimes causes allergic reactions in some people (to get over the habit of salt and pepper shakers on the table, the judicious use of herbs in the kitchen renders them obsolete.) If you have an adventurous group to feed, small glasses with bunches of culinary herbs in water,

Frozen Herb Cubes

one kind to a glass or paper cup, may be set out on the table. Have small scissors handy for snipping fresh leaves over salad or soup, letting the guests choose their own seasonings. There are enterprising gardeners who have found a ready market for surplus fresh Chives, Dill, Chervil and Basils by offering them in bunches to chefs in nearby restaurants. In the 1940's, we mailed such herb bouquets to individuals who received them the next day. The packets of mail went by train from New Jersey to New York City. It wouldn't work today.

Herbs In The Freezer

Our experience with freezing herbs began during World War II, when we purchased our first deep freezer. We still have it and it's never been without herbs, green and fresh-tasting all winter. At the time we first tested herbs in below zero storage, it seemed sensible to blanche them, as we did vegetables, before packing. Some authors took the description of this culinary 'first' from *The Herb Grower Magazine* and made whole chapters of it in cookbooks. Now, we know that the natural oils in fresh herbs have a preservative effect. They do not need blanching to overcome the enzymes which break down the flavor of vegetables. Herbs hold their savor and color without this step, which makes it easier to handle sprigs with small leaves as they are packaged for the freezer.

How To Freeze Herbs

Some herbs such as Parsley or Chives may be chopped fine before placing them in plastic margarine containers of small size. Others are left on the stem to be put in packets of waxed paper, each to its own kind. Waxpaper sandwich bags may be filled, labeled and stapled together to make a handy file of herbs in the freezer. The greens slip out of them more easily than out of pliofilm bags. Waxed paper envelopes should be enclosed in a freezer container or larger film bag to protect the aroma of the contents. Put a list of different herbs enclosed, with them. They will be harder to recognize when frozen.

When steam blanching green beans or other vegetables, have small bunches of appropriate herbs at hand. Just lay a few sprigs on top of the produce before closing the container. Note on the outside, 'beans with Savory' or with 'Marjoram' or peas with 'Mint' before storing in the deep freeze.

Frozen Herb Cubes

After washing the leafy herb, there is no need to pat it dry before placing in the freezer packet. Chervil is especially good when frozen as it does not keep its delicate flavor with drying. The added moisture from a cool water bath does not harm the herbs. In fact, one of the neatest ways to freeze much-used species, such as Chives or Lovage, is by chopping them with water in the blender. Lay washed herb leaves, pulled off the stems, in a 2 cup measuring container. Fill it with water (about 1½ cups to a cup of leaves, loosely packed). Then pour contents into the blender. Whirl them for 2 minutes, or until it is a green puree. Empty an ice cube tray and fill with the herb liquid and leaves. Put in the freezing compartment of the refrigerator or in the

Herb Table Arrangement   *House and Herb Garden*

freezer until solid. Takes less than 24 hours of freezing. Remove cubes and place in a freezer container or stout plastic freezer bag. Label and date it before placing in the freezer. It is surprising how similar green ice cubes appear. While frozen, even the aroma does not tell the kind. Basil, Chervil, Chives, Cilantro (Coriander), Dill, Fennel, Lovage, Mints, French Sorrel, Lemon Balm, Sweet Cicely and other leafy herbs keep their out-of-the-garden taste when frozen this way. Here again, variations are invited. Fresh lemon-scented herbs can replace citrus fruits. Under each plant described there will be suggestions for preserving. A block of ice, from herbs frozen in water in a special mold, is an attractive punch bowl chiller. Sweet Woodruff, with white flowers of the plant and violet blossoms, makes a lovely ice block for May Wine. Borage blooms and Calendula petals with mixed fruits laid in the bottom of a ring mold and put in the freezer will turn out to be at the top of the icy circlet.

Drying Herbs

Drying herbs will be discussed under individual species as well as in general later on. There are many ways of dehydrating the pungent plants to package them for your own use and for gifts. Herb vinegars are the most fuss-free, attractive and mysteriously flavorful products of the sweet herbs. They are made from fresh leaves, flowers and seeds, each according to its kind, such as Tarragon vinegar, or in combination. Both harvests are gifts from the garden which have a personal association. Fortunes have been made with dried herbs, such as poultry seasoning and mixed herb salts.

There is something about the fragrance of plant foliage which stimulates the imagination. Over more than 32 years in which we have published a magazine on herb growing, the wide range of craft and gift ideas that have been shared with us by our readers is astonishing. Early herb gardening books used to speak of "grandmother's garden" with its spicy smelling herbs. Today, those of us who never remember grandmother (and do not long for the inconveniences of her day), are none-the-less excited about making things with herbs. We are not pressed to go shopping when an unexpected occasion for a gift arises. There is always something in the garden with which to make a 'tussie-mussie' or a baby blessing bouquet with flowers and herbs that have had their language and sentiments expressed in books, both old and new.

Conversation Pieces

If you have herbs you will have friends. You will need them, because many of these *official* species of various genera thrive so in the garden that you will want to share them. Whenever a small bouquet of scented Geraniums and herbs is worn as a boutonniere, it will attract comment. Hostesses on airplanes are particularly observant. One took time to sniff of a small plastic heart-shaped pin vase filled with French Lavender flowers and a sprig of Rosemary plucked from the window garden before a flight in winter. Watch the stream of visitors at a spring flower show. The roses, daffodils and violets forced out of season may elicit ooh's and ah's. But where the green spears of Chives, the ruffle of emerald Parsley or crisp look of French Sorrel are noticed in a dooryard scene, people will stop to exchange recipes. The sweet herbs, as opposed to strong-smelling spices, stir memories.

17

As people collect antiques, the ancient species of medicinal herbs and dye plants are now popular in gardens for old houses. They are antique plants with lovely flowers, such as Digitalis, Christmas Rose and Anthemis, which are modern in their uses, too. Nothing could be more appropriate than plants with a purpose growing around a newly finished solar home. Herbs are not dried in the sun, except for those whose seeds are used, but they manufacture their flavors and aromas from sunshine upon their leaves.

Pronunciation

If you are going to talk about herbs, and serious herb gardeners generally end up doing so, you have to decide how to pronounce the word. Will it be *'erb* or *herb?* It really doesn't matter because *either* or *eyther* is right. The dropped 'h' is older than the aspirated 'h' in the word herb. An explanation given to us by a British botanist, scholar and historian, is that, "In Middle English the word was spelled *'erbe';* in Latin it is *'herba'* with the 'h' mute until the 19th century. Whenever you see *'a'* herb rather than *'an'* herb, you know you are likely to be reading a British author. In the United States, today, the 'h' is not stressed as often as it is in England. New Englanders sometimes get around it by saying *'yarb'* while in California the heritage of the Spanish missionaries is heard in the word *'herba'.*

Pot-Herb Dates Back

Pot-herb brings us to the early garden writers in England. Thomas Hyll is one who wrote *The Gardeners Labyrinth,* 1577. His definition of a pot-herb would have been the same as that of the *Oxford English Dictionary,* which dates the term as in vogue in 1538. "A plant cultivated for food; especially an edible herb or root used for human consumption and commonly eaten, either cooked or raw, with meat and other articles of food."

The same authority expands this to "a herb grown for boiling in the pot, any of the herbs cultivated in the kitchen garden." The word vegetable did not come into use until 1767, states the O. E. D. In that volume, we find the word *herbaceous* (1646) 'of the nature of a herb, not forming wood.' This, to the botanist, means 'a plant which dies down to the ground in winter,' such as a *herbaceous perennial,* which grows again the next year. There are many culinary herbs which do not fit this picture - Rosemary, Sage and Thyme, to name a few. *Herbage* meaning herbs collectively, or pasture (1390) may have been the reason for the translation in modern Bibles of the word *herb* to *grass.* They are quite different things to anyone who knows herbs. "I have given you every *grass* growing seed" would be pretty poor sustenance for man.

A *herbist* is the same as a *herbalist,* who may be one of the early botanical writers (1592) or a man who deals in medicinal herbs (1594). In many of these words the 'h' is pronounced in the United States and England.

The Herbalists

The herbalists of the 16th and 17th centuries were men who described more than a thousand plants in one huge volume. John Gerard, whose great work *The Herball,* published in 1597, included the words 'it groweth in my garden', following many of the plants, had a large garden in High Holborn, London, England. The surgeons and apothecaries of his day were also the first botanists. It was their role to supply the medicines from the earth for the populace, or at least to provide sufficient knowledge of them for recognition and use. John Parkinson, another very readable author of the time, also wrote from a garden of herbs. Thomas Johnson, apothecary-botanist, took Gerard's *Herball* and amended and enlarged it after the author's death. It is known as the *Johnson edition,* 1633 and 1636. The story of how this happened is the subject of a book published by The Herb Grower Press, 1968. It is called *The Friends Of John Gerard* by Robert H. Jeffers, Fellow of the Linnean Society of London. The volume was printed in England and published in Falls Village, Connecticut. Copies are located in libraries of medical colleges and botanical gardens in the U. S., the United Kingdom and Sweden because of the new light it sheds on the production of both editions of Gerard's herbal.

In the 18th century, an interesting character named Nicholas Culpeper decided to take the writings, in Latin, of ancient physicians and put them into plain English. His herbal, *The English Physician,* 1652, has been reprinted through the centuries right up to present day. At the time he was considered a renegade in the ranks of healers. Professional men hated his scathing comments on their practices.

The Herball by John Gerard

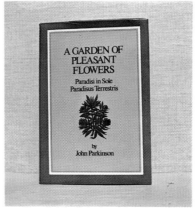

Paradisi In Sole by John Parkinson

Elizabeth Blackwell

The *herbals* are fascinating reading. They mark the dramatic change in the study of plants. Botany was born from them and medicine separated from them in the 19th century. There was only one woman, Elizabeth Blackwell, who produced such a book, in two volumes, called *A Curious Herbal*. It was illustrated by the author from live plants that she studied in the Chelsea Physic Garden. She made the copper plates for the first edition of 1737. Hundreds of exquisite etchings of herbs, were accompanied by text with their 'vertues' (as the medicinal action of herbs were called at the time). Her story is a tragic one but her great name has been repeated, perhaps without direct relationship, as the first woman doctor in the United States was also an Elizabeth Blackwell.

Herbals As Gardening Books

To hold an original folio volume herbal, with its leather binding, in one's hands is an awesome experience. They are found in rare book rooms of large libraries. We have the good fortune to own those of John Gerard and John Parkinson and are still hunting the second volume of Elizabeth Blackwell's. Reading the old type with its 'f's for 's'es is more exciting than doing crossword puzzles. The observations of the authors on plants they grew are more descriptive than the short-hand language of today's botanical works. It was our dream to make parts of the herbals in our library available to others. The Herb Grower Press reproduced fascicles of *The Herball,* 1597, by John Gerard, and *Theatrum Botanicum,* John Parkinson's herbal of 1640.

To do so, Philip W. Foster built a special camera to photograph the pages of the folio volumes, without taking the binding off the books. Then Dover Publications, Inc., whom he had helped with reprinting of Rosetta Clarkson's *Magic Gardens and Green Enchantment,* brought out the facsimile of the Johnson edition of Gerard's *Herball,* 1633. The 1975 Dover reprint is slightly smaller in size than the original. It is printed on fine paper with stout library binding to last a long time. The book weighs 9½ pounds and has 2706 illustrations. They also published a reprint of *Paradisi In Sole, Paradisus Terrestris,* 1629, by John Parkinson. It is retitled *A Garden Of Pleasant Flowers.* Parkinson made a pun upon his name in the original title. His book is considered the first book describing plants for the flower garden. When his herbal was produced 11 years later, Parkinson remarked that if he had been Thomas Johnson, he could have done it in a year. This referred to the controversy over Gerard's *Herball* as redone by Thomas Johnson.

The herbals are garden books today. They are becoming scarce in the out-of-print and rare book trade. There is something immensely reassuring to be able to say, of a particular plant that you never knew was used as medicine almost 400 years ago, that, like Gerard 'it groweth in my garden.' Through all the wars over the centuries, they have endured. Some of the plants in the herbals are now serving man as warnings of his dangerous doings on earth. The Tradescantias, or Spiderworts, which are native American wildflowers, are being planted in Japan near atomic power sites. They take up radiation in their systems and can be used as gauges to detect leakage into the surrounding area. The special way of studying plants, that we like to call 'the humanities of horticulture', is a never ending education to the herb gardener.

Chamomile Tea   *Rose Geranium Tea*

Harvesting Herbs   Leaf Herbs To Dry For Seasonings And Teas

Pick leaf herbs early in the day, but after the dew has dried on them. To wait till noon, when the sun has drawn out some of the essential oils, is to lose a bit of their essence. If possible, wash the plants where they are growing the night before harvesting. Then they will not have to be soaked to remove soil or dust. A hose or sprinkler can of water used carefully, not to splash earth, but to get up under the leaves will cleanse most any plant. There will be more detailed instructions for preserving particular species under the description of the plant. If it isn't feasible to process herbs without washing after cutting, do so with care not to bruise the leaves. They are as delicate as leaf lettuce or Basil plants. If creased, the essential oils will spill out and the bruised spots will darken. Pebbly gray-green Sage, narrow-leaved Thyme and Rosemary are not so fragile. But work quickly to drain the foliage so that it will lose surface moisture before being hung up to dry or spread out on screens. Patting droplets off the surface with paper towels is sufficient when dealing with a small quantity. If a half bushel of Peppermint, for instance, were to be dried for herb tea, this would be a tedious job.

The job should be done quickly as cut leaves will 'heat up' if piled on top of one another. We have found that constant harvest is better than one big effort to get the crop in. Summer Savory, for instance, is easily clipped off at 4 inches down the branching stems. Then it will branch out and give another crop and perhaps a third. The plants show their readiness for harvest when flower buds begin to form. If you can catch Basil then, it will need pinching out to produce more side shoots. Take the tips down to the first set of side shoots. Don't wait until flowers begin to open and the stems elongate. That gives less herbage to dry and more stems to sift out later.

For herbs with woody stems and strong flavor such as the Thymes, Sages and Rosemary and even Catnip or Lemon Balm, gather the clean, cut branches into small 'hands' (as the tobacco trade speaks of their plants when hung up to dry) to tie in bunches. If you have a place that is both airy and out of bright light, such as an attic with a ventilator, or pantry (also an obsolete term today) bunches that are not pressed together will dry well. In England, the directions say, "place them in an airing cupboard". We do not have such convenient, warm, dry closets winter and summer. There the hot water heater, without insulation around it, provides the right amount of heat for rapid drying without driving off the essential oils. Gentle heat is another term for it. Of course, the airing cupboard might have towels hanging from a rack in it as well as jugs of wine brewing on the floor. There is no translation for it in our country; we found when asked to edit the American side of a British "complete book of herbs."

Long before that, we had devised our own method of hanging small bunches of leafy herbs such as Mint, Oregano, and even Basil inside, but not touching the sides and bottom of brown paper shopping bags. It evolved from the days of placing stale bread in such a bag and having it ready for bread crumbs. The paper absorbs the moisture without taking up the precious oils of the herbs. The bread did not get moldy when it was not overstuffed in the bag. Both could be left for any length of time before final use. The bag keeps the light from robbing the leaves of color. We have seen various spurious reprints of this method over the years. One says to hang the wet herbs to 'drip dry' in a brown bag. Well, that would end up in a wet bag and moldy herbage. We

| Drying Herbs—Brown Bag Method | Drying Herbs on a Sweater Dryer |

did write 'drip dry' when speaking of hanging bunches that had been shaken of washing water and hung on a clothes line for an hour or so to drip dry before enclosing in the paper. Another suggests cutting the bottom out of the bag. This is said to be the way to keep the dust off. It simply nullifies the drying process that the paper bag effects.

Brown Bag Method

Take the stems of the leafy herbs that have been washed, and tie them together. Then place them inside the large brown bag. Pull the mouth of the bag around the stems and tie it. Leave a loop of string so that the bag may be hung from a hook or nail. The herbs should not be stuffed into the bag in such quantity as to touch the sides or bottom. In a week or two, depending on the amount of moisture in the leaves and stems, the bag should be opened to check on drying. If the leaves are crisp enough to crumble when touched, then the outside of the bag, with herbs in it, may be gently rolled between the palms of your hands. This will let the leaves fall to the bottom of the bag. Next take the bunch of stems out. Spread the leaves on a cookie sheet or metal tray. Pick off remaining leaves and spread them all out evenly on the sheet.

Finishing Off

They will need finishing off with gentle heat. An oven that is cooling down after baking works well for this. Instead of putting the whole bunch of herbs in the oven, the stripped leaves take up much less room. If there is an aroma of Peppermint, Lemon Balm or Sage that immediately greets the nose, after the herbage is placed inside, the oven is too hot. Leave the door open or remove the tray until it cools down. The ideal temperature is 100° F. (38° C.) As a wise Vermont native, who conducted garden interviews on radio, said to one author, "You mean if it smells good, it is bad!" That is true because the essential oils are very volatile. The accounts of drying herbs in minutes in a microwave oven, usually include the wonderful fragrance in the house. Though they keep beautifully green and become crisp rapidly, might it be there is less oil in the dried leaf or flower? A colleague of one author wrote the following description of drying in microwave oven for the United States Department of Agriculture's 1977 Yearbook - *Gardening For Fun* "Place sprigs on a paper towel and cover with a paper towel. Put in the (microwave) oven for one minute. Take out of oven and cool. If not completely dry put back into oven for a few seconds. When crumbly, store in jars."

Trimming and Turning

Herbs with leaves too small to strip off the stems, are trimmed across the top of the plant with a grass shears, before spreading on a screen. Hold the tray, box or pan under the plant and cut into it by tipping the shears toward it. The terminal tufts of leaves of Summer Savory, Thyme and Sweet Woodruff take a little longer than individual leaflets to dry when spread on muslin or screen frames. They require frequent turning, especially the first day or two. Those with woody stems, such as Thyme and Rosemary, may be hung in small bunches in the kitchen in the old-fashioned way. The "new" way of heating with wood stoves is helpful in drying herbs. On a damp day, in summer, when it is nice to have a fire in the stove, chances are you will be indoors anyway on such a day. Then you will remember to stir and turn the pungent leaves every few hours. Don't place a stew or soup under them as the steam will prevent dehydration. Where

21

summers are hot and humid, drying herbs can be difficult without some heat and possibly a fan to speed up the process. The paper bag method may not work under such conditions.

Packing and Storing

All herbs and flower petals that have been dried will absorb moisture if they are not bottled soon after they are ready to crumble when touched. They must be allowed to cool, after the final heating to crisp them, before placing them in air-tight jars or tins. Working with a small quantity at a time insures better results. A nylon sweater dryer stretched on its own frame is a neat device on which to lay rose petals or leaf herbs which have been stripped off the heads or stems. Chives may be cut with a scissors to spread on the nylon mesh. After use with onion-scented leaves, be sure to wash the netting. One variety of herbs dried at a time is a good rule. The dried herbage looks quite different from fresh leaves. Label the bags in which you have hung bunches. Put a note with the finished-off leaf herbs when they come from the oven. The question of whether to leave the dried leaves whole or to crumble them through a coarse wire strainer will be answered by their intended use. Tea herbs, such as Mint, Sage, Rosemary, Lemon Balm and Lemon Verbena are packed whole without scrunching the leaves.

Kitchen Drying

Those same herbs may be hung in small bunches as kitchen decoration. They may absorb moisture from cooking kettles, after partially dehydrating, but they look pretty and add herb ambience to the room. Many ingenious people have devised ways to use existing gentle heat to hasten drying a small wire tray of herbs. One spreads them thinly on a rack and places it over the back of the refrigerator motor. Another uses the warmth of the furnace when it is on for heating hot water in summer. Solar power is not ideal for drying herbs, unfortunately.

Car But Not Garage

A garage is not a good place in which to hang herbs for drying. If the door is left open they will become damp at night. If it is closed, some of the fumes from starting vehicles may reach and be absorbed by the foliage. An outdoor shed is not advisable, for the same reason of humidity on damp days. The more succulent a plant, such as Basil, which is rich in oils, the longer it takes to dry. One stunt reported to us by a lady in Alabama, consisted of putting the herb on paper towels on the shelf above the back seat of a car. The foliage was spread on two layers of towels and covered with another layer of single sheets. The owner left her car in a parking lot while at work. When she returned to it at the end of the day, the herbs were crispy and the car redolent of their oils.

Dehydrators with heating coils and fans are helpful but expensive. Unless there are fruits and vegetables to process all through the summer, the cost of one would be excessive just for home use of herbs. The green herb takes up so much room, at first spreading, that the narrow space between shelves of the drier would not allow much air circulation. The figure of one pound of dried herb to 6 to 8 pounds of fresh material shows how cramped a small electric drier would prove. It works well for finishing off the mostly dried herbage at the Berkshire Garden Center, in Stockbridge, Massachusetts. A small group of volunteers package herbs and herb products to sell. Their labor of love provides a good part of the budget of caring for the wonderful gardens, (which are open to the public free of charge all summer), in the Berkshires. The herb shop is run on the honor system, with an untended box in which to put payment for herb jellies, salt-free seasonings, mustards and mayonnaise sold there. Its location near Tanglewood, where the Boston Symphony is in residence in summer, may account for some of the sales.

Choosing The Time

The appropriate time to harvest herbs varies with each variety. It will be discussed along with the plant. A general rule for leaf herbs is just before they flower. That may not be possible because of being away, or necessary, if the planting is large. Certain strongly scented herbs such as Sage, Rosemary and Thyme will keep their flavor whenever they are cut. Sage produces its flowers in May of its second year. Its harvest may be deferred until after the inflorescence fades and is cut back. The new growth of summer is cut, without the flower stems, anytime before September. In the North, late cutting after frost may make the plants vulnerable to winter kill.

Seed Herbs

Herbs which are saved for their culinary seeds require different treatment. Each one has its special requirements. Anise is sweet tasting so that insects are attracted to its fruits. When seeds are removed from the seed heads, boiling water may be poured over them in a sieve, before spreading out *in the sun* to dry. It is a difficult plant for a beginner to grow. Seeds take up to four

Herb Bread

Herb Coffee Buns

months to ripen. They turn grayish when mature, rather than the tawny color associated with most seed herbs. Small stems remain attached to the ovate, slender ribbed fruits at the point of attachment to the umbellet. These can be sharp if the whole seed is used in food.

From New Jersey south, it is possible to mature Anise but it is a problem to harvest insect-free seeds. There are bugs, called tarnished beetles, or Lygus bugs, which visit the ripening heads of any of the Umbelliferae, or Parsley family, as the fruits mature. Their chewing may inject a hormone into the seed which makes the inner part cease to ripen. The effects are not visible to the naked eye but germination may be impaired. Aphids on the umbels of Angelica and Lovage are another problem. They may be washed off with a strong spray of cold water.

Drying In The Sun

Some seed herbs are easily collected and quite free of problems. Coriander is a fine example. The round, beige balls that are the seeds, can be hand-picked as soon as ripe. They will fall and self-sow if not taken as they turn color from green to light brown. When most of the fruits may be pulled away from the stems easily, coax them into a brown paper bag. The whole plant may be cut and placed in the bag, without expectations of a mass of minute insects crawling away from the seeds when they are spread out in the sun to finish off drying. Under each herb, a discussion of the harvest for different purposes will be taken up.

The main thing with the umbelliferae is to watch for aphids on the flowering stems and minute insects amid the seeds when they are cut. If the seeds are to be eaten, use a spray recommended for vegetable plants according to the directions on the package and timing recommended, if there is a bad infestation. A hand glass which magnifies plant parts, as for botanical indentification, is helpful in the harvest of seed herbs.

Dill heads with green seeds are put into a crock with cucumbers to make Dill pickles. For dried Dill seed the dry, flat, brown fruits are collected by hand as they mature. On each plant, there will be one prime center umbel and several smaller ones branching out but not as well-formed. Dill seeds shatter easily when the stems begin to dry, so care must be taken in cutting. Lay the heads on an old sheet or in an open, shallow cardboard box, weighted down so it won't blow away, but up off the ground. The sun will finish off the ripening. Even after four or five days airing in the sun and bringing in at night, seeds may need finishing off in a warm oven. It should not be over 200° F. to dry them thoroughly and kill any insect larvae. Another way to prevent bugs in the dry seed product is to cut the stalks and dip the heads in boiling water. Then hang them while still on the stalks, to dry in the sun. If insects float off in the water in the pan, pour them off. Some ripe seeds may go with them but most are likely to fall to the bottom. We do not advise cutting the whole plant of a seed herb and hanging it upside down in a brown bag. The tiny insects on the fruits may go right on eating the heart out of the fruits in the dark environment. Seed herbs take at least a week of drying to be ready for bottling. Do not put them in jars or tins while still warm. Seeds to be saved for planting should not be subject to heating or dipping in boiling water. They must be spread out in the sun and examined for aphids or crawling insects. Angelica and Lovage seeds attract the former more than most. When heads of seed herbs are collected for sowing, instead of cooking, they may be placed in a brown paper bag and dusted with rotenone insecticide. Cold storage after drying will help to preserve the viability of planting seeds.

23

Herb Garden on a Slope

Herb Garden with Lilies

Making The Herb Garden

The most important considerations in choosing a site for the herb garden are the amount of sun and the drainage of the land. The sunniest part of the yard, in the North, should be given over to it because a majority of the aromatic plants need full sun to develop the maximum of flavor-bearing essential oils. There are some fragrant and culinary herbs which will tolerate shade and others that need it for protection of their soft foliage. Therefore, the ideal herb garden might have a southern exposure with one end receiving the broken shade cast by tall trees at the rear of the garden proper. In the South, the perennials need more shade and may have to be replaced annually, while annuals may self-sow or be perennial in some cases.

Choosing The Site

A sloping terrain with sandy or gravelly soil which can be terraced into beds is more suited to the growing of pungent plants than flowers. Where the ground is level or not too well-drained, it is advantageous to make raised beds, with boundaries of steel or aluminum curved to fit the design, or weathered boards if the plots are square or rectangular. Herbs have such individual foliage patterns that they are most interesting and stay healthier if not crowded together or overshadowing each other. If the garden space is entirely exposed to the sun, some provision must be made for finding a place for shade-loving Angelica, Sweet Cicely, Chervil and Sweet Woodruff. They will endure some sun if the roots are kept cool with a mulch of compost through the hot weather. Rose bushes, fruiting shrubs or small trees make partial shade for these special plants. Otherwise a separate bed can be made for them on the north side of the house where shadows predominate.

It is more difficult to accomodate the sun-loving herbs in a sunless garden than to simulate shady areas in the open. If no spot in sun can be found for the half dozen or more indispensable seasoning plants, they might be grown in strawberry jars, pots or window boxes on a bright terrace or porch. But in planning the herb garden, we are not only considering the make-shifts, because happily, most gardeners have at least a small area which is well suited to making the herb garden.

The first year, there is not too much to do to prepare the soil for planting herbs. The beds should be spaded deeply and all the clods broken up by raking. *Do not dig in manure or fertilizer.* Few situations are too impoverished of fertility to support an herb garden. Any enrichment of ordinary loam will result in an excess of foliage with a loss of flavor in the leaves and seeds. In the following year, it may be necessary to divide and shift the hardy perennials with spreading or bulbous root-stocks. This will keep them from exhausting the soil in any one bed. Chives and Leeks, to be used for cooking, can be grown in the vegetable garden where they may benefit by occasional side-dressing of fertilizer. Try to keep manure out of the herb garden. It is likely to harbor a fungus which causes rust on the Mints. However, this is seldom seen in this country except in large commercial plantings of Mints grown for their oils. The small spots of brown that appear on plants of the Labiatae or Mint family in mid-summer are caused by striped beetles which scrape off the chlorophyll or leave holes in the leaves. These can be cut off after the insects have finished their cycle, and the plants will grow new fresh green tops.

Herb Garden in Snow   *Herb Garden in Planning Stages*

Design And Motif

Every garden needs definition. In choosing a design, it may be possible to make use of some existing wall or hedge to serve as a portion of the frame for the planting. Often an old foundation wall of a former outbuilding will prove just the suggestion for a sunken garden. The authors had the pleasure of replanting such a garden on an estate for many years. The owner had a beautiful pink brick manor house and a patterned herb garden in a brick-lined old foundation. The bricks were beautiful and had their own patina. What we did not know for a long time was that the whole thing filled up with water and ice every winter. It took much questioning to discover that was why no Lavender, Santolina or Golden or Sweet Marjoram survived in what seemed to be a most sheltered spot. Even the historic interest of the bricks having been made on the site in the 18th century could not overcome the folly of a lasting herb garden in such a spot!

It had a wonderful layout which was looked down upon from the level of the lawn, two feet above. If a sunken garden is not practical, at least place the garden where its design can be observed season by season from windows of the house or a higher level terrace. If no permanent perimeter of lasting beauty can be constructed before the garden is made, some of the shrubby perennials such as Hyssop and Germander can outline the design. Later it may be feasible to plant flowering shrubs, evergreens or climbing roses as a fitting enclosure for the perfumed air created by the plants. Low fences are better than high wooden walls; herbs need air circulation as well as sunlight.

The selection of the herb varieties will depend, in part, upon the role which they are to play in the household as well as in the garden scene. There may be a theme or motif for each bed. Certain beds might be set aside for seasonings for the kitchen, others for tea herbs, others for dye plants and so on. The collector of rose jars and potpourri recipes would reserve several plots for fragrant plants. Physicians and students of pharmacology often enjoy assembling the important drug plants in their herb gardens. Full consideration must be given to the individual requirements of each plant as well as the pattern to which it must conform. There is no more unattractive sight than an unhapply plant languishing in too much shade or one shriveled by unwelcome exposure to sun and wind. We found out in California that planters, window boxes and strawberry jars are popular for mini-herb gardens. They can be moved out of the sun in hottest, driest weather of summer and protected from the ever-present climbing snails that can consume a whole flower box in one night. Since snails are said to have been brought there by some foolish gourmand, they seem to have a special appetite for Sweet Basil and other culinary herbs.

Soil Buffers

Well-rotted compost and garden lime are the most likely needs for a new herb garden. Where the soil is heavy or too sandy the compost will provide humus. Where there are pine trees, blueberries or other acid requiring plants growing in the environs, lime should be mixed with the earth to the amount specified on the package. Bone meal, a slow-acting fertilizer has an alkaline reaction and can sweeten up soil to be used for Lavender and Rosemary. It should be added a month before planting out seedlings or new perennials and annuals. While seaweed fertilizers,

Seeds Sown in a Jiffy Flat   *Seedlings in a Jiffy Flat*

both liquid and as a meal are excellent for herbs and give less chance of burning than the commercial mixes of 5-10-5, we do not advise fish emulsion for foliar feeding. Any plant which has had fish emulsion from seedling stage to potting will attract skunks and raccoons as long as there is a trace of it in the root ball. They dig up the plant or turn out the pot hunting for fish dinners. Even a window box that has been watered with a solution of fish fertilizer will be fair game for climbing coons. They will turn out all the plants, time and again. The same is true of wooden tubs where the fishy smell remains.

Start Plants From Seed

The greater part of the plant material for the herb garden can be grown from seed sown in the spring. For reasons of economy, as well as for the experience of watching the plants unfold leaf by leaf from seedling stage, starting from seed wherever possible is most advisable. When the garden is under way, the first summer is time enough to purchase roots of clones (plants propagated vegetatively) such as French Tarragon or plants which never set seed such as Horseradish. These may be placed in a nursery bed for propagation the second year. By taking cuttings or making layerings, a few purchased plants may provide enough offshoots to border a bed with Germander or carpet a flagstone terrace with Thyme another year. It is well to make an alternate plan for the placement of herbs in the years to come. If the ultimate goal is a formal garden such as the knot garden of Elizabethan days, it will be necessary to purchase or propagate a number of perennials such as gray and green Santolina, Artemisias and Thymes to delineate the intricate patterns. While working toward this goal, a very satisfactory herb garden can be produced in one season from seed.

First There Was The Seed

Seeds have great fascination when you realize what is in each tiny grain or toothlike nubbin, such as a Safflower seed. Within lies the root and one or two seedling leaves, called cotyledons. No matter how you place them in the ground or on a sowing medium in a flat, the root will try to grow down. It sprouts first and has great strength to push out of the hard seed coat which has kept this miniature plant safe and viable.

Cotyledons As Clues

The cotyledons (seedling leaves) are different from the *first true leaves* of the plant. It has been our observation that each plant family has recognizable seedling leaves. The Mint Family, called *"Labiatae"*, show it most plainly. A Basil seed will put out two spade-shaped leaves. They could not be confused with the single leaf, or monocotyledon, of a plant of the Amaryllidaceae (formerly called Allium Family, in the case of all the Onion clan) which has but one single spear-like leaf. The Umbelliferae or Parsley or Carrot Family, which represents many of the culinary herbs and some poisonous wild herbs, is typified by two strap-shaped or linear leaves quite a bit taller than the first true leaf. Not so easy to see is the common connection in the very complicated Compositae with its daisy-like and button headed flowers. Seedlings of this Family are usually first roundish in cotyledon. When you begin with seeds of herbs, you have a handle on the mysteries of classification accorded to plants, both cultivated and wild, by botanists and taxonomists. The herbs are often the type plant in the various genera.

26

Jiffy 7's—Peat Pots　　　　　　　　　　　'Bio—Gro' Seed Starters

Convenience In Pellet Pots

So we tend to say that plants of the *umbelliferae,* with their carrot-like roots, are better sown where they are to remain in the garden. Fortunately, the great advance in convenience sowing of seeds makes that no longer a hard-and-fast rule. There are neat peat pots with fertilizer in them into which you can simply press one or two large seeds and let them grow. The pellet-like "One-steps" take up little room to store and require warmth, not too much moisture and light to grow a Dill seedling or Borage which you would not otherwise start indoors.

These pellet pots soak up water to expand to the size of a small pot. Expansion is faster if the water into which they are dropped is warm; in fact, the secret of total success with them is to keep them warm. Peat stays cold when wet. If the temperature in the room is not above 65° F. most seedlings will not germinate: There is little chance of their overheating as the small, smooth plastic pots will when in a sunny window. In preparation for seed sowing inside, note that the windowsill may be 10 or more degrees colder than the room because the glass transmits cold which drops to the wooden sill.

Large seeds grow fast when started in the compressed peat pots. However, with the fine dust-like particles of Sweet Marjoram which develop slowly, they may be too moist and too cold. Each herb will have its suggested culture along with it. The netting on the One-Steps sometimes fails to disintegrate in dry soil. Roots may be bound by it even though the Borage seedling is a foot tall. Now there is another model which is called "Bio-Gro", meaning that it has longer peat fibers but no nylon holding them together. They should be better for some plants. As with Jiffy-Pots, the peat composition of One-steps and Bio-Gro requires constant warmth and moisture even after planting directly into the garden. Peat has a way of taking the water it needs out of the soil with its wick-like action.

Types of Flats

Jiffy Seed Flats are very handy and economical of seed sowing medium. Plastic flats of similar depth and size have a way of buckling with handling which cracks the soil substitute and lets air in to the roots. They are reusable after washing in a pail in which some chlorine bleach has been added. Jiffy Flats are better put aside for giving plants dug from the garden, rather than sowing seed in them again. With seedlings in sphagnum moss or even the Cornell type seed substitute, frequent feeding is available from compounds such as Hyponex, Rapid-gro and others. But, for herbs, use ¼ the strength recommended by the packagers in every watering. Keeping the seedlings too wet is one of the greatest causes of failure.

Seeding Onto Sphagnum Moss

Years ago, we used milled sphagnum moss by itself in a flat for sowing fine seeds. The tiny grains of Sweet Marjoram, Thyme or Wormwood were lightly and evenly tapped out of a packet or folded paper trough onto the wetted material. A smooth block was used to press them down into the soft sphagnum which had been soaked with water and then drained. It has a sterile

Park's Indoor Hothouse   Park's Milled Sphagnum Moss

quality and helped to prevent damping off, a fungus condition in which new plantlets sometimes keel over at the point of contact with the soil in a seed flat. Filling with sphagnum alone avoided that problem. But the shredded or milled sphagnum dried out quickly. Even if covered with a pane of glass or plastic film, control of moisture was tricky. When the leaf sprouts appeared the cover had to be lifted or removed. Little seedlings need as much light as possible. That reduces the amount of humidity around them. The straight sphagnum soil substitute had no reservoir of water on which to draw, nor did the rootlets. The material becomes light tan when dry and darker when wetted but the difference is not easy to see at a glance.

A compromise is to fill the flat up to an inch from the rim with potting soil. Then top it off with a half inch of the shredded sphagnum. This gives a sterile layer around the stems. Sphagnum moss is considered an herb. It was used as dressing for wounds in World War I under battlefield conditions. The roots of the plants can reach through it to soil beneath to take nourishment from it. Potting soil, consisting of 1/3 sandy loam, 1/3 compost or vermiculite or peat and 1/3 sand (not salty sand from the road), is sufficiently rich for seedlings. They should not be started in material which is prepared with more nutriments than that in which the transplanted seedlings will ultimately grow.

A relative, who is a noted rock gardener, H. Lincoln Foster, devised a combination which enabled him to start millions of alpine and ericaceous plants from seed with great success. His collection, which covers the side of a mountain in our village, and attracts serious rock gardeners from all over the world, is increased by plants he has hybridized, which means growing from seed. He uses small flats, filled to within half inch of the top with potting soil over drainage material. Seeds are spaced as evenly as possible to avoid crowding. Then they are covered with a light layer of fine stone chips or grit, such as poultry suppliers offer for chicken and turkey farming. When germination is delayed, the moisture is held more evenly with this material on the top of the flat. It permits watering from above without washing out fine seed. The plantlets get support from it as they grow, especially where thinning is necessary. Some of his species do not sprout for a year or two. The flats are placed in open cold frames to freeze and thaw until dormancy is broken. Herbs cover so many plant families that various techniques are needed for aiding germination. Fortunately, a wide range of helpful materials is available from the people who supply seeds.

Heating Coils And Trays

Even moisture and warmth speed up germination of the tender annuals and perennials. Cooler temperatures spell success after the seedlings are up, in the case of Chervil, Parsley and Angelica. Under each plant species there will be more specific instructions. Materials such as vermiculite and perlite are helpful. The first is expanded mica. It holds a great deal of moisture but is best used mixed with other things such as peat moss, rather than alone. Perlite and peat are good in combination for rooting cuttings. The bottom heat which speeds up the process is easily provided by heating cables. There is a special tray that has a cord attached and heats by means of a conductor sheet of graphite. It is attractive and clean for seed flats or cutting containers. The directions for using it are in the catalog of the supplier.

Park's Sow 'n Grow Mix   *Vermiculite*

Greenhouse growers appreciate most the soil substitutes which give them light balanced material for sowing and potting up. To produce top-soil or even compost for a continuous nursery operation would mean mining the land and sterilizing tons of earth. The Cornell type mixes available now bring us better, less expensive plants which do not get set back on putting out in the garden. You can mix your own with equal parts of peat moss and vermiculite grade 2, measured dry. This is blended together with the addition of 1 level tablespoon of commercial fertilizer 5-10-5 and 1 tablespoon ground horticultural lime to four quarts *each* of peat and vermiculite. Place in a large plastic dishpan or bag. Pour in water and stir with a spoon or squeeze in bag until thoroughly moist. The material should be soaked but not so wet that water runs off when you squeeze a handful. Variations on this soil substitute medium are available under different trade names.

The risk to transplanted seedlings is much less in the ready mixed material. However, it should not be reused. The moist, peaty material attracts fungus gnats and can be a problem in greenhouse or window garden. Fungus gnats are as small as white flies but of darker color; in casual observation they look like fruit flies. But the flying insects are not the culprits, it is the larvae which work just under the surface of the potting material. They feed on root hairs and can be very damaging to seedlings. Home remedies for ridding the pot of the microscopic herbivores are few. One tablespoon household bleach to a quart of water, used as a drench, is the most effective. It is hard on seedlings. So the best defense is prevention.

Do Not Reuse Soil-Less Medium

Greenhouse growers do not have to worry about the soil-less mixes because they are moving their plants into other hands at point of sale. The material is pleasant to work with and has a neutral pH which suits many genera of plants. Feeding is done at the same time as watering to keep growth from being stopped. The minor drawback of fungus gnats is balanced by the helpful qualities of the mix. It eliminates the need for fungicide in the flat when sowing seed. Benomyl, often suggested for addition to the water in which seedling flats are soaked or sprinkled to wet them, is not something we like to use on culinary herbs. It remains in the tissues of the plants to continue its work. That is not the kind of additive wanted when a plant is edible. It may be helpful for the ornamental and scented herbs which tend to go black suddenly in a wet, muggy period in summer. Hyssop is one which may develop fungus stem-rot disease. This can be seen when an old plant remains in the same spot in the garden. A few branches will die back. To control it, the plant has to be removed at first sign of the disease and a plant of a different family, such as *Compositae* for a *Labiatae*, substituted.

On the whole, the problems of herb growing are few compared to the care needed for hybrid tea roses or many other fancy flowers. They are the official species which means 'of the shops' or herb species, formerly gathered from the wild to be sold as seasonings or medicine. If their native lands are considered with such varied climates and soil, the wonder is that most take to any condition in gardens anywhere in the country. That means they have the same needs as our common vegetables, with which they have natural affinity in the culinary species.

Vegetable and Herb Garden

Raised Bed Herb Garden

A Little Kitchen Garden

Sometimes it is not advisable to plant perennial herbs, such as Sage, Lovage and Thyme, among the vegetables because they will be in the way of spading up the patch another year, or rototilling or cultivating. One way to solve the problem of having herbs near enough to pick along with vegetables, or to waft their pungency over the pot-herbs (vegetables) in a protective way, is to put them in a raised bed at one end of the garden.

In such a planting, designed for weekend gardeners who need to fence in the area with snow fence and electric fence wire to keep woodchucks and rabbits out, the slightly elevated herbs provide beauty. A framework of cement blocks holds the raised beds in place. They are set so that soil and plants' roots may fill them. Wooden strips edge the paths which are covered with limestone chipping. This helps to overcome a naturally acid soil. If the earth is more limy, peastone would fill the paths instead.

The garden-within-a-garden is designed for utilitarian purposes and consists mainly of culinary herbs except for the Chamomile which is used to make a tea or hair rinse for blond hair. The garden has a two-year plan. The first year such things as Parsley may be picked, dried or frozen. The second year the perennial Chamomile will fill in where the Parsley has been pulled as it runs to seed. All pushy types are left out, such as Mint or Lemon Balm. While the first is useful it would do better elsewhere in partial shade. The second has a tendency to self-sow which would fill a small bed with pretty lemony scented plants but if they were not weeded out or transplanted, they quickly form a dense mat of roots.

The entire garden measures 9 x 15 feet with 18 inch paths making a cross in the rectangle. It will take over 150 plants, representing 25 species, most of which may be started from seed. The soil should be sandy loam and the location in full sun. Conditions that satisfy vegetable planting will produce handsome herbs the first season.

Plants for the first season:	2 Sage	1 French Sorrel
25 Perennial Chamomile	2 French Tarragon	1 Lovage
25 Parsley	2 Rosemary	2 Peppermint Geranium
4 Chives	2 Oregano	8 Sesame
2 Garlic Chives	6 Bush Basil	2 Lemon Geranium
5 Borage	6 Sweet Basil	2 Copper Fennel
4 Salad Burnet	4 Winter Savory	Seed of Dill, Angelica,
6 Sweet Marjoram	2 Rocambole	Perilla, Caraway
25 Shallot bulbs	20 Purple Basil (Dark Opal)	and Chervil
30 Thymes - ½ upright Thyme; ½ Caraway Thyme	and/or Perilla	

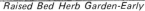

Raised Bed Herb Garden-Early   *Raised Bed Garden-Fully Grown*

The snow fence at the end of the whole vegetable garden will give a bit of shade to the back part of the herb planting, making it easier to set out seedlings. If water is available, plants can be washed where they grow, the evening before harvest. Basils and Sweet Marjoram should be watered *when* the sun is on them, so they dry off before cool of night.

Two-Year Plan

The long paths are edged with boards set flush with the level of the soil. Just inside them, Parsley and perennial Chamomile seedlings are placed alternately so that one can supplant the other the second year. As the Parsley runs to seed, it may be pulled to allow the pretty Chamomile plants to spread out. The latter may be clipped when the daisy-like blossoms appear if they are not going to be dried for tisane or cosmetic use. Behind the Parsley, rows of Shallots are planted giving nice contrast with the curly greens. Shallots die down in the autumn. The brown, garlic-like clusters are dug for winter use. A portion of each multiple clove may be reset in the same or a new place if the hole is dug deeper and a teaspoon of bone meal is placed under it. Let some of the soil fall back before planting the Shallot. It will not need to be buried, just slightly cover; the bulb is hardy and will over-winter for early spring greens to use like Chives.

The short paths, making a cross of the garden, may be edged with Sweet Marjoram, with accents of silver Thyme in the indented corners. Marjoram is treated as an annual in the North. So Salad Burnet seedlings are placed behind it to fill in the second year when the Sweet Marjoram has been pulled. Where two steps lead up to the raised bed at the long end of the center path, 2 clumps of Chives are placed at either side with one each of Garlic-Chives behind them. The lavender pompom flowers of Chives in bloom, will give color in May. The leaves should be cut carefully around the outside of the plant, instead of being bobbed off leaving stubble. Garlic-Chives benefit by the same trimming and will produce fragrant white star-shaped heads of flowers in August. Both herbs are used after flowering in making vinegars.

Purple Basil, variety Dark Opal, and Perilla with mahogany leaves, are attractive if alternated at either end of the long beds, three plants of each. They may be used as dot plants in any arrangement of contrasting foliage. Closer to the path, the aromatic Rosemary, Lemon Geranium, and Peppermint Geranium are set out in the middle of both beds, which have Bush and Sweet Basil alternating just inside the Parsley border. The latter may be trimmed often to the 12 inch height of the Bush Basil, for use in cooking and for a neat effect.

When the Rosemary, which is not hardy north of Zone 7, is removed the second year and the Pelargoniums (Peppermint and Lemon Geranium) are lifted to bring in for the winter, Sage and Oregano will fill in the spaces. They will give a complete look to the front beds in the spring. The rear beds containing Oregano, Rocambole (French Garlic) and French Tarragon, in the middle of one and seeded Coriander and Caraway in the middle of the other, may also have Borage (an annual) and Sesame towards the back. Copper Fennel, Lovage and Angelica will provide a tall background close to the fence. Summer Savory should be seeded between bush beans in the vegetable rows. Winter Savory, a hardy perennial, may replace the Purple Basil, the second summer.

31

The Foster Herb Garden

Foster's Garden Spirit House

Plants For Next Year

Sweet and Bush Basil may be replaced with Summer Savory next season. For best results it is well to sow different herbs in different parts of an established framework of an herb garden just as you rotate vegetable crops. Thus the Basils can replace the Chervil or Caraway seeded in the first year behind the Chamomile edging along the paths. Parsley can take the place of the Sweet Marjoram. Compost, mixed with a small amount of lime if the soil is on the acid side, should be used as a top dressing for the perennial plants in the fall. Dill may self-sow if planted at the end close to the snow fence.

This garden, based on the plan and plants described, had an 18th century sundial in the middle of the crossed path. It could have any sort of ornament or none at all. It was not a place for strolling with friends; the paths were too narrow. But it kept its delightful verdure all summer, even as harvesting went on from month to month. The second year, the creeping Caraway Thyme covered the rough cement blocks. The Angelica bloomed with stately head of round umbels. It and the Lovage stood over 5 feet tall. Copper Fennel was cut back so the flowers would not cross pollinate with Dill. That was allowed to seed for pickling cucumbers and for volunteers the second year. Even without the silvery Artemisias and Lamb's Ears, a purely culinary garden can be a charming planting. Another season White and Silver Horehound could be set in for their foliage color and flavoring for homemade cough drops.

CHAPTER II
THE
HERBS

Allium pulchellum

Allium Christophii

FLOWERING ALLIUMS   PERENNIAL
Allium Species   Zone 4
Amaryllidaceae, native to Asia and Europe

HABIT: *Allium pulchellum* is a bright spot of color in the garden in late summer. Seeds may be planted where they are to grow outdoors, in autumn, for a quick start in the spring. Plants take up little space for the showy effect of the bearded, rosy purple flowers on blue-green 18 inch tall stems. They sway gracefully atop the slim tubular stems, making one of the showiest flowering Alliums.

CULTURE: Start seed in a flat. Space them evenly, half an inch apart, so that the whole mass may be set out without breaking up the rooting material. They are easily transplanted when up to 6 inches tall. Plants do not die down after flowering. The twin species *Allium flavum* blooms a few weeks earlier, in July, with yellow pendant florets of a smaller size. It has the same attractive bract at the top of the flower stalk. Both purple and yellow types self-sow around the garden. Excess plants are easily pulled as the bulb at the base is smaller than most Alliums and single. *Pulchellum* means pretty. Both plants are attractive in bloom and almost evergreen in nature.

USE: The onion odor in both plants dissipates when stems are cut for fresh or dried bouquets. The florets will dry on the stems upright in a basket or other container which keeps them straight. The gardener is not likely to have too many clumps as friends are always asking for a start. Ours came from Helen M. Fox, author of three books on herb gardening. She collected many species of ornamental Alliums which she grew from seed. These two do not form thick clumps or need dividing.

HABIT: *Allium Christophii* is one of the startlingly beautiful flowering onions which can be started from seed. The quick germination of Allium seed is a cheering sight to any herb gardener. Though the bulbous plants take 2 to 3 years to come into flower, their economy of seed is worthwhile. The single bulb, planted in the fall, will bloom the following May. It then is possible, if the flower stalk is left on the plant to dry, that it will shed some seeds to show up the next year. *Allium Christophii* produces a head of purplish, star-shaped flowers with a metallic sheen. The inflorescence is 12 inches across on a hollow stalk that may be up to two feet tall. It flourishes in full sun and loose, rich soil.

CULTURE: Sow seed in a flat or furrow in the garden and mark with a permanent label. Germination will occur in two to three weeks. Since the plant is a monocotyledon, that is, it has one seedling leaf, it will not grow two leaves the first year. The young plants tend to die down in late summer and would be forgotten if not in a spot that is well marked. As with most bulbs,

Aloe barbadensis

Aloe barbadensis

multiple leaves are a sign that flowering is near but sometimes this does not occur for three years. *Allium Christophii* has a single bulb which goes even deeper into the soil—it is possible to transplant when young but difficult to lift after years of blooming. The leaves stay flat against the ground when the flower scape develops. They are 6 to 10 inches long by a half to an inch wide with reddish hairs along the edges. Soon after flowering, leaves disappear but the wonderful head of maturing seeds remains intact. It is a lovely round ball of spokes with knobby seed pods on the ends. The whole thing turns a tawny beige. It will stand on the drying hollow stem for weeks, attracting comment, then suddenly the weight of the ripening seeds may cause it to break off. Even then it may be saved.

USE: The seed head is durable. It can be attached to a wire stem or other stiff-stemmed plant stalk for using in dried arrangements. It has no onion scent in its dried state and very little when fresh. It would be a pity to cut the dazzling inflorescence when fresh because the plant needs to mature its leaves and fruits to survive. Seeds may be removed from the dried capsules, without spoiling their shape, and planted for spring germination outdoors. They are black when ripe. If the head blows off the dried stem, seedlings may appear at some distance from the original bulb. As with any onion plant, *Allium Christophii* flourishes in full sun and rich soil.

ALOE, MEDICINAL   TENDER POT PLANT
Aloe, barbadensis, formerly *Aloe vera*
Liliaceae, native to Mediterranean region

HABIT: Where the "First Aid Plant," *Aloe barbadensis,* may be planted in the ground in frost-free areas, it develops spikes of yellow flowers seldom seen on potted specimens. It is used for landscaping in dry, semi-tropical areas and its long-lasting, bell-shaped blooms are attractive to humming-birds. Under such conditions the herb seems to be impervious to full sun. When in a container, after wintering indoors, the plant will turn brownish when first exposed to sunlight.

CULTURE: Aloes may be started from seed collected from plants growing in warm places such as Florida or California. Propagation is easier by young shoots which come up around the original fan of leaves. The herbal Aloe is quite different from the spiny, rather stiff-toothed species. It was brought to the West Indies by early traders from islands in the eastern Mediterranean. Now it is grown as an economic crop in the southwestern part of this country. The healing gel, just under the cuticle of the leaves, is in great demand for burn remedies, radiation damage treatment, shampoo, sunburn relief and cosmetics. Aloe has been known for centuries to be easy to grow if allowed to go almost dry in winter, but may take plenty of water in warm weather. *Aloe vera,* the former name, was described in the *Herbal Of Dioscorides,* written in the first century A. D. As pot plants, Aloes survive benign neglect and need very little feeding. Watering must be gauged so that the roots, which are very small for the size of the plant, are not

Ambrosia/Chenopodium Botrys   *Ambrosia Wreath*

allowed to remain soggy. Small 'pups' or offshoots, are the source of new plants. If they are not removed from the 'mother plant', they will push the old stock almost out of the pot. So there is always something to share if you have a good Aloe plant.

USE: One could write a book about the uses of *Aloe barbadensis.* They are so numerous that a fine monograph on its history and medicinal applications has been published. It has the simple title, *Aloe Vera,* and contains 18 pages of medical and historical references as well as growing instructions. Unfortunately, the reputation of Aloe's gentle gel, which dries without stickiness, as a topical herb, has been extended to other species. This is too bad—applying some of the hard-leaved, prickly Aloes to burns or cuts would result in pain with little positive effect. This is not the 'bitter aloes' of the Bible. The inner part of the leaf is used fresh. Its gel has been stabilized to make ointments, shampoo, and burn relief. To have a plant of the 'First Aid Herb', as *Aloe barbadensis* has been called, on the kitchen windowsill is pretty nearly standard practice with herb gardeners. It serves the cook for small emergencies at the stove and the gardener for relief of poison ivy rash's itching. A broken leaf heals over after a tip has been cut off. The gel may drip onto paint in the meantime causing a yellow stain. It is also a dye plant.

AMBROSIA   HARDY ANNUAL
Chenopodium Botrys
Chenopodiaceae, native to Europe, Asia and Africa

HABIT: The name of the genus means *goosefoot.* The species name describes the clusters of greenish flowers as *grape-like* in formation. A popular name, 'Oak-leaf Geranium', comes from the shape of the true leaves when young. They are reddish underneath with wavy margins resembling those of an oak leaf. Ambrosia develops feathery plumes of flowering stems up to 2 feet tall. The whole plant has a strong scent which comes from the glandular hairs. Where it touches the skin, it leaves a warm perfume, both sweet and spicy.

CULTURE: Seeds need light to germinate, taking 20 to 25 days, even in a special flat of sterile soil substitute. Once established in the garden, the hardy annual self-sows readily. Seeds will not sprout until the ground is warm. Plantlets may be thinned to stand 10 inches apart. Even seed planted directly in the garden does not need covering. Simply ready a spot by raking the soil to a fine tilth, then broadcast (scatter) the dust-like seed upon it. Transplanting is not helpful as the root is thin and unbranching. In poor soil, or where crowded volunteers from previous years seed have come up thickly, Ambrosia may run to seed at half its normal height. The absence of petals on the blossoms does not interfere with seed formation. The herb is wind pollinated. Once Ambrosia flowers in a garden, seed will last over the years to sprout whenever it is turned up to the light by cultivation. Frost does not affect those which have not gone from green to beige as seed matures on the plants.

Angelica Archangelica Leaves   Angelica Archangelica Flower

USE: Ambrosia is harvested for its flowering stems that become arching with the weight of many florets. A few of the feathery stalks, placed in a flower arrangement of annuals, such as zinnias and asters, will keep the water sweeter. If green dried material is desired for Ambrosia wreaths, cut the whole plant before if changes color. Wreaths of Ambrosia are formed by bending the trusses of flowering tops and lacing them into a circle. Paper ribbon or green thread will hold the curves. Putting a wreath in a large brown paper grocery bag will retain the desired circular position of the stalks while drying.

Seeds of Ambrosia ripen over a long period. They may fall out while the wreath is drying. The storage helps to eliminate fall-out of the seeds when wreath is hung. Seeds collect in the bottom of the bag. They may be scattered where plants are desired for another year. Decorating the sweet Ambrosia wreath can be done at any time if it has been held in shape in the meanwhile. Bits of dried flowers such as Golden Baby Helichrysum, Statice florets, Lavender sprigs, pink Chive flowers that have been dried may be tucked into the wreath between the grape-like bunches of the green blooms.

Angelica Archangelica	**BIENNIAL**
Umbelliferae, native to Lapland, Northern Europe	Zone 3

HABIT: Angelica makes a low basal clump of broadly segmented leaves which come directly from the root on hollow stems. Garden Angelica has broad leaflets with a hint of gold along their incised edges. Flowering is delayed until the second, or sometimes the third, year. A central round stalk will shoot up to six feet in height when the plant is ready to bloom. Atop the main stem will form one main round umbel of whitish blossoms opening out of a fat bud which looks like a rolled-up pair of socks. The flower stalk has few leaves or side shoots except right at the top where there are small satellite umbels. In New England, native *Angelica atropurpurea* grows in watery ditches in full sun in limestone valleys. The stems are reddish rather than mainly green as in the cultivated herb and the leaflets are narrower.

CULTURE: Angelica has to be grown from seed. It is best suited to moist, limy soil. Sow seed thickly in a small pot on sterile soil substitute. Keep the moistened pot in a plastic bag in the refrigerator for 6 to 8 weeks. After this cold treatment, the seeded pot is brought into the light and 60° F. temperature. Germination may take up to a month. Discard seed which molds without sprouting. Sowing seed outside in moist soil with plenty of humus in late summer, right after it ripens, is most satisfactory where the ground freezes. The best plants come from seed that has fallen from a flowering plant. If seeds are fully ripened, there may be seedlings that volunteer that same year. Others will come up the next spring, if moist conditions have kept them viable. Angelica may be grown in a deep, large pot or wooden planter in which it will flower at 2 to 3 feet the second year. It is a hardy herb except where conditions are hot and dry. Even there it may be

Angelica in a Pot

Angelica Syrup on Ice Cream

grown on the north side of a wall or building or along the edge of a stream. Seedlings may be potted up or set out 3 feet apart when they have 4 true leaves. The plant has a deep tap root which makes it hard to move when more than four inches tall. Flowering is sometimes delayed by cutting off the main blossom stalk before it forms a bud. But this is defeating if you want more plants another year. Angelica dies after flowering. The seed heads should be watched for aphids which are attracted to the sweet scent of the whole plant. Spraying with a non-persistent insecticide, allowed for vegetables, is acceptable to insure viable seeds. The seeds have no culinary value.

USE: The first summer, small side stems and leaves may be picked for flavoring. They are tender and have the aroma of Juniper berries. The whole herb suggests the liqueurs and gin to which Juniper and Angelica have given subtlety for centuries. The digestive and healthful qualities of Angelica are famous. In Lapland, where it is native, the nomadic people use the leaves of Angelica to wrap fish which is being carried on long treks. It is a preservative. In cooking rhubarb, if Angelica is added to the cut up fruit, less sugar will be needed. As with rhubarb, Angelica stems may be cut up and put in freezer containers for storage in deep freeze for later use. No blanching is needed. However, rhubarb should be covered with water, brought to a boil and the water poured off before adding sugar or using in baking, to avoid oxalates. The Angelica is added during this blanching period and then removed. The rhubarb is almost cooked by this method.

Angelica In Syrup

A delightful cordial syrup of Angelica with the stems in it can be made to keep for a year or more on the shelf or in the refrigerator. It is more useful and less laborious than candying the stems. The pieces of Angelica stored in syrup may be drained to place on baked coffee breads or further crystallized by rolling in sugar for decorating iced cakes. The syrup is an exotic topping for ice cream or sherbet. It also spices punch or lemonade.

To make Syrup—cut young stalks of Angelica in four inch lengths. Wash, peel off the thin outer skin by scraping with a knife. Soak overnight in cold water to which 1 tablespoon salt and 1 tablespoon white vinegar have been added. Drain, cover with water and parboil until stems become somewhat translucent. Make a syrup of 1 cup water to 2 cups granulated sugar. Bring to a boil and add a few drops of green vegetable color. Drain Angelica stems. Add to boiling syrup. Turn down heat and cook until tender. Place in a sterilized glass jar, covering with syrup to exclude air. Seal tightly. The Angelica in syrup should be kept in the refrigerator or freezer after opening for use. Pieces of stem may be taken out, drained and rolled in powdered sugar. If left in the air on waxed paper they will dry enough to slice for decorating a frosted cake. For placing on sweet rolls before baking they may be simply drained and cut up.

ANISE   ANNUAL

Pimpinella Anisum

Umbelliferae, native Greece to Egypt

HABIT: A slim plant that flowers at 2 feet in height, Anise has two kinds of leaves. The first leaves are rounded with toothed edges; the ones on flowering stems are linear. Lacy blossoms in pure white umbels top the herb in flower, sometimes weighting the plant down. As seeds form they turn greenish gray when ripe. A bit of sharp stem clings to each one even after removal from the seed head. Maturation of seed take up to four months of growing in a warm climate.

CULTURE: In Guatemala and Mexico, Anise is grown as a commercial crop for seed. Seeds are sown in shallow drills where plants are to grow. Transplanting Anise is not worthwhile. For a small patch in the herb garden, start seeds indoors in pellet pots in March. Two or three seeds to a pot may be thinned to one when the seedlings are 4 inches high. Then set out in the garden but first remove the nylon netting so the tap root may go down. Anise needs 70° F. temperature to germinate. The plants may be thinned to stand 4 inches apart so that one will support another. A line of string each side of the row will help to keep the flowering heads from being muddied.

USE: When Anise seeds may be pulled gently from the heads they are ready for cutting. Pull up or cut off the whole plant. Trim roots and main stem away. If plants have accumulated dirt, wash gently over a fine mesh screen to catch the seeds. Spread a sheet in the sun, up off the ground. Scatter seed heads over it. Bring the cloth or box indoors at night or in case of rain. Three or four days in warm sunlight will help to dry seeds. When stems snap, finish off seeds by rubbing over a screen of mesh to let them through. Spread them on a cookie sheet and place in a warm oven, not over 100° F. to become really dry. This will kill any insect larvae in the seeds. Anise seeds are distilled green for the flavorful oil. It is used in beverages, candies, and medicine. Licorice confections are flavored with it which leads to the impression that true Licorice plant, *Glycyrrhiza glabra* is scented. It is not. The root has a sweetness but it is incorrect to describe plants with Anise aroma as licorice-scented. Star Anise is the source of much oil of Anise used in the trade. The fruits of the Chinese tree, *Illicium verum,* which is grown as a pot plant or tropical perennial in Florida, are star shaped and keep their perfume for years. They may be used instead of Anise in flavoring. A spice necklace, strung with bits of Cinnamon stick, whole Nutmeg drilled, whole Allspice pierced through, will gain its long time sweetness from bits of Star Anise between the other spices. Anise seeds are reasonable to buy; plants fun to grow and there are other herbs which offer much the same flavor for foods and teas.

Whole Anise seeds are the most familiar parts of the herb to cooks. The distilled oil is used in commerce. Anise seed is often called a *spice.* If it is ground before packing much of the flavor of the essential oil is lost. Use a mortar and pestle to pulverize it if the recipe calls for ground Anise. In cooking, you don't have to limit Anise seed to cookies, though any sugar cookie base may be

Ansie Seed Cookies   Anise—Hyssop/Agastache Foeniculum

improved with a tablespoon of Anise seeds added just before the flour in the recipe. The German Christmas cookies, called Pferrernuesse, depend on Anise for part of their sweetness, thus saving sugar. They are dropped rather than rolled, which saves time.

Anise Cookies

2/3 cup sugar	2 eggs
1½ cups flour	½ teaspoon Anise seed

Beat eggs until thick and lemon-colored. Add sugar, continue beating. Fold in sifted flour and crushed Anise seed. Drop from a spoon or put through a press onto a greased cookie sheet. Let stand overnight. Bake in a slow oven, 20 to 30 minutes, until firm but not browned. Store in a tin box for several days before using.

Quite a different use, created by Isabella Gaylord, is that of Pork Roast with Anise Seed

1 pork roast	1 cup chicken stock
1 Tablespoon minced Parsley	1 Tablespoon Anise Seed
1 minced clove of Garlic	½ cup white wine

Season roast with salt and pepper. Cut 5 deep gashes in it with a sharp knife. Fill them with combined Parsley and Garlic. Rub outside well with flour. Put in a 350° F. oven for 30 minutes. During that time make a baste of the stock (this may be done by dissolving 2 chicken bouillon cubes in boiling water) wine and Anise seed. Simmer 15 minutes. At the end of the half hour, reduce heat in oven to 300° F. Allow 40 minutes to the pound, baste every 15 minutes. When baste is exhausted, use the gravy in the pan. Sweet Cicely's green seeds may be used in stock, instead of Anise seeds, in the above recipe. There is a German way with roast pork that achieves somewhat the same flavor. The meat, which has been rubbed with salt and a lot of pepper, is wrapped with Fennel leaves, tied on with string, before roasting.

ANISE-HYSSOP   PERENNIAL
Agastache Foeniculum,
Labiatae, native to United States and Korea

HABIT: The herb is decorative enough for the flower garden. Roundish leaves on upright plants have a distinct 'Anise' scent and flavor. It does not begin to branch until about a foot tall and grows to 3 to 4 feet when in bloom. Spikes of small purple flowers remain in bloom for months. It is a fine plant for color in late summer through autumn. Interestingly, the plant was introduced to the herb trade as 'Korean Mint'. It is in the Mint family but does not spread by runners as do the true species of the Mentha genus. A seedsman was in the Korean War and brought seed of the handsome plant he saw growing there back to this country. He called it 'Anise Mint' or 'Korean Mint' and it has been passed around under those names. It also grows wild in the heartland of America and in Texas.

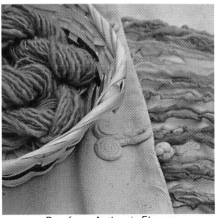

Dye from Anthemis Flowers   *Golden Marguerite/Anthemis tinctoria*

CULTURE: Anise-Hyssop is generally grown from seed. It can be transplanted at any time during its growth, right up to flowering. The fine seeds sown in a flat will germinate in 7 days. Temperature of 68° to 86° bring them on quickly. In the garden they will self-sow under a plant that has seeded the previous year. Allow 12 inches between plants by thinning or transplanting seedlings started in the ground. Full sun and rich soil are their delight but they will grow in partial shade without leaning for sunshine.

USE: Leaves may be dried for flavoring herb tea, also can be used in place of Anise seed by steeping in water or other liquid to be used in cakes, muffins or cookies. Anise-Hyssop is considered a fine bee plant. It yields nectar all through the day rather than just part of it as many flowers do. Beekeepers like to grow it near their hives. When fresh, the aroma is not as strong as when the foliage is dried. To choose between blossoms and herbage is difficult. If it is to be cut for leaves, the greatest amount is available before blooming. But as Anise-scented plants are numerous, we wait until Anise-Hyssop has bloomed to cut the whole plant down. Then the stems are put in a large brown paper bag, tied at mouth of bag to enclose stems, and hung up to dry. If some seed is included in the dried material when it is stripped for finishing off in the oven, it is set aside for scattering in the garden. Anise-Hyssop is unobtrusive, modest in the garden, but lovely in bloom and in herb tea or potpourri.

GOLDEN ANTHEMIS   PERENNIAL
Anthemis tinctoria   Zone 4
Compositae, native to central and southern Europe

HABIT: A satisfactory perennial which flowers the first season. Fat daisylike heads of bloom range in color from butter yellow to orange. The most popular form is cultivar *'Kelwayi'* with finely cut foliage and lighter flowers. A little help from small twigs to 'brush' the plants will hold the heads up when covered with bloom. It is a plant for long flowering in summer; spent blossoms must be removed to keep it so. Grows 2 feet tall and spreads as widely. Dried flowers saved for use as a dye or adding color to potpourri. Finely cut gray foliage is aromatic.

CULTURE: Anthemis may be started from seed in the garden as soon as the soil is workable. Cover with just enough earth to hold them in place when it is firmed down. It is a good plant for a slope as the herb needs good drainage. Will grow best in full sun but can stand partial shade. May be started earlier indoors in soil substitute in a flat. Seeds germinate at 68° to 86° F. They are easily moved when small. Even the plantlets that self-sow in the garden may be picked up to place in more favorable position. The herb Chamomile, formerly named *Anthemis nobilis,* has been moved to its own genus in *Hortus Third. Chamaemelum nobile* is a hard name to remember when you've grown Roman Chamomile as Anthemis for 40 years. The Bailey Hortorium, Cornell University, has made many changes in plant names in this third edition of

| *Cudweed/Artemisia ludoviciana* | *Artemisia 'Silver Mound'* |

their manual of cultivated plants. It is the botanical authority being used by nurseries, gardeners and taxonomists. Three decades of work went into it.

USE: "Tinctoria" in any plant name identifies its early use. *Anthemis tinctoria* has richly colored petals and florets which are steeped in boiling water to yield a dye for cloth. Various shades of yellow to gold are obtained from the dye bath depending on the mordant which is used. This is a chemical solution that insures lasting color. The material dipped in it before the dye process will hold the color after drying. *The Brooklyn Botanic Garden Handbook #46, Dye Plants and Dyeing* details methods of using plant materials for natural dyes. As a garden cut flower Golden Marguerite is nice to work with in making arrangements. The foliage is silvery gray and feathery. Even without its bright blossoms, Anthemis would deserve a place in the sun in any collection of herbs.

HISTORY: *Anthemis tinctoria* was considered a garden flower in 1629. John Parkinson, author of *Paradisi in Sole, Paradisus Terrestris,* wrote that it was put to different and sundry uses, both for pleasure and profit. This sounds familiar to those who grow herbs for gift-giving, crafts, plant sales and natural dyes. In the 17th century it was grown for 'the sick and the sound, in bathings to comfort and strengthen the sound, and to ease the pains of the diseased, as also in many other forms applied outwardly.'

ORNAMENTAL ARTEMISIAS   PERENNIAL
Artemisia species   Zones 4
Compositae, native to United States, Europe and Asia

HABIT: Plants with white, gray and silvery foliage which make good foil for bright flowers, background for green herbs and the material for wreaths and crafts. Species vary from spreading plants of tall, white-leaved branching nature, to shimmering silver tufted rounds which do not invade the area. All have a distinct aroma, bitter quality and limit the growth of plants around them by their own exudations in the soil.

CULTURE: *Artemisia ludoviciana* is a true American plant with two very hardy varieties. Both must be started from root divisions. The Cudweed, or White Sage, has entire leaves, slightly notched at the ends, on the lower part of the 2½ foot tall clump. Its heavy inflorescence of small yellow to brownish flowers in panicles usually becomes lateral rather than standing straight. Plants in full sun will be more erect than those in partial shade. As the thick nap of whitish or silvery hairs on the Artemisia suggests, they are plants for dry soils, withstanding heat and winds. 'Silver King,' *Artemisia ludoviciana var. albula,* is easily distinguished from Cudweed when it reaches 3 feet in height and begins to bloom. Stems are stiff, panicles much slimmer and less weighty so the plants do not sprawl. It has spreading roots, with tufts of whitish leaves which are dissected. These tend to disappear as the clump comes into bloom. 'Silver King'

Artemisia Wreath   *Artemisia Pine Cone Tree*

is the most desirable variety of the species for perennial borders and accent plants. It has branching stems with leaves white on both sides. *Artemisia Schmidtiana 'Silver Mound'* is a dwarf, round clump of soft, silky leaves in tufts that make a perfect bun. They stay less than a foot tall and grow best in full sun and dry soil. Root divisions are made by lifting a clump as soon as the new leaves appear in the spring and literally breaking it up. Each piece with a good mass of roots will make a new plant if replanted at once. 'Silver Mound' is difficult to keep in a pot and late season transplanting can be fatal. The glistening 'Mound' tends to fall apart when flower stems develop. Fred McGourty, editor of the Brooklyn Botanic Garden's *Plants and Gardens,* trims his border of this Artemisia in mid-summer, cutting off the budding stems. His fine perennial garden is in a cool climate in northern Connecticut, where hardy plants stretch out their blooming period. The leaner the soil for 'Silver Mound' the better it looks. But the fluffy, spreading inflorescence yields material for the prime use of the ornamental Artemisias: wreath making. The medicinal species and green forms of the genus will be described under their common names, 'Southernwood', 'Sweet Wormwood' and the true 'absinthe', Wormwood, *Artemisia Absinthium.*

USE: The species of Artemisia with silvery leaves and curling heads of small yellowish blossoms are ideal for making herb wreaths. They were an old tradition to give sweet smells where 16th century households sometimes had dirt floors. Strewing the hardpacked earth inside the house with Hyssop, Pennyroyal and Wormwood chased out fleas. Hanging garlands of Tansy, Thyme and Mints perfumed the rooms. Indoors and out people have always decked their abodes. Dryden suggested that 18th century housewives "With Laurels wreath your posts and strow with Flowers the Pavement." Sounds a bit like Christmas decoration in the suburbs, today. The great thing about Artemisia wreaths, besides their beauty, is that they are bug proof and can be saved from year to year. The aroma is not evident unless the hanging garland is touched but it is there, protecting itself and the house from moths. To make your own version of the expensive silver and pewter colored wreaths requires a few materials—

A. Artemisia Silver King, Silver Mound or White Sage tops, cut as the plants begin to bloom.
B. The curling ends of stems may be worked while still fresh. If time does not permit, hang bunches to dry and dampen them with a mist of water before working.
C. A wreath base of wire. Twisted wire circles may be bought. Vines of grape or self-braided Hop stems are easily tied into rounds.
D. Fine wire or nylon thread on a spool.

Method. Take several tips with their fluffy heads. Tie them into small bundles, slightly spread so they will project an inch or two beyond the wreath base. Fasten each one to it with heads over lapping stems of the one laid on before it. See that the curves go in the same direction. Go round the circle with the Artemisia to make a sturdy but light wreath. It may be decorated at a later time or stuck with small flower heads on very short stems, such as yellow Yarrow blossoms which dry well, too. There are other wreath bases such as straw, wire framework, and styrofoam but they do not give the same halo effect and are heavy to hang. The wreath of Artemisia on wire or natural vine wood is light and graceful.

43

Bush Basil/Ocimum Basilicum *Creamy Basil Dressing*

BUSH BASIL   TENDER ANNUAL

Ocimum Basilicum cv 'Minimum'
Labiatae, cultivated herb

HABIT: Beautiful Basil delights in warmth. It grows easily from seed. Bush Basil is one of the prettiest of more than a half dozen varieties. It makes a scented, miniature bush, not more than 12 inches tall. Half-inch or smaller leaves on branching stems are ovate and shiny. Small white, two-lipped flowers are mostly in the axils of the leaves.

CULTURE: Sow seed indoors in a flat at temperatures betwen 68° to 86° F. If kept moist, seeds will sprout in a week. They must be covered to twice the depth of the seed when planted outdoors but in a flat, enough soil substitute to cover lightly is sufficient. It should be well pressed down. Basil seeds develop a mucilaginous coating within the first hour of wetting. If this dries out, germination is apt to be inhibited. Bush or other Basils transplant readily as they have branching roots. Set seedlings out a foot apart, protect from wind and keep moist until established. This should be done only after the ground is thoroughly warm and nights are no longer chilly. Basil likes 'corn weather' - hot and humid. It develops black spots on the leaves if cold dew drops settle on the foliage. Use the thinnings in salads when pulling seedlings of garden sown plants to give 12 inch space between them.

USE: Bush Basil is a good subject for a pot or container. A miniature form, known as 'Greek Basil', seldom flowers or sets seed. It is perennial if kept in a warm greenhouse. All Basils are blackened by the first frost in the garden. It is well to lift some Bush Basil plants to bring indoors a week or two before that sad occurrence is expected. Tops of branches may be pinched back to set of leaves two inches lower. The herb is generally used fresh because other forms have larger leaves which afford more harvest for drying, freezing or putting down in oil. The little Bush Basil has more stems in proportion to leaves, Along the Mediterranean Sea, the Basils are grown in pots in open windows. As screening is not common on windows and doors in the rest of the world as it is in the U. S., Basil plants set on balconies deter flies. Tomatoes and Basil make a happy marriage, as does—

CREAMY BASIL DRESSING FOR GREEN SALAD

1 clove Garlic	1 teaspoon salt
1 cup salad oil	½ teaspoon sugar
½ teaspoon powdered Mustard	¼ teaspoon ground pepper
1 teaspoon water	1/3 cup vinegar
1 egg white	2 Tablespoons fresh Basil leaves chopped

Put all ingredients in the blender and blend on low for 15 seconds. Pour over salad and toss lightly. For salt-free diets, omit salt and enjoy a diet-light dressing.

Well Sweep Basil Garden   Camphor Basil/Ocimum kilimandscharicum

BASIL, CAMPHOR   TENDER PERENNIAL
Ocimum kilimandscharicum
Labiatae, native to Africa, especially Kenya

HABIT: A truly perennial Basil which grows in Africa is named for Mount Kilimanjaro. It is not one of the culinary Basils. The leaves are longer and narrower than those of Sweet Basil. Fine hairs give the foliage a gray look, while small white flowers in spikes top the 3½ foot tall plants. Stems become woody when plants begin to bloom in July. The herb is used medicinally in its native land. Fresh or dried, it is steeped in boiled water to make a tea to reduce fevers. Possibly it has anti-malarial effects, as Basils have been used to keep mosquitoes away by their scent.

CULTURE: Seeds need alternating temperatures of 55° at night and 72° daytimes to sprout in sterile soil substitute. Transplant seedlings to pots before setting out in the garden. As seed is not generally available, propagation by cuttings from a plant obtained from a nursery specializing in herbs is the usual way to obtain Camphor Basil. It roots quickly with bottom heat, either in rooting medium or spring water. Mature plants are difficult to repot to return indoors. While not as frost sensitive as the culinary Basils, Camphor Basil will not live over where the ground freezes.

USE: Foliage is dried by hanging stems upside down in bunches in a dry room. The brown bag method of inverting stems into a large paper bag and closing the mouth of the bag around them works well for it. During World War II, Camphor Basil substituted for true camphor from the tropical tree *Cinnamonum Camphora.* A pot of the herb on a patio will help to keep mosquitoes away. Camphor tree is used as a container plant in Florida for the same purpose. Dried leaves of Camphor Basil may be added to anti-moth mixtures of herbs such as Wormwood and Southernwood made up into small bags to hang in closets.

HISTORY: In literature and legend, Basil represents love and hate according to the locale. The origin of the name has been related to words meaning *royal* as in *basilica,* the royal palace, (in Rome applied to seven principal churches founded by Constantine), and *basilisk,* a legendary lizard. Always the stories involve fears or contrary emotions. It was said that Basil bred scorpions or incited romantic passions. There is a lizard in Australia which enjoys eating Basil grown in gardens. Not the true basilisk which was said to be able to kill with a look. The Camphor Basil was used as a febrifuge in Western Africa; in Sierra Leone it is called Feverplant, as the tea was a remedy for the prevalent fevers.

Ocimum sanctum
Labiatae

HABIT: Holy Basil has much the same hairiness as Camphor Basil. Leaves are broader at the base, wider and stems branch more freely. Candelabra-like flower stalks bear small pink flowers. The whole plant is strongly pungent. Its scent has been described as that of walnuts, or ripe bananas, or spice. A recent monograph on *The Cultivated Basils* by Helen H. Darrah, retired biology professor, suggests that the Holy Basil in this country is a hybrid of two species. There is another form, called "Tulsi" in India and By-Krapow in Thailand, with a muskier flavor. The latter is sold as a dried herb in Chinatown, New York City, as an import from Thailand. The Holy Basil of which seed is available in this country has been recognized by visitors from India as the sacred herb of their Hindu religion. It may be used in cooking for a different flavor.

CULTURE: Holy Basil requires the same alternating temperatures as Camphor Basil for germination; 55° by night, 72° F. by day. Under such conditions it may come up as volunteers in the garden from seed of previous year's plants. It is one of the few species of Basil to have seed hardy enough to survive in frozen ground. The way to start it is to sow in a flat indoors. Transplant seedlings to the herb bed after all danger of frost is past. Self-sown plants may be lifted to space 10 to 12 inches apart when three to four inches high. Seed sown directly in the garden should be covered lightly and thinned at the same size. Once Holy Basil comes into bloom at 18 inches in height the stems become woody. They are not worth moving when the main stalk hardens, thus are not good houseplants.

USE: If the dried herb is to be used in cooking, trim plants before blooming. Wash the leafy tips carefully and pat dry. Spread on a screen, turning several times a day. When edges begin to crisp, the leaflets may be spread on a cookie sheet and finished off in a cool oven, not more than 100° F. They will need stirring during this process also. Let them become thoroughly cool before storing. For potpourri, for which Holy Basil acts as a fixative of the perfume of other dried herbs and rose petals, it may be dried on the stems. Cut the whole plant, even if it is forming seed. Hang up to dry or upside down in a paper bag for a week or more. Strip flower heads and leaves and finish off as for drying the culinary herbs. Basil seeds are fragrant. The seed heads also have strong aroma which is useful in mixtures of sweet herbs for sachets. Heads have to be crushed to remove the seeds which seem to become tighter in their calyces after removal from the plant. In Asian countries, Holy Basil is also a culinary herb. The following recipe was given to the authors by the wife of a native of Thailand. Karen Sriuttamayotin calls it

Chicken By Krapow (Holy Basil)

3 Tablespoons peanut oil	2 Tablespoons Soy Sauce
2 large cloves Garlic	2 large Chinese dried mush-rooms or ½ cup of sliced
2 fresh Chili peppers (if desired)	fresh ones
Meat from 2 chicken breast shredded into bite size pieces	2-3 Tablespoons By Krapow (dried Holy Basil leaves)
(Equal amount of mussels, scallops or zucchini squash may be used instead of chicken)	Fish sauce or salt to taste Pepper to taste

Heat the oil. Add Garlic and Chilis which have each been mashed. When Garlic turns golden, add chicken. Brown quickly. If using Chinese dried mushrooms, prepare by soaking them in warm water for ½ hour before cooking. Then slice them thinly. Add mushrooms to chicken. Cook a few minutes longer. Add Soy sauce to taste. Put in By-Krapow, fish sauce and ground pepper. Lower heat and cover. Allow to cook five minutes more. Serve with rice.

Holy Basil/Ocimum sanctum   Lemon Basil/Ocimum Basilicum

A typical Thai meal might include this dish, a curried meat, fish or vegetable dish and a pungent soup, all served at the same time with each person helping himself from the bowls at the center of the table. The donor of this unusual recipe has grown herbs and vegetables in a neighborhood allotment garden in the heart of New York City. She found the herbs the most productive of flavor for the small space allowed.

BASIL, LEMON   TENDER ANNUAL
Ocimum Basilicum cv 'Citriodorum'   Culinary Herb
Labiatae, native to Thailand, East Indies, Australia

HABIT: The lemon-scented Basil was introduced from Thailand to the United States by the U. S. Department of Agriculture in 1940. At that time it was known as *Ocimum citriodorum.* It was distributed by a small herb seed business known as Laurel Hill Herb Farm during World War II. The combination of lemon and Basil flavors made it popular with herb fanciers. When the authors' seed business gave way to *The Herb Grower Magazine* in 1951, seed was difficult to find. Now the largest flower and herb seed concern has included it in its full color catalog. So to us it's a welcome back, old friend. Seed of Lemon Basil has come to the writers from India, recently. The plant has been in cultivation since the 16th century in England and was described by John Gerard in his *The Herball,* 1597. He called it *Ocimum citratum.* John Parkinson, a third of a century later, considered it a fine plant to put in nose-gays for its lemony fragrance. They did not seem to know it as a culinary herb in England in those days. Even today, Basils are difficult to bring to seed maturity in the cool summers there.

CULTURE: Lemon Basil grows to 18 inches tall with more open branching inflorescence and narrower, lighter green leaves without the glossiness of those of Sweet Basil. It is scarcely worth starting Lemon Basil indoors, 6 weeks before the last frost, as is done with Bush Basil, Lettuce Leaf and Sweet Basil. The plants tend to run to seed when first set out even if grown in pellet or peat pots to go right in the ground. Seed sown where it is to grow, after the ground is thoroughly warm, produces fuller plants. Make a shallow furrow, tip out the seed from the packet as well-spaced as possible. Cover with a quarter inch of fine soil. Firm it down with a brick or short flat block to prevent washing in heavy rain. Transplanting seems to retard this hybrid Basil where all the others take it in stride. Growth is not as stiffly upright as in the Sweet Basil and other culinary types. Scattered hairs on stems and undersides of the pointed oval leaves on short stems are typical. White blossoms develop on 5 to 7 inch long terminal branches with hairy bracts longer than the calyces. Whole plants are gathered for drying the leaves, rather than taking several clippings from the same plant. They are more scattered on the stems and do not make much herbage. Plants can stand 6 to 10 inches apart, after thinning seedlings, without being crowded.

USE: Lemon Basil is used in cooking, especially in pea soup, where the lemon-citron overtone is most welcome. Some people find it delectable. Others may miss the clove-like Basil savor. For lemon-scented pot-pourri this Basil adds its special perfume. The whole plant may be cut before frost and hung up to dry in a large brown bag. No need to wash the leaves that are not for culinary use. Simply trim off the roots, tie the stems loosely in a hand-size bundle. Put heads down in the brown bag but do not let them touch bottom. Then tie the mouth of the bag around the stems. Leave a loop of string to suspend the bagged herbs from a nail or clothes hanger. When convenient, take the bag down. Shake it to see if leaves are ready to drop off. Open and feel the foliage. If it is crispy, remove the bundle from the bag. Depending on weather, Basils will dry this way in 2 to 3 weeks. Roll the individual stalks between your palms to remove leaves from stems. Finish off in a cool oven, not more than 100° F. by spreading the herb on a cookie sheet. Cool before adding to mixed herbs for sweet bags or packing in a jar for adding to herb tea mixtures.

John Gerard, who called this species "Citron Basil" said of the whole genus—"the smell of Basil is good for the heart and for the head. That the seed cureth the infirmities of the heart, taketh away sorrowfulness which commeth of melancholy, and maketh a man merry and glad." Good medicine!

BASIL, LETTUCE LEAF   TENDER ANNUAL
Ocimum Basilicum cv. 'Crispum'
Labiatae, Culinary Herb long in cultivation

HABIT: Called "robust" by Helen Darrah, author of the study of *Cultivated Basils,* Lettuce Leaf Basil offers the most harvest. Leaves are 3 to 4 inches long and just as wide. They have smooth edges with puffed or crinkled centers. Stems are heavier, also, with short flower spikes. The inflorescence is removed before cutting begins. The white flowers are nice in bouquets. Some forms have spotting of purple on the crisped leaves.

Flavor of Lettuce Leaf is pungently pleasant. Plants grow 2 feet tall and almost as broad. They are affected by the first frost but are pretty well cut back by then for Basil's many uses. If is the best type for making into pesto, Basil in oil, freezing in cubes and drying.

CULTURE: Sow seed indoors in a flat. Keep temperature in the soil substitute close to 72° F. Germination begins in 5 to 7 days. Seedlings have large, spade-shaped cotyledons. Grow to 4 sets of true leaves before setting out in the garden. The ground must be thoroughly warm for Basil transplants. Adding garden loam to sterile soil mix for a potting medium will get the plantlets off to a good start. The two smallest leaves at the top of the plant may be pinched out to encourage branching even before they are set out 18 inches apart.

Outdoor sowing of seed in a shallow furrow should have not more than twice the depth of the grains firmed over them. Seed is mucilaginous when wet and may float up in a heavy rain and then dry out before sprouting if it is not covered and patted down. Lettuce Leaf Basil is not easily propagated by cuttings or suitable for potting up to return indoors before frost. Seedlings may be thinned to 12 to 18 inches. The large leaves should not touch other plants. They have a specific design on the stem so that they will shed the early morning dew or rain. Each pair is at right angles to the one below it. Droplets of cold water that collect on the plant towards the end of the season cause black spots on the leaves. The early herbalists advised watering Basil with sun-heated water when the sun was on the plants. Spray from a hose of cold well-water late in the afternoon causes leaf spots.

HARVEST: Make continuous cuttings of the leaves throughout the summer. First cutting may be taken as soon as square flower buds begin to form. Prune back to a second set of leaves right across the plant. Do not leave unsightly stubs that will blacken and disfigure the tops which you want to branch and fill out again. Lettuce Leaf Basil dries better off the stems. The leaves are spread on a screen so that they do not overlap. They should be turned several times a day while air drying. Handle them gently both when washing them and patting them dry, as you would lettuce itself, and when turning over. The anise or clove aroma comes from oil glands on the surface of the leaves. If these are broken when the foliage is fresh, black creases or lines will show up.

Basil Frozen in Cubes   *Basil with Beans*

USE: BASIL FROZEN IN CUBES

Big Lettuce Leaf Basil supplies leaves for chopping in a blender. Lightly fill a 2 cup measure with fresh, washed leaves torn apart. Place in the blender top. Add 1½ cups water. Whirl until it becomes a green puree, in about one minute. Pour into empty ice cube tray. Freeze in refrigerator or freezer. Remove cubes when solid. Pack into pliofilm bag or freezer container. Attach a label and place in freezer. The green herb cubes look very similar when frozen. Good labelling is a great time-saver. One Basil cube will flavor a pint of tomato sauce. Two will provide enough moisture for reheating pasta that is left over. Herb cubes can be made out of French Sorrel, Chervil, Mint, fresh Coriander leaves (Cilantro) and other leaf herbs. They are as close to chopped fresh leaves as you can get in winter when put in hot soup, stew or sauces. French Tarragon, especially, keeps its extraordinary taste when stored in this way.

BASIL WITH BEANS

1½ lbs. green beans	½ cup boiling water
¼ cup oil	1 teaspoon salt
1 clove Garlic, crushed	2 Tablespoons fresh Basil minced
1 Tablespoon chopped	or 1 teaspoon dried
Chives	½ cup grated Paremesan cheese
¾ cup diced green pepper	

Beans may be left whole if they are very fresh and stringless or cut up frozen beans. Heat oil and Garlic in a large fry pan. Add green pepper and cook slowly for 3 minutes. Add the beans, water, salt, Basil and Chives. Cover and simmer until tender but still crisp (about 5 minutes). Mix in ¼ cup cheese and sprinkle ¼ cup on top for garnish.

PURPLE BASIL VINEGAR

Purple Basil gives a fine pinkish red color to the vinegar as well as the pungency of Basil. Start the colorful vinegar with clear "white" vinegar. For each quart of finished infusion allow one closely packed cup of leaves and stems. Put the leaves in a glass quart container. The local delicatessen or grocery store may give you wide mouth large mayonnaise jars, if you ask. For each quart of liquid put at least one cup of leaves. More will add to the strength but perhaps not the color. Do not use earthenware crocks. Stoneware is alright, however. If a low-fired glaze contains lead, the acid of the vinegar will draw it out. It may make a vinegar that looks and tastes fine but it will possibly contain dangerous levels of lead.

The glass container is good, for the gradual process of change from white vinegar to ruby color vinegar can be watched and enjoyed. After leaves and stems fresh from the garden are put in the jar, pour vinegar over to cover them and fill it. The top of the jar may be closed but not too tightly. If a screw top is required, stretch wax paper over the mouth of the jar. Then screw down the top but not too tightly, to avoid sticking later. Place the jar on a windowsill in warm sun to hasten the process. Or the bottle may be put away in the cupboard. Inspect it after a month to see if the color is taken up by the vinegar. Then it is time to bottle off in fancy containers. The

Basil Dark Opal   *Dwarf Purple Bush Basil*

herb leaves will look wilted. Acid in the vinegar breaks down the plant material but takes up its oils. Therefore it is more attractive to bottle off the vinegar at its peak rather than to keep the herb forever in the container. Color will keep even after the vinegar is decanted. Use a strainer and a funnel to pour the vinegar into small-necked jars.

BASIL, PURPLE   TENDER ANNUAL
Ocimum Basilicum cv 'Purpurascens'
Labiatae, Cultivated form Dark Opal

HABIT: Most Basils have been carried about by migrant populations for three thousand years. The form Dark Opal is a modern introduction. It was developed at the University of Connecticut about 30 years ago. In the past there have been other Purple Basils but most have reverted back to green or partially purple and green after several generations. There was a miniature Purple Bush Basil in the 1930's. Seed of it has not been available for two decades but one herb specialist in New Jersey is trying to breed back to it. It, like the dark Purple Lettuce Leaf form or typical Purple Sweet Basil we used to grow, seems to be a recessive trait. The coloring would not remain true from seed. Dark Opal has pink flowers in purple calyces on branching plants not more than 18 inches tall. It is a delicate herb which requires warmth and full sun to show its true beauty. Dark Opal is usually allowed to flower because it is too pretty to cut for drying or freezing. The color is against it in the matter of seasoning with the dried herb. It is delightful in contrast to annual flowers in an arrangement or sprinkled on salad or yellow tomatoes when fresh.

CULTURE: Sow seeds in a flat. Cover with sterile soil mix to a depth not more than twice the size of the seed. Space seeds ⅜ to ½ inch apart in the flat. Maintain a temperature of 70° to 72° degrees. Keep moist all the while the seedlings are growing but do not water from above. Flat may be put in a pan for the water to soak up from below and then drained. Bottom heat helps to stimulate sprouting in less than a week. The seedlings do not need transplanting before setting out. If they are not crowded in the original container, they will do better if allowed to grow 3 to 4 inches tall before further handling. Pellet pots suit the plantlets well if they are kept thoroughly warm. Just one night of chill will set the plants back. Without the green chlorphyll in the leaves, Dark Opal is more vulnerable to shock at the beginning of its life. As with all seedlings, it should be picked up by the leaves rather than the stem. Of course, the roots must be lifted from the flat with a spatula type stick before any attempt is made to remove a seedling.

USE: Dark Opal makes lovely purple Basil vinegar. It's flavor is not as sweet as that of the other Basils so this is a fine use for it. Putting herbs in vinegar captures their flavor for the months when fresh herbs are not available. The chore of making herb vinegar is simple and joyful. It can be done only on the beautiful harvest days when the hot sun and matured oils of the leaves make them ready to infuse in the acid medium. Dried herbs do not give much flavor to vinegar.

Sweet Basil/Ocimum Basilcum

Greek Basil/Ocimum minimum

BASIL, SWEET   TENDER ANNUAL
Ocimum Basilicum
Labiatae, cultivated culinary herb

HABIT: It has been said that as many as 60 named varieties of Sweet Basil were known to 19th century gardeners in Europe. Many of the variations have been lost to cultivation. Leaving to last on our list of seven Basils the most commonly known form, is just a matter of alphabetical order. Sweet Basil has the typical clove-like Basil flavor. Plants are usally 24 to 30 inches tall at time of flowering. Leaves are opposite on square stems. The height at the time of flower bud formation is approximately half of its full growth size at the end of summer. The flowers are white, in 6-flowered whorls. They, too, are in opposite groups. Before blossoms open, the bracts between them have a square shape, rather like the roof of a Chinese pagoda. A gardener would be lucky to locate and grow seed of all 7 Basils. They would make a pleasant picture with varied foliage, color and shape, each with its own usefulness. Basils are most successful, in warm, moist climates. Some are almost perennial in Florida.

CULTURE: Though grown commercially in California, Sweet Basil is so much in demand for flavoring that over 300 metric tons per year are imported into the United States. Oil of Sweet Basil is used in many commercial products. California's climate with adequate irrigation is ideal for Sweet Basil production. Plants need a long season to mature seed.
Six weeks or more before last frost date, is a good time to start Sweet Basil seeds indoors. They germinate quickly in a soil substitute if kept at 70° F. It is one of the better herbs to grow under lights indoors. Temperature and adequate moisture for rapid growing make it a fine leaf crop. In the light garden, flowering is not the object. If seeds are sown once a month, there will be greens to use even before transplanting. Once germination begins, at 5 to 7 days, the plantlets must be kept warm, at 70° F. or above. Losses in transplanting seedlings from flat to pot or larger container, often occur because of temperature changes or drying out of the potting soil. The love-hate relationship which is part of the legend of Basils shows up in any neglect of plants grown indoors. You can't neglect them, even for a day. When the ground is thoroughly warm, Sweet Basil is a satisfactory seed for the beginner. It will appear in a short time after sowing in a shallow furrow. But, here too, care must be taken to firm the seed down. If it is not covered to twice its depth, heavy rain may float the gelatinous seeds out of the earth. Perhaps, this is why Basil was supposed to be sown with cursing and stomping!

USE: Among the ways to preserve Sweet Basil's inimitable flavor for winter use are those described for the other six varieties: drying (least likely to preserve the color), freezing in ice cubes (nearest to fresh taste when added to cooked foods), putting fresh leaves in vinegar (most useful in salad dressings), blending with oil and cheese and pine nuts (Pesto). To capture the essence of Sweet Basil there is another way.

Sweet Basil in Oil

Sweet Basil/Ocimum Basilicum

Sweet Basil in Oil

A most convenient way to have Basil flavor in winter, is the Sweet Basil in Oil, either with leaves left in at final bottling or just one or two added for mysterious atmosphere when looking at the bottle. The oil is used anywhere salad oil is an integral ingredient; such as in French dressing, spaghetti sauce, or for underlying sauce on pizza. It can be spread over fish before broiling. The method is very simple but requires the fresh herbs.

Fill a pint, glass-top canning jar (or a powdered coffee container with plastic cover) with leaves of Sweet Basil. They should be cut just before using. If washing is needed, pat dry with a paper towel. The herb may be bruised but should not be limp. Pour over it enough salad, olive, safflower, sunflower or other favorite oil to fill the jar almost to the top. Run a knife down the sides of the jar so that air bubbles will be released. Add 1 Tablespoon of wine vinegar. Place the cover on tightly enough so that the jar may be shaken without spilling. The leaves are not packed in the jar because the oil must reach all of them at all times. A gentle shaking each day will help to assure this distribution. As oil has a way of creeping out of almost any capped container, a plastic bag around the Basil in Oil jar will prevent spoiling a window sill on which it is set. Sunlight streaming through the jar warms the herb enough to promote further infusion of the oils of the leaves in the covering oil. If you wish to do this in winter, to use up a Sweet Basil brought into the house or raised there, the jar may be put in a pan of hot water (not boiling) for an hour each day. A warm radiator or furnace top which will keep it moderately hot works well.

After three weeks, the Basil leaves will have transferred their essence to the oil. The strength of its aroma and flavor may be tested by putting a drop on your wrist. If it has a strong Basil scent, further steeping may not be needed. If it does not seem characteristic of Basil, draw off the oil, remove the Basil leaves and replace them with new ones. Add the tablespoon of wine vinegar again and procede as before.

The vinegar adds to the keeping quality but when the oil is decanted it does not mix with it as it sinks to the bottom. The leaves taken out of the first infusion may be used in cooking immediately, as an addition to tomato soup, and then removed before serving.

52

Box for Rooting Cuttings

Sweet Bay /Laurus noblis

BAY SWEET   TENDER PERENNIAL

Laurus nobilis   Zone 8

Lauraceae, native to the Mediterranean region

HABIT: Where it grows wild, the true laurel or Sweet Bay may attain 40 feet in height. The leaves are oval, stiff, without sheen, bright green when young and duller when held on year round. The plant is evergreen and may be put in a large pot or tub for enjoyment as a houseplant in winter. There are a number of forms with crinkly, variegated and more linear leaves. Roots are brown and stems dark green growing only a few inches a year when potted, but three or four feet when planted in the earth. One author has had a plant for over 30 years in a deep coldframe pit. When glass is taken off in summer, it puts up new growth to three feet above the frame and has to be cut back so that the protective glass can be replaced before freezes.

There are several plants called "Laurel" and it is important to know the Sweet Bay which has leaves used in cooking from the poisonous native Mountain Laurel. In cold situations, *Laurus nobilis* seldom flowers. *Kalmia latifolia* has masses of pink blooms in the spring but it is toxic to most animals except deer. The true Laurel has a delicious aroma on crushing a leaf which Mountain Laurel does not. California Laurel, *Umbellularia californica* is narrow-leaved, tall tree in its native heath. The foliage is packaged as Bay leaf by one spice firm but it is not as satisfactory for cooking as Sweet Bay. Species of Prunus have one poisonous member which is wrongly called "Laurel" but does not grow wild in this country. Bayberry, *Myrica pensylvanica,* has leaves which curl under slightly and are not as broad and flat as true Laurel. Early colonists used the leaves for a Bay leaf substitute and made candles from the wax of the gray berries.

CULTURE: Sweet Bay is propagated by cuttings where it does not set seed. They take up to three months to root under the best conditions of mist propagation. In Europe, seeds of *Laurus nobilis* are planted in sand outdoors to await germination when the pulpy material surrounding the seeds rots away. Germination takes 6 months to a year. The plant grows slowly at first. Cuttings may put on just a few inches of new growth while in a pot the first year. Wood that is just beginning to harden makes the best slips. A strong hormone powder dusted on the cut stem helps to speed rooting. Without a misting device, rooting can be done in sand with a cover of a plastic bag over the bulb pan of slips. One of the plastic boxes called "sweater boxes" which lets light through, filled half way with a mixture of perlite and peat, makes a good rooting container for Sweet Bay. Keep it in the light but not where sun will cause dripping inside the box.

USE: Bay leaves formed the original Laurel wreaths used to crown poets and scholars. They are still used for decorating winners of the Boston Marathon and honoring athletes and symphony conductors. Sweet Bay is a bit different from other leaf herbs. While most herbs give off all their flavor in a short cooking time, the Bay leaf enriches a soup, stew or long cooking dish for a

Bee Balm/Monarda fistulosa   *Bee Balm/Monarda didyma*

number of hours. That is why Bay leaves go in at the start of the spaghetti sauce and the Basil or Oregano at the end.

It is good to use the leaves whole. They do not reduce in volume and if chopped can be unpleasantly tough to try to chew, and Heaven forbid, accidentally get stuck in someone's throat. A good cold weather dish that takes 2 Bay leaves whole is

Minestrone Soup

1 lb. plus 11 oz. cooked red kidney beans	½ cup uncooked elbow macaroni
1 teaspoon salt	1 teaspoon dried Basil
1 clove Garlic, pressed	¼ teaspoon pepper
¼ cup chopped Parsley	1 Tablespoon oil
1 small zucchini, cut up	1 carrot, diced
2 stalks celery, chopped	4 or 5 leaves Swiss chard or spinach, chopped
3 Tablespoons butter	½ cup Sherry
2 Bay leaves	1 can (8 oz.) tomato sauce or stewed tomatoes
2½ cups water	Grated Parmesan cheese

Crush two-thirds of the kidney beans and leave the rest whole. Put everything in a large cooking kettle EXCEPT wine, macaroni, cheese and Basil. Bring to a boil and turn down to simmer an hour or more. Bay goes in at the start; Basil, Sherry and elbow macaroni are added during the last 15 minutes when soup is returned to boiling. Serve with a dusting of grated Parmesan.

BEE BALM   PERENNIAL
Monarda didyma and species   Zone 4
Labiatae, native American herbs

HABIT: Bee Balm, also called "Bergamot", is recognized by its red tubular florets arranged in whorls. Their deep throats attract hummingbirds to sip the nectar; a much better food for them than a sugar-syrup in a plastic tube. There are varieties with pink, white and maroon blossoms. Unless the oval, pointed leaves are pinched or brushed against, their pleasant minty aroma is not discovered. *Monarda didyma* thrives in moist, somewhat acid soil. Its 3 foot tall flower stems produce terminal heads of bloom in mid-summer that remain attractive for many weeks.

A lavender-flowered species, *Monarda fistulosa*, covers the abandoned pastures in limestone areas of New England. It stands drought and competition with the native grasses, making it a good subject for naturalistic meadow planting. A sweet fragrance is evident in the blossoms as well as the foliage. The lovely lavender florets are shorter than those of red Bee Balm. They can be pollinated by bumble bees and large moths, causing them to set seed. In the Southwest, *Monarda fistulosa "menthaefolia"* is collected in the wild for its foliage. When dried it smells and tastes like Oregano and is packaged under that name. The Lemon Bergamot, *Monarda citriodora,* grows in the Appalachian mountain area. Flowers are white, foliage and florets have a distinct lemon scent. It will cross with the lavender species in a garden. Seedling plants may or may not have the citrus overtone. Blossoms may be either lavender or white. All of the Bee Balms tolerate partial shade, but clumps are thicker in full sun.

CULTURE: All three of the Monardas increase by runners which spread out from the original clumps after flowering ends. The stolons benefit from a top dressing of compost after the seed heads are cut back to the ground, before it freezes. It is possible to grow Bee Balm and other species from seed. Sow in soil substitute and keep temperature of the flat between 68° and 86° F. Transplant to pots or a deeper flat when seedlings have 4 true leaves. Put out in the garden after the last frost leaving 12 inches between plantlets. Do not let them dry out for the first month or two. Flowering may begin on the indigenous species late in the same summer that seed is started. The showier *Monarda didyma* does not set seed as readily. Its deep-throated blossoms have few pollinators.

USE: The red florets of Bee Balm have a delightful lemon flavor. Scattered over a green salad they are meant to be eaten. With lemons costing like gold, any of the lemony herbs are a great value. Dried leaves of this Monarda make a pleasant tea, either by themselves or mixed with Mint leaves. Jane Colden, the 18th century botanist, called it "Red Mint" and noted that it grew in the Mohawk's country. She may have learned from them its other familiar name "Oswego Tea". The other species of Monarda described here also add zest to herb tea. During the days before the Boston Tea Party, the patriotic ladies collected wild Mints, Mountain Mints and Monardas to make a good substitute for the imported tea. Today, we collect and dry them by hanging the stems upside down to use for the same purpose. Extra leaves left-over at the end of winter are added to potpourri made of rose petals and scented herb leaves.

BETONY, Woundwort   HARDY PERENNIAL
Stachys officinalis   Zone 4
Labiatae, native to Europe and Asia

HABIT: Betony plants are grown for beauty of their flowers and foliage. Their historic applications of staunching bleeding and healing wounds has been largely forgotton. The hardy perennial plants form rosettes of attractive leaves before the 2½ foot-tall flowers develop. After the spent blossoms are cut off, the clumps rejuvenate with new basal leaves. Flowering period lasts for a month or more in mid-summer. *Stachys officinalis* is the 'official' medicinal plant of old, but to modern gardeners it is a reliable hardy flower with pink or reddish purple blossoms in spikes on tall, leafless stems. Leaves are bright green, heartshaped at the base, heavily veined. Woolly Betony, *Stachys byzantina,* called "Lambs' Ears" or "Lambs' Tongues", has furry, oval leaves. They make a dense mat of silvery white, lying close to the ground. It lasts through the winter as a border plant of interesting foliage where drainage is good. Both species need full sun to thrive. Woolly Betony develops 18 inches tall flower stems in July or earlier. Small purple blossoms are almost hidden by the cottony covering of dense hairs on stems and calyces.

CULTURE: The hardy Betony species are easily grown from seed. Sow in a flat of prepared potting soil or soil substitute, covering seeds slightly. It will germinate at temperatures of 55° at night and 72° daytimes. Future plants may be made from root divisions. Green Betony forms a thick clump of tight roots which have to be lifted to pry apart with a fork. Woolly Betony creeps along with side shoots which are easily lifted and broken up to make new plants in early spring. If seed heads are cut off in late summer, plants can be separated then.

USE: A surprising thing about Woolly Betony is that the flower stems and leaves develop an apple scent when they are dried. Fresh leaves are used in making the natural trimming for a tussie-mussie or nosegay, especially for someone who is blind. Usually used fresh, some people press the flat, furry tongues to surround a dried nosegay. The plant is a delight to children as the texture of leaves appeals to the touch. Usually it is presented with the idea that here was a prototype of a 'band-aid', a plant whose leaves were used to stop bleeding of a cut and also provided the absorbent dressing. To someone who cannot see, the contrasting softness of its leaves along with the more crisp feeling of those of scented Geraniums or the pungent Thymes, adds up to enchantment in hand.

Borage/Borago officinalis

Pimm's Cup with Borage Flower

BORAGE   ANNUAL

Borago officinalis
Boraginaceae, native to Europe

HABIT: Borage is one of the herbs with hairy leaves and rather sprawling habit when in bloom. A whole family of interesting plants takes its name from this herb. It is the species whose name means 'sold in the shops' meaning apothecary shops where medicinal plants, edible and otherwise useful herbs, were dispensed. Other members are the Forget-me-not, Hound's Tongue, Lungwort, Anchusa and Comfrey. A good many have pink and blue flowers. In Borage the buds may be pink opening to skyblue stars encircling a cone of black anthers. Some have pink circles of petals. Stems are succulent, reaching 2 to 3 feet tall, studded with glistening hairs. The foliage and flowers do not have fragrance but develop a cucumber-like flavor.

CULTURE: The seeds of the herb are large enough to plant each one separately. They are sown in ½ inch deep furrows where they are to grow. Cover with finely tilled earth to a depth of twice their size. Seedling leaves are fat and round with a pair of fuzzy true leaves protruding from them. The plant has a tap root, which makes it difficult to transplant when past seedling stage. Seed may be started in a one-step peat pot indoors. It germinates quickly at 60° to 70° but may be grown on at cooler temperatures and put out as soon as heavy frosts are past. Borage self-sows freely to make even larger plants a second year. When flowers fade, ripening seeds drop from the calyces as soon as they turn black. Members of the Borage family are hard to cultivate for seed because of this characteristic. Small volunteer plants may be potted up in autumn to enjoy their cheerful blue blossoms in a window-sill garden.

USE: Borage is considered 'cooling' in its effect in fruit and wine drink. It takes the place of cucumber in salad or in a Pimm's Cup. For such usage, fairly big stems are scraped free of hairs and cut up into lengths to add to salad or steep with gin or wine beverages. Charles Dickens is said to have delighted his Bostonian hosts with his Cider Punch made with Borage. He called it "a European herb used in France for its soothing properties. You'll find it sometimes in French Salads." The drink included 2 wine glasses of Sherry and a wine glass of brandy, stirred with a bottle of cider, and a good handful of Borage. A little boiling water was first poured over a little sugar and lemon peel, left to stand while assembling the potables. John Gerard, in 1597, quoted the motto "I Borage, bring always courage," in his great study of herbs called *The Herball, or General Historie of Plants.* It's fun to know these things and even more fun to candy the blue petals of Borage for cake decorating or dry them in silica gel for placing on a wreath.

Burnet Sour Cream

Salad Burnet/Poterium Sanguisorba

BURNET, SALAD   PERENNIAL
Poterium Sanguisorba   Zone 4
Rosaceae, native to Europe and England

HABIT: Little about Salad Burnet suggests its membership in the Rose family except its picot-edge leaflets. It is a singular plant that makes a tussock of leaves close to the ground. In May of the second year, wiry stems raise thimbles of bloom, about 12 inches above the basal rosette. They have no conspicuous petals, just pink tufts of stigmas with dangling stamens, which are tossed about the flower heads as the wind pollinates the herb. The flowers are interesting but usually are cut off by the gardener who grows it for the cucumber-flavored leaves. Some may be left to produce seed which insures tender young plants for next year. Burnet lives longer in dry soils which are on the sandy side. Rich and moist conditions cause the rosette to rot in winter.

CULTURE: It is another herb which must be started from seed which may be sown in the spring or late autumn whenever the ground can be worked. These odd-looking bare seeds are brown with diamond shaped markings, somewhat rough feeling. They are planted in shallow furrows or scattered over a small area where they are to grow in the herb bed. Cover lightly with soil but do not bury them. In the wild they volunteer where the land is chalky and too poor for lush grass. As a forage crop for quail, Salad Burnet has been planted in the sandy barrens in New Jersey and along the coast of California. Though it has a deep root when mature, the salad herb may be transplanted when young. Seeds started indoors may be put in pellet pots to germinate. Remove the nylon netting when setting them out in the garden after all danger of frost is past. Germination is faster at 70° F. but seed may be planted outside long before such a temperature is reached. Salad Burnet makes an attractive edging for a garden when grown from seed. The second year the plants will not be as pretty if allowed to go to seed so it is just as well to start new ones annually. The basal rosettes spread out to 12 inches across during the growing season so should be spaced that far apart.

HISTORY: Salad Burnet was one of the first herbs to be brought to this country by the colonists. It was thought to protect against infections and reduce the possibility of gout if put in wine or beer. The number of botanical names which it has had show how great was its reputation among herbalists. It has been called *Pimpinella* and *Sanguisorba* but taxonomists have gone back to the older name of *Poterium. Sanguisorba* means to 'soak up', whereas *Poterium* is derived from the Greek word *poterion,* a drinking cup. Mrs. Grieve says this indicates that the herb was added to numerous beverages, mostly wine-derived, in which Salad Burnet was placed.

USE: Fresh young leaves of Salad Burnet, formerly called *Sanguisorba minor,* contribute a nice cucumber savor to green salad. Strip them off the stems to add to the greens. Long before cucumbers are ready, second year Burnet plants are lush and asking for picking. They are best in the spring and fall as, when in flower, the stems get tough and leaves are fewer. Flower buds or seed heads should be cut back to encourage new growth from the crown. A few plants supply more than enough for salad, so use the trimmings for making delicious Burnet Vinegar.

SALAD BURNET VINEGAR

As the herb does not keep its flavor in drying or freezing, it is preserved in vinegar. Gather a handful of Burnet to place in a pint bottle. No need to remove the leaves from the stems. If they are muddy, wash them and pat dry with a towel. A lettuce dryer may be used here. Place the herb in the jar, pour over it enough cider vinegar to cover and to fill the jar. Other vinegars can be used but the cider blends well with the Burnet's delicate cucumber quality. Place the jar or bottle in a sunny window, or outdoors in the sun by day. When it has developed the distinctive aroma and taste, pour off the vinegar. This can take up to two months or two weeks according to the warmth in which the infusion is kept. You can leave the jar as long as you like but a fresh sprig of the herb in a gift bottle is more attractive than the rather sodden mass of leaves to be found in the original container.

SALAD BURNET SOUR CREAM

Chop ½ cup Salad Burnet greens and mix with one pint of sour cream. Refrigerate overnight or longer. Serve as a dip for potato chips or crackers or as a garnish for baked potatoes.

BUTTERFLY WEED   PERENNIAL
Asclepias tuberosa   Zone 4
Asclepiadaceae, native American herb

HABIT: This glorious orange-flowered plant is one of the showiest for late summer bloom in the garden. Unlike common Milkweed, it does not romp about, but has a deep root which does not put out suckers or runners. The difficulty of lifting the root has been the cause of its destruction by foolish attempts to transplant it from the wild. Some parts of the country have Butterfly weed on their protected plant lists. Cutting the 3 foot tall flowers, where it grows wild, reduces the stand because it would self-sow if allowed to produce its pointed pods. These are narrower than the ordinary milkweed and all of the plant has less milky juice. Asclepias needs perfect drainage and full sun to bloom freely.

CULTURE: Fortunately the herb, which the Indians called "Pleurisy Root", is easy to grow from seed. Park's specially selected color strains are the only improvement made on a most ornamental herb. They have come from collecting color variations in the manner that Luther Burbank used for his introductions. The bees and butterflies do the crossing and then a discerning eye chooses the nuances of shades of orange to yellow to collect for further sowing. Seeds may be planted outdoors where the plant is to grow. Fall sowing allows it to keep at optimum degree of moistness until germination begins in the spring. Indoor sowing in sterile soil substitute kept at 65° to 72° F. takes longer than most people want to wait for sprouting. It may be three weeks or a month. Plants grown in peat or pellet pots will not need transplanting if one good seedling per pot is left. They will need at least a foot between mature plants in the garden. Butterfly Weed is the last plant to show in the herb garden. Care must be taken not in injure the crown of the root with cultivating or planting something on top of it in late Spring. Full sun and sandy soil suit it best though it may be found growing and blooming in a piney woods near the shore.

USE: If you grow your own plants it may be possible to indulge in the luxury of using some for cut flowers in a few years. It takes at least 3 years to come into full glory of inflorescence from seed. The use of the root for treating pleurisy, the lung condition that makes breathing difficult, is something only the Indian medicine man was allowed. In the case of a beautiful flower which attracts its own matching monarch butterflies, it would be a foolish sacrifice of a plant for a dubious treatment. The blossoms will dry in silica gel for winter color, but only if you grow your own, should you try that.

Butterfly Weed/Asclepias tuberosa   South African Milkweed/Asclepias physocarpa

SOUTH AFRICAN MILKWEED   ANNUAL OR POT PLANT
Asclepias physocarpa
Asclepiadaceae, native to South Africa

HABIT: A tender herb with intriguingly different milkweed pods, grown as an annual or greenhouse plant in England and the U. S. It makes a shrub in its native land. Flowers are white and not showy but the fruiting bodies are popular with flower arrangers. When floated on water in a crystal bowl they look like green, slight hairy swans. Seed was given to us in 1967 by the late Helen M. Fox who introduced many herbs to collectors in this country. She grew allees of dogwood trees from seed at her home, Foxden. To her, there was nothing so thrilling as discovering a new herb through obtaining seed and growing it.

CULTURE: The species from South Africa was more of a vine than shrubby specimen in our greenhouse. It was quick to germinate at 72° F. in a sterile soil substitute. The wand-like branches with narrow leaves up to five inches long gave no idea of the excitement the seed pods would cause.

USE: George Kalmbacher, taxonomist at the Brooklyn Botanic Garden, took one from our garden in 1967 and described it in a letter. He said the plant is a weed in South Africa. As the pod lay on his desk he saw that it had split down the middle. The lower half is the silk attachment for the seeds, packed into a tail-like mass, shines under fluorescent light like quicksilver. In its native land the shrub is used for intestinal troubles in children or as a remedy for colds. The powdered leaves were dried for snuff. W. G. MacKenzie of the Chelsea Physic Garden in London, liked the herb for its pods launched on water in a crystal bowl set over a mirror for a centerpiece.

CALENDULA, POT MARIGOLD   ANNUAL
Calendula officinalis
Compositae, native to Europe

HABIT: The single and double flowered forms of the herb were known to gardeners and apothecaries in 16th century England. John Gerard, in 1597, described the way in which some forms of the plant with fat buds opened to form small blossoms growing out of larger ones. He said that vulgar sort of women called it *Jacke-an-apes-a-horsebacke.* The hardiness of the herb and long season of bloom make it valuable to gardeners today. Leaves are spatulate with a rib down the middle and more or less clasp the stalks. Eighteen-inch tall blooms have butter yellow to orange rays up to 3 inches across in overlapping layers. The center disk flowers are almost obscured by them. The blossoms close at night or on dark days, opening to the sun again each day. The buds and leaves have a glandular stickiness but the petals are smooth with a slight notch at the tip.

Pot Marigold/Calendula officinalis

Martha Ann's Marigold Buns

CULTURE: Calendula was called Pot Marigold because it was grown in cool greenhouses to bloom in winter. Some plants may be dug from the garden and kept on a glassed-in porch or bay window to continue flowering most of the winter. Better still, start seed in July for more shapely specimens to pot up. The seeds are rounded and curled at the edges. They may be started indoors at 55° to 68° F. in peat pots or pellet starters to be set in the garden as soon as the ground is worked. In the South, it is a plant for fall sowing as snow does not daunt it, if it comes up early in the spring. Hot weather is inimical to it. Heat if accompanied by drought causes the plants to sprawl and attract aphids. Seeds should be planted either in a flat or pot or in a shallow furrow in the garden. Seedlings transplant readily and often volunteer where last summer's spent blooms have ripened on the plant. Calendula needs 12 to 18 inches between mature plants in full sun. The flowers are not discouraged by partial shade which may help to keep them cool. Always connected with the sun, Calendula is the perfect plant for the solar home. Ill-fated Charles I, wrote in his diary when England turned against him, "The marigold observes the sun/more than my subjects me have done." The Latin name refers to its blossoming on the first day of every month, which actually happens in England.

USE: The petals of Pot Marigold may be used fresh or dried to give color to soups and custards. It could take the place of rare and expensive Saffron for giving a yellow hue to rice. The flowers were even taken off the heads and put in vinegar to have their salubrious effects in salad. White vinegar would be used to preserve them in pickling. A salve made from the flowers of the herb was used in the Civil War for treating wounds. It is still available for external use. A better way to enjoy the flowers that need picking anyway is to use the petals in a British type of tea cookie called

MARTHA ANN'S MARIGOLD BUNS

½ cup sugar	2 eggs, beaten
½ cup butter	2 cups flour
2½ teaspoons baking powder	¼ teaspoon salt

Petals from 2 or 3 fresh Calendula blossoms, not Mexican or French Marigold petals or *Tagetes*. Pour boiling water over petals in a strainer to remove any minute bugs. Cream sugar and butter; add the beaten eggs, Marigold petals and dry ingredients. beat to distribute petals throughout the dough. They give a good color and delicate flavor which may be enhanced by ½ teaspoon Vanilla extract. Drop dough by tablespoonfuls onto a greased cookie sheet. Bake at 350° F. for 10 minutes or till lightly browned but not hard. If cookies are to be used immediately, a whole blueberry may be put on top of each one before baking. They may be stored in a tin box when cool, if the berries are not put on top. Makes 2 dozen soft cookies or buns. Where blueberries, which contrast with the flecks of orange in the buns, are added, keep in freezer.

Caper Bush/Capparis spinosa

CAPER BUSH   TENDER PERENNIAL
Capparis spinosa
Capparaceae, native to dry Mediterranean regions

HABIT: Caper plant is not hardy in the north but may be grown from seed as an annual. Leaves are round with a notch in the middle of the outer edge. They may be up to 3 inches in diameter on spiny stems which spread out along the ground. Showy 2 to 3 inch wide yellowish white flowers are long stalked with many anthers. The garden flower Cleome is closely related to the Caper Bush. The seeds form berry-like pods but it is the unopened flower buds which are picked to make pickled capers. It must be quite a job to gather them from the prickly plant which grows along the Mediterranean and other sandy shores in warm places around the world.

CULTURE: When growing Caper for the garden, it is well to remember that the plant is tender. Its companion plants in its native area are the Rosemary and Marjorams of the Greek islands such as Crete. This gives a clue as to the plant's need for good drainage and dry soil. Keeping Caper Bush plants in pots in the North means bringing them into the greenhouse in winter. The buds may not develop the first summer. Seeds may be started in peat or pellet pots kept at 65° to 75° F. Cuttings also need bottom heat at that temperature. Compost of two parts turfy loam, one part leaf-mold and sand will give the proper drainage for potting up the Caper Bush. It may be planted outdoors in summer but if desired to carry over in the greenhouse, sink the pot in the earth rather than putting roots directly in the garden. Water should be only moderate in winter indoors, or even out, where temperatures do not go below 40° to 50° F. Free watering in the spring may be resumed as temperatures rise to 65° F. In the south of England the plant will endure winters in a sheltered position. In the Mediterranean region, rains come in the autumn, but for pot culture the spring and summer is the time the plants put on more growth and need watering.

USE: Your own Caper Bush would be quite a curiosity to other herb gardeners. If you take the buds for pickling for use in Tartar Sauce you will miss the large and pretty flowers. Better to buy the bottled Capers and keep your plants intact.

Caraway/Carum Carvi

Caraway/Carum Carvi

CARAWAY   BIENNIAL
Carum Carvi,   Zone 4
Umbelliferae, native to Europe, naturalized in parts of N.E. U. S.

HABIT: Much cut leaves resemble those of carrot but are glossier. Caraway remains a basal rosette the first season unless planted in early autumn outdoors. Then it will winter over. At the first spell of heat in the spring a blossom stalk begins to form. It develops 2 foot tall umbels of white flowers, attractive in the herb garden for more than two weeks. The deep tap root enables Caraway to hold up its fruiting heads without support from strings or brush. Seed is half-moon shaped.

CULTURE: Sow seed in shallow drills as early in the spring as possible. Thin seedlings to 6 to 8 inches apart and keep weeded but undisturbed for bloom the following spring. Caraway needs full sun and good drainage. To shorten time to cropping try a late summer planting of seeds. It is possible to start Caraway indoors in peat or pellet pots. They are set out in the garden with some of the peat torn away or the nylon netting peeled away to allow the root to go down. Sowing in place is preferable, but if Caraway must be sold as plants or moved to another place, this is one way to do it.

HARVEST: As Caraway seeds are the main harvest, it is an herb to grow for the flowers. The foliage has a slight bit of the unique flavor that is Caraway's but cutting them will weaken the plant. When seeds are brown, test for ripeness by gently pulling a few from the largest umbel. If most are ready to go without tugging, cut off the whole plant. Turn upside down in a large paper bag. When dry, seeds will fall to the bottom as the bag is rolled between your hands. Spread them out on a screen or box in the sun. Look for any insects among the seeds. If in doubt about their presence, pour boiling water over the seeds held in a strainer. Spread out again daytimes to dry for 2 or 3 days in the sun. Watch for any moisture which may appear in the air-tight jar in which you put them before storing them in a cupboard. The seeds should be dry enough to separate upon shaking the jar. Any webs or musty smell means weevils so throw away. Caraway is worth growing for its beauty in the garden. Seeds are low enough in price to buy as needed for cooking. They are harvested by machine where grown for the trade.

USE: Caraway, the plant, gives its name to a liqueur. *Kummel* is German for Caraway and the name of the cordial. The flavor of Caraway has few imitations in the plant world. Some parts of the oil contain similar fractions found in oils of Dill and Cumin but they cannot be mistaken for Caraway in flavor or scent. It takes 6 pounds of the seeds, which are small, to produce 4 ounces of essential oil. Though it grows wild in Europe and could be grown in many countries, the seed which comes from northern climates is considered strong in flavor. Full sun increases the strength of the oil as the plant grows. Caraway is best known today for its use in baking; cookies, breads and cheeses take the flavor well. It was considered an aid to digestion, so sugar-coated Caraway comfits were eaten as peppermints are today. Caraway cooked with cabbage modifies the mustardy odor it gives off in cooking. It also adds a delightful nuance of flavor to Bob Yndra's—

62

Stewed Bills with Caraway   Castor Bean/Ricinus communis

STEWED BILLS

One small head of cabbage, shredded
One can whole stewed tomatoes
1 tablespoon Caraway seeds
Cook the above three ingredients in a large saucepan for 30 minutes until cabbage is tender.
Slice and fry one medium onion. Add to cabbage mixture. Clean the frying pan and put 3 tablespoons butter in pan over heat. Add 2 tablespoons all-purpose flour. Stir it until it becomes a tan-colored roux. Then, using a little of the liquid from the pot to thin roux, pour it into the cabbage. Add a little freshly ground pepper. Heat through for 15 minutes on low heat.

HISTORY: Where Caraway grows wild on the continent, it has been a pot-herb of choice. The tender leaves are gathered to put into soup in the spring. Well enough, if you have a lot of plants, as in Maine where it has become naturalized. But to eat the roots in preference to parsnips, as John Parkinson did in 1629, means sacrificing flowers and seeds. Saucers of Caraway seeds were placed among the tea things in Shakespeare's day. They still are on special occasions in London. The Scottish custom is to dip the buttered side of bread into the dish of seeds. Mrs. Grieve who described the use of Caraway, said it was called *Salt water jelly,* when eaten this way.

CASTOR BEAN   ANNUAL
Ricinus communis
Euphorbiaceae, native to Tropical Africa

HABIT: It is a surprise to a Northerner to see Castor Bean plants growing as perennials in Florida and California. It shouldn't be really because the well-known Euphorbia, Poinsettia, is also a shrub in Zones 8-10. As an annual, Castor grows quickly to make a stunning screen for a part of the yard or between properties. Leaves on long stems are three feet broad. They are divided into segments palmately. Flowers are close to the stems and separate as male with yellow stamens and female with red stigmas. The stout stem may reach 10 feet in one summer where it is really hot and moist. Leaves are reddish and provide shade above smaller plants. The Castor Beans are the seeds which grow in prickly fruits, each containing 3 mottled beans. It is the poisonous nature of the seeds which must be made known to the grower. Just one bite to break the integument can cause death because there is no antidote for the toxic nature of the bean. Yet, this is the plant which furnishes the castor oil of hospital fame. The oil is safely used as a cathartic but the seed is put in mole runs to discourage the diggers of lawn and garden. Flowers should be removed before they form seeds if children are likely to be anywhere near the plants.

Castor Bean/Ricinus communis   Catmint/Nepeta Mussini

CULTURE: Sow seeds where plants are to grow, as soon as the ground is thoroughly warm. Thin seedlings to stand 3 feet apart. The new peat or pellet pots are a help in starting these large seeded plants because the roots will soon fill the contents of the container. They also will be strong enough to permit peeling the peat sides of the pot or the nylon netting on the pellet before planting. There are now new 'one-step' compressed seed starter cubes which may be placed in the garden without any consideration of whether the edges of the peat pot may dry out or the roots be confined by nylon netting. It takes 2 to 3 weeks for Caster Bean seeds to sprout indoors at 75°-80° degrees and outdoors about the same. Do not slice at the bean or otherwise prick it to hasten germination. The inner substance is highly poisonous (if it should be carried by hand to mouth).

USE: How then, one wonders, can the oil be safe? The oil is given a cold process of extraction when it is for medicinal use. If the seeds are heated, as when the oil is intended for industrial use, as in washing powders which are biodegradable, or for airplane engines, then some of the poisonous substances may enter into it. The oil has a low freezing point so may be used in jet engines. The Castor Bean is an interesting example of a plant with medicinal uses if safely treated and important commercial uses which have made it a valuable economic crop worldwide.

CATMINT   PERENNIAL
Nepeta Mussinii   Zone 4
Labiatae, native to the Caucasus and Iran

HABIT: If you take the leaves of three Nepeta species, put them in a vase and look at them to see how they differ, it's hard to say which is which. The way they look in the garden is always a matter of comment in the case of *Nepeta Mussinii* and *Nepeta x Fassenii.* The first is a low-growing, early-blooming plant that does not exceed 12 to 15 inches in height. Leaves are soft to the touch, with rounded tips and not much indentation of margins. The blue to purple blossom is spotted with dark purple on the lower lip which is slightly ruffled at the edge. Many flowers cover the grayish looking plant for a month in the spring and a few more bloom in autumn. It is a splendid edging herb because the strong Nepeta scent deters pests and attracts bees. The natural hybrid *N. x Fassenii* is taller with 18-24 inch upright growth and larger leaves, conspicuously indented. They are farther apart on the stems which are noticeably hoary giving a whitish look at the ends of the stems. Flowers are larger, more blue-violet, with stems long enough for use in bouquets. This species is sterile so cannot be grown from seed. It has dense roots which may be sliced apart to make new plants in the spring before flowering or in late summer. Both plants are drought-resistant and long-lived with many garden attributes of blossom and foliage.

Catnip/Nepeta Cataria   Catnip/Nepeta Cataria

CULTURE: Catmint is easily grown from seed. It may be started indoors 6 to 8 weeks before the last frost. The soil medium should be 60°-70° F. Pellet pots are useful to start seeds which germinates in a week to 10 days. Remove the nylon netting when placing it in the garden, 12 inches apart. Nepetas need good drainage but will adapt to almost any soil and grow in partial shade. They are not as full of lovely color where the light is lower but they are useful edging and very aromatic. In England, hedges of *Nepeta x Fassenii* are sometimes mistaken for Lavender in bloom. Both species develop woody stems towards the end of summer. These must be removed in the spring before the flower buds start up from the basal rosette. Cutting back the spent flower heads encourages a second blossoming of *Nepeta Mussinii.*

USE: The horticultural species of Nepeta have their usefulness in the oils of the plant. It has been proven to be inimical to ants and other insects. *Nepeta Mussini* is not the great attractant to cats that Catnip, *Nepeta Cataria* is noted for being. The flowers provide an early blue in the low-growing species and a long summer blue-lavender in the taller hybrid.

CATNIP   PERENNIAL
Nepeta Cataria   Zone 4
Labiatae, native to Europe, Asia, naturalized in U. S.

HABIT: It is hard for one living in a limestone area of New England to think of the difficulty some people have in getting common Catnip or Catnep going. The grayish plant with heart-shaped leaves up to 1½-2 inches long with rounded, toothed edges self-sows freely with us. It is found in old pastures or anywhere there has been habitation in the area. Spikes of white flowers keep forming all summer. They are not conspicuous and are somewhat hidden by leaflets along the flower stems. The plant changes appearance from a dense clump of soft green foliage to a rather sparse looking 3 foot tall plant when in bloom. If cut back severely for collection of herbage to be dried for Catnip too late in the fall, plants may die out in winter. It sometimes acts as a biennial. To keep it truly perennial the collecting should be done while there is more leafage than blossom.

CULTURE: One of the easiest herbs to grow from seed, Catnip produces many volunteers once a plant has become established. The only way to grow it is from seed started in a flat indoors at 60°-70° temperature or sown outdoors in a shallow furrow with little soil covering, early in the spring. Either way germination should take place in a week to 10 days. The finest looking plants are those which grow in full sun spaced 18 inches apart. However, Catnip chooses its own site in shade, under a bush or anywhere the seed has found a fertile toe-hold. In limy soils it can be considered a weed if you have no particular use for it. Those who say cats rub it out of their gardens, (this happens even at the Brooklyn Botanic Garden,) had better heed the old instructions of William Coles, 1657 - in *The Art of Simpling* -

"If you set it, the Catts will eat it,
"If you sow it, the Catts can't know it."

It is true that cats may pass right by an undisturbed plant of Catnip but if the scent is released by their passage, they will catch the aroma and start to roll on it, chew it or otherwise have an orgy.

USE: The curious effects of the herb have not been explained by science. Cats are stimulated by the oil of Catnip while women are soothed by Catnip tea made from dried leaves. At Cornell University tests of the essential oil, a terpene called *nepetalactone* showed that its vapors caused insects to turn away. Gardeners have found that steeping fresh Catnip in water and using the infusion to sprinkle plants will dispel flea beetles. If applied frequently the Catnip water will discourage ants and other insects in the garden. For dried Catnip, to stuff toys for kitties or make tea for ladies, collect the leaves and stems, hang up in bags to dry and strip from stems later. Do not leave sharp bits of stem in Catnip to be used for cat tonic lest they cause choking.

CHAMOMILE ANNUAL   ANNUAL
Matricaria recutita
Compositae, native to Europe and West Asia

HABIT: The two Chamomiles known to herb gardeners for use in tea and sweet scented mixtures have had name changes. The annual, formerly called "German" Chamomile has not changed its nature, just its botanical name. It was *Matricaria Chamomilla,* but is now *M. recutita* in *Hortus Third.* We have found no definition of *recutita* as a species name but we can recognize the slim annual by its tall heads of flowers, 2-2½ feet high. They have yellow centers which are conical and hollow in the middle, if sliced through to see, with white rays (petals) spaced a bit apart around them. The leaves are linear and almost disappear as the plant blooms. It is the sweet apple scent which distinguishes them, also that translates into pleasant tisane (tea) when the herb is dried. The perennial Chamomile has a very bitter taste, which suggests it must be good for you.

CULTURE: The seeds may be started where plants are to grow for best herbage. If they are planted indoors the temperature should be between 55° and 60° F. Pellet pots holding 2 seeds will help to reduce the problem of transplanting the slight seedlings. Be sure to remove the netting before placing them in the garden 4 to 6 inches apart. Scattering a packet of seed on well prepared soil with just a dusting of sifted sand or sandy soil will get the annual herb off to a good start right in the garden as early in the spring as possible. It is an herb which runs to flower and seed in hot weather. If allowed to flower without cutting all the seed heads, annual Chamomile will self-sow in sandy soil. The seedlings can be picked up and put in place if detected when they have about 4 true leaves. Later they do not stand moving.

USE: The uses of the two Chamomiles do not differ too much. If you cut the foliage of the annual, you will get no flowers. The flowers of both are dried just as the petals begin to turn back and the golden color of the centers browns. They are cut as nearly as possible without stems and laid on paper or screen in the sun to dry. If, within an hour or so when the heads are stirred, small insects also stir, take the whole mass up. Put it in a colander and pour boiling water over it. Then drain and return to the sun. That day, take the trouble to turn the blossoms so that they dry off. Putting the heads in paper bags to dry may compound the problem of insects that infest the heads. Chamomile is noted for its sleep inducing effects when used as a tea. It also soothes indigestion and fretfulness in man, woman, and child. But anyone allergic to ragweed or other members of the Composite family should avoid Chamomile tea.

Chamomile/Chamamaemelum nobile

C. Matricaria recutita

CHAMOMILE, PERENNIAL
Chamaemelum nobile
Compositae, native to Europe

PERENNIAL
Zones 3-4

HABIT: Old friend Roman Chamomile, which was called *Anthemis nobilis,* remains a delightful spreading plant with bright green, rather curly foliage. It may be grown from seed and has been used for lawns and seats in England. The idea has charm but it also entails having the proper microclimate and, in the case of the lawn, patience to weed it, especially the first year. Perennial Chamomile is not strong enough to fight competition unless it is growing at its best. It is discouraged from flowering the first year, by clipping, to enable it to sprawl. Height is about 6 inches. Blossoms may be 12-18 inches on single, leafless stems. They may or may not have petals, or rays as they are called. They require sun and good drainage. Soil should be slightly acid which can be achieved by covering the Chamomile patch with pine needles as winter protection. They are lifted off in the spring and replaced when the ground freezes. This dream of lawn and seat of sweet smelling tufted Chamomile is one for the English climate or, possibly, our Northwest where there is moisture and little drought. Even at the Royal Horticultural Society's great garden called Wisley, the Chamomile lawn has been worn out where there is constant foot traffic. At the Queen's Garden at Kew, the Chamomile cushioned seat had to have wire laid on it after the first summer. People sat, but also picked at bits of root upon rising, because the air was sweet of Chamomile. There is a form which does not flower, called "Treanague", from the estate where it originated. Double flowered Chamomile is a choice garden plant but seed is very scarce.

CULTURE: Often seed of Chamomile turns out to be the annual which grows faster and sets more seed than the perennial. Experiences with starting seed, in sphagnum moss, or soil subtitute over potting soil, differ in temperature and time. The plant seems to need cooler conditions than most for germination, 55°-65° F. suit it well indoors. Other Anthemis species have germinated at 68°-86° in a seed testing laboratory. Perennial Chamomile self-sows in our garden which never attains such high temperatures until mid-summer. Seedlings are picked up to replace the Chamomile patch much earlier than that in the spring. The low-growing perennial transplants easily when young. Old plants develop a deep root system and spread widely. If lifted, there is a tug of war with the roots as the side shoots do not root down. Flowers may be enjoyed the second year till they begin to lose petals or go off the bright gold color. Cut off stems close to the Chamomile carpet and dry flower heads trimmed from them. Watch for insects as the yellow buttons are spread out in the sun to dry.

USE: The best use for dried Chamomile flowers of the perennial form is as blonde hair rinse made by boiling up the dried heads in water, cooling and straining for use.

Chervil Butter

Chervil/Anthriscus Cerefolium

CHERVIL   HARDY ANNUAL
Anthriscus Cerefolium
Umbelliferae, native to southeast Europe, Caucusus, W. Asia

HABIT: Chervil's lacy leaves are finely dissected. The color is lighter green than that of Parsley, the whole growth more delicate. It is the leaves which are used in flavoring. The plants run to seed quickly in hot weather rendering them useless for mincing and adding to dishes or herb butter. They have a delicious Anise-overtone in flavor. Often substituted for French Tarragon, which cannot be grown from seed, Chervil makes a hardy over-winter crop if seed is planted in late summer. The seeds look like black splinters, have a short storage life and germinate readily where plants are to grow or self-sow under matured ones gone to seed. The root is slight, resents transplanting but supports a foot-wide rosette of the choice leaves through the winter if autumn planted. Flowers are white on 1½-2 foot stems, umbels are restricted but numerous, when well-grown. Soil and temperature has a great effect on Chervil. In poor soil, baked in the sun, plantlets will struggle up to seed in 6 to 8 weeks. The leaves blanch in the sun. A cool, compost soil in partial shade suits it best.

CULTURE: Sow seed in late summer where plants are to grow. Cover lightly and thin seedlings to 12 inches apart. This can be delayed till two sets of true leaves form so that the thinnings can be added to the Fines Herbes that flavor French Omelette. The herb is a great favorite of French chefs. It's possible to have pots of Chervil in a cool room in the house all winter if started in August. The need for light is not as great as in other culinary herbs. It is one for the shade garden, as is Sweet Cicely, which has much the same flavor in leaves more fern-like and fuzzier. Peat or pellet pots work well with Chervil. The 55° F. material promotes growth and with removal of the peat walls or nylon netting, the plantlets can be set right in a larger container with 1/3 compost, 1/3 loam and 1/3 sand. Or plant out in the garden as early as the ground can be worked. To treat Chervil as a biennial, let seed form on some plants. They will survive the winter, storing up strength in the root for a really good harvest of foliage in the spring.

USE: Chervil does not retain its flavor in drying. Making cubes of the foliage by whirling 1 cup of leaves with 1½ cups water in a blender and then freezing it in ice cube trays preserves the fresh taste. These are packed in containers, labeled and stored in the deep freeze. For Fines Herbes, freeze Chervil, Chives and Sweet Marjoram in a small container to chop while frozen when making omelette. Chervil butter is made by mincing 2 or 3 tablespoons of fresh leaves. Cream the 2 sticks of butter or margarine; blend in the minced herb. Let sit for an hour or two before spreading on crackers; broiled fish just out of the oven, or hot biscuits or bread.

Chicory/Cichorium Intybus

Chicory/Cichorium Endivia

CHICORY
Cichorium Intybus
Compositae, native to the Mediterranean

HABIT: The cheerful Chicory which gazes at us with blue eyes in early morning and goes to sleep by noon along the road-sides may have arrived as a stowaway in grain or hay that came with the Pilgrims. It also escaped from gardens where it was well-fed for the fat roots. From the ground to the leaf-clasped stems, to the blossoms, which were placed in floral clocks for their dependable timing, the herb has been beloved by man. We seldom think of the wild herb as being the same species as the expensive 'Endive' or "chicons" which appear in the market as pale, pointed, slightly bitter but delicious salad makings. John Parkinson in 1629 understood the differences between it and the Curly Chicory, *Cichorium Endivia* which forms broad heads of crisped or widely ruffled leaves.

> *"I put both Succorie and Endive into one chapter and description . . . They are both of one kindred; and although they do differ a little . . . yet they agree both in this, that they are eaten eyther green or whited of many."*

CULTURE: Both Chicory (also called "Succory") and Escarole, the broad-leaved salad plant, thrive in cool weather. At times in winter they are the most thrifty buy in greens. The forced roots that make Belgian Endive or "chicons" are costly because the plant has been grown all summer for strengthening the root; flower stalks cut off and roots dug before the ground freezes. They are dried and laid down in a root cellar in sand. Then, as needed, they are put in a forcing box. The growing ends stand up in a moist mixture of peat and sand in a large flower pot or packing box. The growing mixture must cover the tops which are then kept moist but dark for three or four weeks at 50° F. to produce the folded buds. They may be snapped off, recovered and possibly produce a second crop. Too much heat will bring them on faster but with less success. Light should be kept from roots and shoots or they will turn greenish and bitter. Seed of Chicory is planted in furrows in the garden in early spring. Soil should be rich, well-spaded and kept free of weeds. A sowing of *C. Intybus* in spring, followed by a planting *C. Endivia* in July, will insure greens for a long season. The Succory grown for roots to dry as a coffee additive can stand closer than the heads to be picked for salad. The latter should be thinned to a foot apart. Crowded plants will not head up. More than twenty kinds of cultivated Chicories have been developed in Italy. A custom of gathering the greens of the wild Chicory, to be soaked, chopped and cooked in the water clinging to the leaves, as with Dandelions, persists there.

USE: Chicory had a reputation as a medicinal herb. The flowers were distilled to make a water that was considered soothing to the eyes. They were also candied, along with Violet blossoms to

69

Chicory—Witloof

Chives/Allium Schoenoprasum

make decoration for cakes. But too much Chicory was warned against as causing loss of visual power in the retina of the eye. Something of the homeopathic wisdom, that a little may cure but a lot may cause the trouble or some other disease. The leaves have been used to produce a blue dye, according to Mrs. Grieve. It is for coffee flavoring that Chicory is still widely used today. The cultivar 'Magdeburg' is sold for growing the root to dry for ground Chicory. Seed is planted in June in the North. If started earlier, the plants run to seed in hot weather and that reduces the quality of the root. In late fall the roots are dug, or pulled, and scrubbed. Some people put them through a slicer before spreading the cut roots out for drying. This makes it possible to bring them to the brittle stage in one day in an electric food drier. Spreading them in the sun, as for seed herbs, requires constant turning and bringing indoors at any turn of weather towards dampness or humidity.

After the Chicory roots are dried to snap easily, they must be roasted. This is done in a slow 300°-325° F. oven. The moisture has to escape but heat needs to be constant. It is a process that requires constant attention. Slight scorching to look like cocoa powder enhances the flavor. One herb grower, uses smallish pieces that have been roasted to almost black in her coffee grinder, just as she does coffee beans. A teaspoon of Chicory to a quarter cup of ground coffee suits her taste. She finds it cuts the amount of coffee she uses in half and makes a drink comparable to decaffeinated coffee, thus cutting costs too.

The salad green Chicory is blanched by gathering the outer leaves together over the crown and tying them with twist-ems or rubber bands several weeks before harvest. If the plants get wet in that time, they must be opened and allowed to dry off before tying up again. They can rot if sodden while the leaves are constricted. There is also a warning in *A Modern Herbal* that eating Chicory in excess can cause congestion of the blood in the digestive organs. But when boiled in broth it helped 'those that have hot, weak and feeble stomachs . . .' Today there is a popular soup brand which has Escarole (the Italian name for salad Chicory) in its chicken broth.

CHIVES   PERENNIAL
Allium Schoenoprasum   Zone 3
Amaryllidaceae, native to Europe and Asia

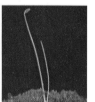

HABIT: This familiar seasoning herb with round spears of onion-flavored leaves is grown for its foliage and flowers. The tightly clustered bulbous roots are not used, so it grows into ever larger clumps. There are several forms of Chives. One has fatter leaves, more than the usual 12 inches in height. It is one of the herbs that Luther Burbank improved by natural selection. Bees visit Chive blossoms, causing them to set seed plentifully. Under the right conditions, the herb will self-sow. The roundish purple heads of bloom consist of many individual florets. The whole inflorescence has several uses. If Chives for the kitchen are sheared straight across, the gardener misses the beauty of the spring flowering. There is a small-leaved form with flowers no taller than the thin spears; one with white flowers and one with pink. All have the lovely onion scent which spurs the appetite.

Making Chive Blossom Vinegar   *Cutting Chives to Dry*

CULTURE: Sow seeds indoors 6 to 8 weeks before the last frost. They will sprout in 10 days to 2 weeks at temperatures of 60°-70° F. Plant in potting soil in a deep container such as a flat or pot. Cover with soil enough to hide the black seeds. Seedlings may be set out in clusters rather than transplanting thin spears, one by one. Plant seeds in furrows in the garden or broadcast them where the plants are to grow into typical Chive clumps. All members of the Onion family benefit from full sun and rich soil. Chives will survive in partial shade but do not grow as fully erect. If you don't want to do anything with the blossoms, then the shy flowering, without full sun, is not a detriment. Clumps will last 4 or 5 years, then should be taken up and divided if grass gets through the root cluster, or to help avoid root maggots. It does not work to pot up plants to bring into the house for winter. The leaves begin to die down in the heat of summer. If clumps are fed after the flowers are cut back, they will send up new spears in autumn. However, the roots need to rest before another growing season. Where the ground freezes they enter dormancy to store up for new growth. Potted Chives lifted from the garden should be sunk in the ground for 3 or 4 months to be chilled before bringing indoors in a January thaw or February mild spell. Popping them into the below-zero freezer is not the same as nature's gradual cooling. It might kill the bulbs or dry them out. It's more satisfactory to sow a second lot of seed in pots in late summer. The young plants will afford some harvest in the window garden in 2 or 3 months. They in turn may be put in the garden in the spring. The forced plants found in markets in late winter will grow on for years in the garden if they are watered and fed with liquid fertilizer after being set out. Of course, if they are cut off straight across they will have no leaves to help the plant recover. The plant is under enough stress indoors without bobbing it all at once.

USE: Chives not only look terrible when reduced to stubble by cutting but they lose their means to manufacture food for the roots. The leaves are vital for photosynthesis. Select a few outer hollow leaves to cut right down to the base. You can have leaves and flowers, too, this way. Single florets of Chives are pretty and delicious when scattered in a green salad. The older heads, just as they finish the first flush of bloom and begin to get a rosy color, make beautiful Chive vinegar. The flowers also dry well, at this stage, for winter bouquets and wreath decorations. Cut the stems down as far as possible for dried flowers. Put heads in large brown paper bag. Leave the mouth of the bag open to let the onion smell evaporate. Do not tie the stems in bunches lest they rot instead of drying.

CHIVE BLOSSOM VINEGAR

Place mature flower heads of Chives, which have not started to fade in color, in a glass bottle or jar. Do not pack them down, but fill loosely, leaving room for the white vinegar to completely cover each set of small blossoms. Make sure that all are surrounded with the acid liquid. Cap and set in the sun on a window sill. The delicate pink color will soon appear in the liquid. In a week or two the blossoms will have transferred their rosy glow to the vinegar. Strain it off and dilute with more white vinegar if you find the flavor too strong. Herb vinegars are the most popular of gifts or sales items at a bazaar or food sale. Saving pretty bottles from liqueurs or wine and putting sealing wax over the corks gives them an added air of elegance.

Garlic Chives/Allium tuberosum   *Garlic Chives/Allium tuberosum*

DRYING CHIVES

For many years we thought Chives could not be dried successfully. When the late Pat Winter, of the first stylish herb packaging firm, proved it coule be done, we and other herb gardeners found it did not require special equipment. The trick is to snip the fresh leaves as you would for use in salad or omelet. Spread the cut leaves on a nylon mesh drier or fine screen. Place them in a warm situation, out of bright light and stir them regularly for several days. The whole house may develop a rich onion aroma if you use the guest room but it soon dissipates. The dried green herb is colorful and some people find it a way to enjoy the flavor of onions without digestive upsets. Dried Chives are much to be preferred to Onion salt or Garlic salt or powdered Garlic. They are also an unusual gift from the garden.

CHIVES, GARLIC	PERENNIAL
Allium tuberosum	Zone 3

Amaryllidaceae, native to East Asia

HABIT: It is a curious thing that many of the garlic-scented Alliums have flat, rather than round leaves. That is one of the distinguishing features about Garlic Chives. The relationship to Chives lies in the fact that it is the leaves and flower heads that are used, rather than the roots. The bulbs come in sets of three small ones attached to a rhizome. Thus they grow horizontally rather than forming rounded clumps of roots. The leaves are a quarter inch wide, shorter than the 12 to 18 inch flower stem which bears many flowered umbels of white, star-like blossoms. The flowers have a sweet scent which does not suggest the garlic strength of the cut leaves. Later green knobs of seed pods form on the scape. They have a culinary use, as does the almost evergreen foliage. The plant self-sows if the heads, which turn an attractive tissue papery color, are allowed to remain on long enough to drop their seeds.

CULTURE: A most obliging plant, Garlic Chives will grow almost anywhere. In Japan, it is called "Nira". Sow seed as for regular Chives. But seedlings should be set out individually because they will form a clump more quickly than ordinary Chives. Seedlings that volunteer in the garden may be lifted for pot growing. Garlic Chives is more satisfactory as a window herb because it does not die down or go into dormancy. Sometimes called "Chinese Chives", *Allium tuberosum* has its origin in the Orient. Plants should be placed at least a foot apart. They will bloom in late summer the first year. The flowers are so attractive that it is a pity to cut off all the leaves for seasoning. The blossoms cause comment in the garden as they are seldom suspected of being members of the Onion tribe. The species of Chives properly called "Chinese Chives" is *Allium Bakeri,* with thin, rounded leaves, tender roots, grown mostly in California. Garlic Chives are hardy and easily divided by pulling apart the rhizomatous roots.

Sweet Cicely/Myrrhis odorata   Sweet Cicely/Myrrhis odorata

USE: Leaves are snipped into salad; added to soup, or sauces, either whole, to be removed before serving, or cut up. They would probably dry as Chives do, but being almost evergreen we haven't had the need to try it. The herb is really a fine landscape plant for its capacity to hold soil on banks and provide a glorious flowering time from August through September in the North. Unless the foliage is disturbed, its secret aroma is not noticeable above the fragrance of the blossoms. The green seed heads make fine Garlic Vinegar. They are put in wine cider or malt vinegar, without breaking up the heads. No Garlic to peel, no struggling to mash the cloves with salt to make the vinegar less likely to be detected on one's breath. Garlic Chives do it all, without bother. Their only drawback may be too much self-seeding but off with their heads if they do.

CICELY, SWEET   PERENNIAL
Myrrhis odorata   Zone 3
Umbelliferae, native to Europe

HABIT: Sweet Cicely is a plant for the North. It is hardy and deep-rooted with all the appearance of a fern, but softer foliage, finely segmented, resembling a much enlarged Chervil. The plant has been called giant Chervil and used in the same way for its Anise-scented leaves and green fruits of strong Anise flavor. If it were not an herb it might be in every shade garden for its beautiful white flowers in May which form dense umbels held above the 2 foot tall foliage on branching stems. When the seeds form, some of the leaves begin to yellow. While pointed fruits, with conspicuous ribs, are still green they are soft enough to chew on, somewhat like licorice candy, which is so often flavored with Anise oil. If a little boiling water is poured over them, they can give a good imitation of Anise seed infusion. Later the pairs of seeds, attached to the spokes of the umbels at their tips, hang loosely and drop to the earth. There the long germination period begins to take place. Sometimes it takes a whole winter and spring to bring the seed of Cicely to sprouting. Which is probably the reason the plant is not among the shade-loving perennials at nurseries. The root goes down a foot or more and is difficult to transplant. Seedlings are the only means of distribution of the plant at any reasonable size. The herb is a handsome one for foundation planting. It will stand northern exposure and poor soil but yellows and withers in bright sun and summer heat. The fresh leaves that come out from the root after the flower stalks are cut back give the plants a new look through the autumn.

CULTURE: Sweet Cicely was one of the most difficult herbs to grow in heavy clay soil in our first herb plantings in northern New Jersey. We didn't realize at the time that it had best be treated as a woods plant, with humus around the roots and a ready place for the seeds to fall. We sent seeds to the Boyce Thompson Institute for testing. They were able to hasten the germination time to two or three months by cooling the seeds in a moist medium at 40°, before bringing them into the greenhouse. Precooled seeds germinate twice as well as those not cooled, as for

73

Blue Comfrey /Symphytum caucasicum   Russian Comfrey /Symphytum x uplandicum

Angelica seed. We still find the best means of starting Sweet Cicely is by fresh seeds that are planted in the garden as soon as they ripen in August and September. Aphids may injure the embryo in the aromatic seeds which means some are not viable.

USE: The herb is used fresh for seasoning and foliage in bouquets. It needs conditioning before putting in arrangements. It could be dried and still keep its scent. Sweet Cicely lasts so long in the garden from first appearance in early April to snow cover that spreading the ferny leaves to dry off their stalks doesn't seem in the picture. A few leaves cooked with rhubarb reduces its need for sugar. Those who like Anise flavor will find use for the herb's foliage and stems to cook with broiled fish or any use to which Fennel or French Tarragon may be put.

COMFREY   PERENNIAL
Symphytum species   Zone 3
Boraginaceae, native to Russia and Caucasus

HABIT: The various species of Comfrey are united by the genus name which means "to grow together". This refers to the capacity of the plant to cause broken bones to heal. 'Knit-bone' is another name for it. The roots go deep and flower stems reach 3 feet above clumps of hairy, rather folded leaves on stems which contain a mucilaginous substance. The typical Borage family inflorescence is curled over in bud. *Symphytum caucasicum* has showy pink buds which open to blue flowers, rather like those of Virginia Bluebells. It is used in flower borders in England though a large plant needs some staking to keep it in full beauty. The curled-back edges of each Comfrey flower, when seen in magnification, look like a petticoat. The Russian Comfrey, *S. x uplandicum,* may have its flowers in hues of purple, rose, yellow or white.

CULTURE: Seed of Comfrey is planted in half-inch deep drills where plants are to grow. It is such a hardy plant that autumn is as good a time for sowing as is early spring. Cover seeds to a depth of twice their size with soil firmed down well. Root divisions will give larger plants the first year. Allow three feet between clumps. Plants thrive in wet places. Some have become natural-ized beside ditches in the East. Because of the permanent nature of a deep root system, do not plant a large area until you see how much room they take. In dry situations the plants will persist but never have the vigor of those getting plentiful moisture. Flowering Comfrey drops its ripe seeds over a long period. The seedlings may be lifted when small, as in the first year, and placed where they are desired. Red-flowered and variegated forms and sports with white blossoms that appear sometimes in a planting of *S. caucasicum* are smaller in stature and easier to manage in a garden. Drought is about the only condition which will discourage Comfrey. Plowing them out spreads the pieces of roots, as it does with Horseradish.

USE: The herb is no longer used internally for greens or animal fodder. It had a few decades of modern popularity due to its vitamin and mineral content. Now the medicinal usage is confined

Coriander Seeds

Coriander/Coriandrum sativum

to external application of leaves on wounds or broken bones, as it was described in the early Herbals. The people who first promoted it for internal medicine still find it helpful in compost making but are no longer advocating eating the leaves or drinking tea or juice made with them. As with many remedies the pendulum swings one way and another through the ages. Those who find themselves with too many plants, will put their Comfrey leaves upon the compost pile, after enjoying the flowers, but before the plants seed themselves.

CORIANDER ANNUAL
Coriandrum sativum
Umbelliferae, native to Eastern Mediterranean

HABIT: One of the few plants known by its botanical name, rather than its common names of Cilantro or Chinese Parsley, Coriander is used in culinary but different fashion on several continents. It is very hardy in that it will self-sow even where temperatures fall below zero. The greens are better known in hot countries, the seeds used in northern ones such as Germany, Scandinavia and North America. In description of the plant emphasis has been put upon the meaning of the genus name which is defined as coming from a Greek word meaning *bug.* The foliage resembles Anise in its early stages. Then when the graceful umbels of pinkish flowers develop on 2½ foot tall stems, the leaves are more linear. It is a pretty plant in bloom and interesting in seed as the fruits are round and dry to light brown right on the stems. They are about ⅛ inch in diameter. If rubbed they separate into two halves and the thin rough textured outside shell drops off. It is the inner heart of the seed which is edible and also the viable part for growing. They are planted whole but ground or steeped in water from which they are strained out, for use in baking. Rosetta Clarkson, author of many herb books, called attention to the beauty of the flower umbellets with their enlarged petals but suggested Coriander was not a subject for decorative planting. Now with the emphasis on herbs protecting other plants by their scent, the peculiar aroma of Coriander or Cilantro's foliage is valued. No insect attacks the plant, no aphids suck on the green seeds. In Eastern, Latin American, Spanish, and Oriental cuisines, the green leaves are enjoyed as we use Parsley.

CULTURE: Coriander is one of the easiest herbs to grow. The seeds are large enough to plant individually in a shallow furrow spaced 3 to 4 inches apart. They may be covered with soil or scattered in a patch on tilled soil in the garden. If broadcast, they should have finely ground compost or sandy soil over them. They germinate at 55°-68° in a flat or in soil at that temperature. If you don't turn over the ground where Coriander has grown during summer, you may have seedlings coming up in the autumn, some of which will live over till spring. Seedlings lifted and potted will provide *'cilantro'* greens for winter wok cookery. Coriander may be started in pellet or peat pots indoors and set out early in the spring. They run to seed faster than garden sown plants but the herb is worth successive sowings for its dual purposes.

USE: The fresh foliage of Coriander (Chinese Parsley or Cilantro) is available in Chinatown, Spanish, Thai or Vietnamese markets in large cities. Americans are just discovering its value in meat loaf, tacos, chili, and other well-favored foods. The seeds were mentioned in the Bible as a comparison in size to manna. They have been the better known part of the plant until wars and jet travel brought new ways to use familiar seasonings to this country. In Rosetta Clarkson's *The Herb Journal,* to which *The Herb Grower Magazine* is the successor, there was never a thought of Coriander having an alias. Actually, the first articles on use of the greens and knowledge of their other names, came in our magazine twenty years ago. Coriander is one of the spicy flavored seeds which develop into a now very stylish green herb. The name is seldom used in the plural. Few people speak of Corianders. In northern India the fresh herb is blended into a beautiful green chutney which is used fresh, with rice dishes. It may be steeped in oil, in the same way that Sweet Basil is done, to preserve the Cilantro flavor for winter cooking. Seeds increase in pleasant aroma with keeping. They are also viable for a long time. A nice way to use them is in—

KAY SANECKI'S CORIANDER CAKE

½ cup margarine or butter   ½ cup granulated sugar
1 egg, lightly beaten   1 cup all-purpose flour
½ teaspoon baking powder
1 Tablespoon Coriander seed, crushed in a mortar and
soaked in 2 Tablespoons hot milk

Cream margarine and sugar. Add beaten egg. Sift flour with baking powder. Fold into batter. Add Coriander seed soaked in milk. Spread in a small loaf pan, which has been greased. Bake at 375° F. for 30 minutes, or till firm to the touch but do not brown heavily. It is a tea cake that needs no frosting. Coriander seeds should not be used whole except in pickling. The outer shell, though thin, is not as flavorful as the inner kernel. In grinding it with a pestle in a mortar, it is separated and may be winnowed away by blowing lightly on the seeds. Soaking further removes the sharpness of it and the light bits may be skimmed off. The flavor of Coriander seeds in baking is like that of lemon peel. The scent holds well in sachet mixtures and potpourri, whether seeds are left whole or crushed. It is one of the ingredients in some Indian curries.

COSTMARY   PERENNIAL
Chrysanthemum Balsamita,   Zone 4
Compositae, native to Europe and West Asia

HABIT: Costmary is one of the herbs in the Chrysanthemum genus which is grown for its leaves rather than its flowers. It seldom blooms. Leaves are quite different from those of other "Mums". They are 3 inches long, oblong in shape and have narrow three inch stems. They feel smooth though edges are saw-toothed. Inflorescence of pale yellow button flowers resembles that of Tansy. The flowers may be three feet tall in late summer. They should be cut back rather than encouraged as it is the mint-scented leaves which are used. For more than 30 years, there has been confusion in the botanical name of the herb. Bailey's manuals, *Hortus Second and Third* state that the gray-leaved much smaller form with camphor scent is *Chrysanthemum Balsamita var. tanacetoides.* However, herb gardeners of two generations find that it is the Costmary which has yellowish flowers that lack the "few white rays". The Camphor Plant which is the smaller variety is the one with the white rays. It blooms more freely but is altogether a more delicate plant to grow. We leave the problem to the taxonomists in hopes that they will see the two plants together one day.

CULTURE: A small piece of Costmary root will soon grow into a fair-sized clump if given full sun and fertile loam. Seed is generally absent when the plants do flower. The herb is not easily discouraged. It will grow in shade with less vigor which sometimes pleases the gardener. The Chrysanthemum nature shows in the tendency of clumps to die out in the middle after several years. New plants may be started by prying off a piece of root from around the edge of the tight-growing root system. Top dressing of new soil or compost every third year is helpful in keeping the herb in an attractive condition. The plant is a heavy feeder. For really handsome foliage it needs good husbandry.

Costmary /Chrys. Balsamita   *Costmary /Chrys. Balsamita*

USE: Bible Leaf is another name given to the plant. Flat leaves were often pressed between the pages of a family Bible by early settlers who brought it to this country from Europe. In the English Herbals it was called "Alecost". It is in a list of Medieval herbs grown in England in the 6th to 15th centuries, given by Helen N. Webster in her book *Herbs, How To Grow And Use Them.* She speaks of Camphor Costmary which blooms early with white-rayed flowers, and *C. majus tanacetoides,* which has yellow rayless, Tansy-like heads. Another name in the same book is 'Patagonian Mint' for Costmary or Sweet Mary. Both herbs were used in 'washing waters' which suggests that 16th century soaps were strong on lye and short on perfume. Parkinson mentions the leaves being used in nosegays, as we include them in tussie-mussies or posies made of herbs with special meanings. "Alecost" had a part in the Church-ales held to raise money for the parish somewhat the same as bingo games today. The herb gave a special tang to the ale. The brew was sold to the congregation which may have increased attendance, in 16th century England. It was a novelty plant at that time having been introduced a hundred years before to Europe, from the Orient. Gardeners vied with one another to have the plant growing in their gardens. It was named for the Virgin Mary and the botanical name for spices of the Ginger genus, *Costus.* Possibly the association suggested putting a leaf with prayer book and Bible. One of the authors supplied over 200 leaves from one plant growing in her garden to the church in her town when it was celebrating its 150th anniversary. Parishoners were given a Bible Leaf at the door as they came in. A California gardener puts the leaves among her cookbooks to keep insects away from treasured old volumes. This is similar to the custom of placing a Bay leaf with cereals and flour in the cupboard in summer to keep out grain weevils.

The Italian custom of swishing a Costmary leaf about in butter being melted for an omelet and then removing it, gives a subtle mint-like piquancy to the egg dish. Where gardens are too sunny and dry for species of Mint to grow well, Costmary is a fine substitute. It takes much less water and flourishes in full sun. The scent is something like that of Spearmint chewing gum. A leaf of Costmary will give the same effect as a small bunch of Mint in iced tea or fruit punch.

CUMIN   ANNUAL
Cuminum Cyminum
Umbelliferae, native to the Mediterranean

HABIT: More people eat food flavored with Cumin than know what it looks like. The thin, slight herb of the Parsley family has such fine, linear leaves that it is not very noticed until the small, pinkish white flowers develop. They are not very numerous, and have short rays, or petals, on plants no more than a foot tall. The seeds resemble Caraway seeds but are so different in scent and flavor that they can't be confused. There is an oily quality to Cumin seed which is strong smelling and tasting. In spite of this description, there is a large amount of the herb grown in hot countries and quite some in the U. S. for the spice trade. It is not a successful garden subject in the North, even less so than Anise. Rains will knock the plants down and seed heads cause them to sprawl.

Cumin/Cuminum Cyminum

CULTURE: Seed is sown in drills in large plantings. The slim plants need little thinning as close cultivation helps them to support each other. They need only 4 to 6 inches between them. If started indoors, temperature of 70° F. is required for germination. Pellet or peat pots which can be set in the ground, after removal of their coverings, will enable the tap root to dig in without disturbance. Do not try to grow Cumin without ground as warm as that in which it is sprouted. Harvest of the seeds takes up to four months. It is labor intensive work in India, where the seed is broadcast and plants have to be hand weeded. Iran has been the major world exporter of Cumin which means it may be worthwhile to grow just enough for home use. It has been one of the least expensive of packaged herbs. The seeds are sensitive to drought when they are forming. In producing countries, harvest of 'green Cumin' or seed may vary from 8,000 to 50,000 tons depending on sufficient rain. If the plants suffer hot dry weather, as in gardens in summer, they may just dry up rather than produce seed.

USE: Chili powder and Curry mixtures rely heavily on Cumin seed for flavor. It is powdered for such mixtures but used whole and crushed in home cooking. Ground Cumin does not retain its essential oils for any length of time. Over 4,000,000 pounds of Cumin seed has been imported into the United States in recent years. The fast-food chicken preparation, Mexican take out food places and general knowledge of spicy foods, has increased demand. In Latin-America, the seeds are used for soup and stews. Use a little at first, to see if you can acquire a taste for the strong flavor. It can't be subtracted and tends to dominate in any dish that is not equally highly spiced with chilis.

Beef Tacos with Cumin

Curry Plant/Helichrysum   *Curry Plant/Helichrysum*

CURRY PLANT   PERENNIAL
Helichrysum species
Compositae, native to Mediterranean region and Turkestan

HABIT: The genus has some fragrant species which are ornamental and herbal. A hardy one with a curry scent is *Helichrysum thianschanicum,* from Turkestan. It creeps along the ground with silvery leaves until late summer when heads of golden disk-like flowers rise up to 18 inches. In the early Herbals the species would have been referred to as "Goldilocks", for its fluffy flowers. In Park's catalog the excellent everlasting flower has been called 'Golden Baby'. The Curry plants are named for the aroma of the leaves, especially when growing in full sun. They are not used to make curry powder, which is a mixture of many herbs and peppers. Two tender species,. *H. angustifolium* and *H. plicatum,* have become popular with herb gardeners. They are similar to those described by John Gerard in the *The Herball,* 1597. Leaves are narrow, silvery and scented. Stems of both plants are whitish when young with dense hairs. They become woody the second year and produce 2 foot tall tufts of golden flowers. *H. plicatum* has more pewter-colored foliage as it matures with stems that have grooves along the sides of the wood. Another Helichrysum used in tubs and planted out in herb gardens is the round-leaved one from Africa, *H. petiolatum.* It is called "Licorice Plant" because leaves on spreading stems, that are velvety, have an anise aroma associated with licorice candy.

CULTURE: The low-growing, thoroughly dependable curry-scented 'Golden Baby' is easy to start from seed planted indoors in a soil substitute. It will germinate quickly at 70°-80° F. Seedlings should be transplanted and hardened off 6 to 8 weeks before the last frost. The seed may be started in August and plantlets kept in a cold frame for planting out the following spring. The species has done well as far as Zone 4, surviving 20° below zero in winter. *Helichrysum angustifolia* and *H. plicatum* are more often grown from cuttings. Culture is very similar to that for Rosemary, in areas where the ground freezes. Plants will grow 2 feet across in the South in one summer but may need protection from wet during the winter. *H. petiolatum* is a greenhouse subject. It makes a fine winter hanging plant because in South Africa it would be making growth at that time.

USE: The aromatic Curry Plants and Licorice Plant are pleasant to handle and make refreshing contrast to greens in the garden and window box. The flowers may be used for their everlasting quality in bouquets and to decorate wreaths of dried material. They add to the ambience associated with herbal decorations. In the 16th and 17th centuries they were recommended to put among woolens to keep out moths. Definitely not recommended by the authors for curry or licorice substitutes in foods. They lose their aroma when heated and taste bitter when eaten.

Dill/Anethum graveolens   *Dill/Anethum graveolens*

DILL   ANNUAL

Anethum graveolens
Umbelliferae, native to Europe

HABIT: Though Dill self-sows in gardens where the soil is fertile enough
for vegetables, we have not had a confirmed report of it being a naturalized
plant in this country. Caraway and Fennel do perpetuate themselves as
close to wildlings in coastal areas but Dill needs a lot more moisture than
those other Umbelliferae. Leaves are linear, clasping the ribbed hollow
stems. Their color is bluish green when young, which further distinguishes
the herb from Fennel. Carrot-like roots make the plants difficult to
transplant. Flowers are yellow in broad, flat umbels, 2-3 feet tall, larger than those of Fennel and
more graceful. The fruit is flattened with a conspicuous ribbing, about 1/16 of an inch long. The
most easily identifiable feature that distinguishes it from Fennel is that stems of Dill are hollow
while those of Fennel are filled. We have had experience with the crossing of the two genera,
which occurred in New Zealand and seeds from it were grown in our garden for two successive
years. The first year plants looked like Fennel but had hybrid vigor and strong Dill taste. Their
progeny reverted to the dominant characteristic of Fennel, not only in appearance but flavor.
They were not an improvement on either Dill or Fennel.

CULTURE: Dill is grown for its piquant leaves, as well as flowers and seeds best known in
pickled cucumbers called "Dill Pickles". The fresh foliage may be used from the time seedlings
sown outdoors need thinning to the beginning of branching for flowering. After that the amount
of leaf is much less and tops of plants in bloom absorb all the strength of the plant. Sow in early
spring right where Dill is to grow. Soil should be moist and fertile for a good crop. Make as
many successive sowings as space permits, until very hot weather. This allows for using greens
and leaving lots of plants for seeding. It is possible to start Dill indoors in three weeks at 60-70°
F. in a soil substitute or pellet pots. The small plants should be set out as soon as they develop
true leaves. Remove peat or nylon material cover of the starter pot as roots may go deep. Thin
garden sown plants to 6 inches apart, setting seedlings similarly. The dry weather in midsummer
will cause young Dill plants to loose leaves by yellowing and withering. If enough water can be
applied, the plants will sustain growth. Those which self-sow and winter over make lovely Dill
for early season use. The herb is said to prefer acid soil. We do know of a garden in the Cornwalls
of Connecticut where Dill has volunteered continuously for 30 years. It is a very well tended
vegetable patch where soil is somewhat acid.

USE: Dill is marketed in two forms, the dried foliage called "Dill Weed" and the seed. It is
possible to dry Dill leaves by spreading them on a fine mesh screen, turning them daily and
keeping them out of the sun but in a warm place that is not humid. The lady who said that pinch
of Dill in chicken soup took away the taste of 'the feathers', would never have thought that she
could produce her own Dill weed. A great many gardeners forget to plant the herb before and

during the growth of cucumbers, they then hunt vainly for fresh heads of Dill in flower and ripening seed to put down for pickles, along with the cucurbit. Dill is delightful as a garnish in working a change from plain Parsley. Dilled new potatoes are memorable. Lamb chops sprinkled with fresh Dill just before serving seem less fatty. Everyone knows Dill in connection with cucumber pickles but few but an artist would combine them to make Marina Stern's imaginative—

CREAM OF BEET AND CUCUMBER SOUP

¾ pound beets,
  cooked and sliced
3 cups chicken broth
2 teaspons lemon juice
1 cucumber

2 teaspoons fresh Dill
  or Parsley, chopped
1 cup plain yogurt
Salt and pepper

This bright pink soup with a dollop of yogurt and a sprinkling of green is truly a color sensation. It looks best served in white bowls. Puree the beets and one cup of the broth in a blender. Bring the remaining broth to a boil, added the pureed beets and simmer three minutes. Cool.

Add the lemon juice, yogurt, salt and pepper. Beat with a wire whisk until thoroughly blended. Chill in the refrigerator. Peel, seed and chop the cucumber, add it to the soup right before serving. Serve in chilled soup bowls, place a small dollop of yogurt in the center of each and sprinkle with Dill. Serves six. With the author's permission from *A Book Of Vegetables* By Marina Stern.

EPAZOTE   ANNUAL

Chenopodium ambrosioides

Chenopodiaceae, naturalized in U. S. sometimes a weed even in cities, native to tropical America.

HABIT: A member of the Goosefoot family which has become popular in Mexican cookery made and served in New York City, it is found growing in between sidewalk cracks in the Spanish barrios. 'Mexican Tea' and 'American Wormseed' are other names for it. The first refers to the plants origin and use for external lotion, made as a tea, to deter insects on people and in dwellings, the latter for a former use as a medicine for intestinal worms. A tea of the herb is taken as a digestive occasionally. The plant grows up to 4 feet tall in rich soil but is usually seen going to seed in dry conditions at half that size. Leaves may be 1 to 3 inches on the lower stems and smaller and pointed on the upper ones. The margins are rather bluntly indented. Branching blossom stalks, beginning in the axils of the leaves, have inconspicuous greenish flowers. The herb has been confused with Ambrosia, the ornamental herb, because it has much the same habit of growth. But the strongly scented foliage does not have the glandular quality of that sweet herb. The resemblance is more in the name, and family, than in fact.

CULTURE: Because of its proliferation of seed that has long-lasting viability, Epazote is apt to become weedy in the garden. Those who like the flavor in Mexican dishes or wish to create their own chili sauces, will find it a good pot plant. It is so accomodating that if it finds the soil rich and sun hot enough to enable it to grow tall it will. But through centuries of clinging to life under adverse conditions through self-seeding, it may be kept small enough for 5 or 6 plants in a 4 inch pot. Seeds take 3 weeks to germinate at 70°-80° in any potting soil. If they are to be set out in the garden, there is no need to transplant them. Just put plants and rooted soil down in one spot. In the window garden it deters insects on plants.

USE: Epazote is used fresh. The leaves infused in boiling water for a wash, or strong tea, to rub on limbs to deter insects or relieve their bites. Sprigs of fresh herb are placed with grain to repel insects. They are also ground in a mortar called a "molcajete" for use in cooking. For one recipe of black beans, cooked Mexican style 2 large sprigs of Epazote would be crushed with the pestle in a squat, stone mortar. Seed is available from Mexican grocery and food shops. Years ago it was on Park Seed Company's herb list until we persuaded them to offer Ambrosia. Ever since we have been growing seed of *Chenopodium Botrys* for the company. It was only recently that its relative Epazote came to our attention as a culinary herb. Now seed of that is not generally available. It is a collector's item among herb gardeners.

Epazote/Chenopodium ambrosioides

Fennel/Foeniculum var. 'Azoricum'

FENNEL   PERENNIAL
Foeniculum vulgare   Zone 5
Umbelliferae, native to Southern Europe

HABIT: Fennel is a tall plant with yellow umbels of small flowers on ribbed stems which may reach 3 to 5 feet in height. The finely cut leaves are yellowish green and much denser at the base than those of Dill when plants are young. Plants are often confused by gardeners when seen in bloom. However, although they will cross-fertilize with Dill if planted close together, there is one certain distinguishing feature. Dill has hollow stems; Fennel's are filled with white pith. Usually, they bloom at different times so the problem of crossing is an unusual one. The result of such hybridization is not to be seen until the seed is planted the next season. (See Dill for more details). Fennel has become naturalized in coastal areas of Virginia, in the East, and California in the West. It tolerates sandy dry soil better than fertile loam. In the garden, Fennel does not survive winters if the conditions are wet or poorly drained. It is relatively tender north of Zone 5 and seems to prefer acid rather than alkaline soil. The clasping leaf stems are similar to those of Dill but the umbels are not as broad or even as those of *Anethum graveolens.*

CULTURE: There are several sub-species of *Foeniculum vulgare.* The one called "Florence Fennel", or "Finocchio" or "Anise", formerly *var. dulce,* is now named *F. vulgare, var. 'azoricum.'* It has swollen stems at the base which have the plant's strong Anise-flavor. They are cultivated for use in salads and cooking, as is celery. The leaves are learger than those of *F. vulgare,* in length, particularly. In order to encourage the bulging at the bottom of the plant, seed must be sown in midsummer so that stems will not bolt to flower and seed. They may be hilled up as soon as they become the size of an egg, to blanch the bases. Fennel is sown, as soon as the ground is warm, in drills where plants are to grow. They are thinned to stand 10-12 inches apart and seldom need staking in spite of their height. A decorative form of the perennial herb is called "Bronzed Fennel". The plumes of feathery looking leaves are thicker than the species and of a handsome bronze or coppery hue. As Finocchio is pulled for eating in early autumn, the question of annual or perennial nature of the plant does not come up. It is not a form that persists in the wild, so is probably annual in nature. It takes richer soil and more moisture to produce its bulbous stalk than the type. Any of the Fennels may be started indoors in a deep flat or peat pot. Temperature of 65° F. will produce germination in 2 weeks. It is said that seeds need covering but the way in which Fennel self-sows in the wild suggests that those which fall to sandy soil find a toe-hold.

USE: Bronze Fennel is an attractive garden plant. Where it was interplanted with Borage, one summer at Britain's Kew Gardens, it looked specially fine. The green Fennel is grown for seed as well as foliage. So it goes to the back of the herb garden where it can stand tall and have heads in

Fennel/*Foeniculum vulgare*   Fenugreek/*Trigonella Foenum—graecum*

the sun. Watch for aphids as it ripens as the Anise-flavor will attract the ants which carry aphids for their own use. The herb was grown in a special caged area at Chartwell, the late Sir Winston Churchill's home. He raised butterflies from the Swallow-tail caterpillar which likes to feed on Fennel's sweet leaves and stems. In the case of herbs, there is often a choice of what plant part you wish to harvest. The foliage from Fennel can be put in a blender with oil and chopped. This stores well in a jar in the refrigerator. The same may be done with the herbage in water, then freezing the puree in ice cubes to put down in the freezer. Fennel seeds flavor Swedish Limpa Rye Bread and a number of other sour rye loaves. Fennel leaves may be made into a weak tea for the age-old purpose of soothing a baby's colic. As a change from Anise seed, they seeds make delicious cookie-flavoring—

Fennel Seed Cookies

½ cup soft butter or margerine
1 teaspoon ground Fennel seeds
¼ teaspoon salt

Combine above ingredients. Blend in 1 cup sugar. Beat in 1 large egg. Gradually stir into mixture 1¾ cups sifted flour, plus 1½ teaspoon double-acting baking powder. Refrigerate for 2 hours. Shape into 1 inch balls. Place on lightly greased cookie sheets. Press flat with bottom of a glass dipped in water. Bake at 375° F. for 10 minutes. Cool. Store in a tin box. Makes 4 dozen cookies. Courtesy of Merry Jo Bauer.

Branches of fresh Fennel are used to lay on a grill before placing fish on it to broil. The herb has somewhat the same quality as that of French Tarragon in removing the fishy odor when cooking seafood. It is much easier to grow than the Estragon or French Tarragon which is not started from seed, but by root divisions.

FENUGREEK   ANNUAL
Trigonella Foenum-graecum
Leguminosae, native to southern Europe and Asia

HABIT: This slight member of the pea family has an interesting background of use in antiquity. Leaves, smaller than most members of the group, almost hide the pale pink flowers on 2 foot tall stalks. Plant needs rich soil to form the long narrow pods which contain brown kidney-shaped seeds. They are the source of flavoring, although its foliage has some of the aroma of maple syrup.

"With what rare colours and sweet odours doe the flourishing fields and gardens entertain the Senses? The usefulness of which no judicious man can deny, unless he would deny the vertues of Herbes, which experience itself doth daily approve."
                    William Coles, 1657

Feverfew/Chrys. Parthenium

CULTURE: Sow where plants are to grow in full sun. Cover seeds to a depth of twice their size. Keep weeded; protect from rabbits and deer. Fenugreek needs temperatures of 70°-75° F. to grow. Cold and wet soil will cause it to rot. Seeds found in health food stores for sprouting may be planted in the garden. They germinate in 2 days.

USE: Fenugreek is a subtitute for maple flavoring in cookies, some pancake syrup and medicines. Seeds are among the many ground spices and herbs that comprise Curry Powder. In Idaho, they are steeped in boiling water, strained out and the liquid made into a thick syrup for pouring over hot cakes. The pseudo-maple taste is hard to tell from that of the forest crop. Thomas Hyll, writing in 1652, says that gardeners who would possess a green and delectable garden should dilligently sprinkle all beds and borders with a mixture of water and powdered Fenugreek seed 'tempered together'. In Egypt it was eaten to gain weight to add to a lady's appeal.

FEVERFEW   PERENNIAL
Chrysanthemum Parthenium   Zone 4
Compositae, native to southern Europe and Caucasus

HABIT: Foliage of Feverfew is light, yellow green on upright plants to 3 feet tall. Leaves are soft-textured, broadly segmented, intensely fragrant. Yellow flower disks may have white rays (petals). Where they are double-flowered the blooms are more white than yellow. Roots do not have the spreading ways of most Chrysanthemums. They do not winter well where soil is wet but will tolerate some shade. Propagation is by seed rather than root divisions.

CULTURE: Sow seed indoors in soil substitute at 70° temperature, where they will germinate in 10 to 15 days. Light helps sprouting so seed may just be pressed down on medium. Set plants out a foot apart as soon as they have four true leaves. Seedlings move more readily than mature plants which wilt in hot weather if disturbed.

USE: Pick the naturally bunching flower heads in July and August for bouquets. If left on the plants to go to seed, the roots will not remain perennial. Hang some upside down to dry for winter arrangements and potpourri. Flowers do not shatter when dry. The scent helps to keep insects out of sweet herb mixtures. Feverfew has few insect problems in the garden. It was once thought to cure headaches.

Scented Geraniums/Pelargonium 'Dr. Livingston *Scented Geraniums/Pelargonium 'Apple'*

GERANIUMS, SCENTED   POT PLANT
Pelargonium species   Zone 10
Geraniaceae, native to South Africa

HABIT: It is impossible to describe the many soft-leaved scented Geraniums which are put in the herb garden for their fragrance there and for foliage to be dried for sweet bags and sachets. These imitators of other plants in habit and aroma are a fascinating hobby in themselves. Fortunately, seed is available in the catalog of some that are easy to grow. This increases the choice because Pelargoniums vary from seed. 'Apple Geranium', *P. odoratissimum* has a modest white flower on a cushiony plant of soft round leaves with an intoxicating apple appeal. 'Bode's Peppermint' has larger leaves with furry texture, 'Coconut', *P. grossularioides,* is trailing, with a light perfume, 'Dr. Livingston', *P. radens* is but one of the many fine lemon-scented. Each of these and 'Oak Leaf', in a prostrate form, may be bought as individual seeds or in a mixed blend. The latter is likely to give you an intriguing medley whose pretend aromas you may name yourself. All of the Scented Geraniums smell differently to different people, but none is disappointing. There are Pelargoniums that look like cactus; and huge round-headed flowering Geraniums. Seeding them is an exciting way to start.

CULTURE: Germination is slow. Plant seeds in a sandy mix two months before you hope to set plants out. Perhaps you will keep all the crop in pots, for patio and to give as gifts. The spreading Scented Geraniums make delicious-smelling hanging container plants. Their flowers are not the most important feature, so lower the hanger to height for touching and sniffing. Temperature of 68°-86° F. must be maintained for the Scented types, during incubation. The seeds resemble needles, or beaks which is what the genus name of Storksbill refers to in botanical derivation. Cranesbill was the country name for the hardy Geraniums, which are native to parts of the U. S. as well as Eurasia. They are available to grow from seed also, particularly *Geranium sanguineum,* Bloody Cranesbill. It contrasts nicely with silvery foliage herbs, blooming all summer and growing only a foot tall. A good feature of Scented and other Pelargoniums is their adaptability to indoor growing. Temperatures of 50-55° F. keep them sturdy in winter. They will keep growing, if they are the fruit-scented types, during winter when the large flowered ones go more or less dormant. Those have to be allowed to get pot-bound to flower well, whereas the shy blooming, touchable 'Nutmeg', 'Apricot' and other mimes of the clan offer their sweets without forcing into bloom. Cuttings may be stuck in ordinary garden soil to root over winter. A mixture of peat and sand in a plastic margarine container will hold a dozen cuttings of Scented Geraniums. They may be set on a windowsill and seldom watered. In the early spring they will have rooted. The long, lanky effect of plants dug from the garden to be brought indoors is avoided.

Scented Geraniums/Pelargonium 'Quercifolium'   *Rose Geranium Tea*

USE: The application of sweet, scented-leaved in nosegays, planters and potpourri needs a close encounter with their scents for suggestions. As they name themselves by their subtle perfumes, they also bring to mind ways to put the flavor into food and drink. Rose Geranium leaves yield an essential oil similar to that of Attar of Roses. The leaves are harvested on a grand scale for distillation in France. The same leaves will give the flavor of rose water to powdered or confectioners' sugar used in baking. Fresh leaves are placed in a wide-mouthed glass jar and sifted sugar is poured in to cover them. The sugar and leaves are stirred every few days for a week or two. The leaves may be sifted out when the sugar takes up the flavor or left in until it is used on fruit cup, in cookie making or rose-flavored frosting. The leaves dry as they give their perfume to the sugar.

Rose Geranium Frosting
Separate one egg white into a bowl. Sift 1½ cups confectioners' sugar which has been stored with Rose Geranium leaves. Beat egg white with a whisk until frothy. Add a pinch of cream of tartar or drop of lemon juice. Stir in the sifted 10 X sugar until the icing is thick enough to spread. A drop or two of red vegetable coloring to give a rosy hue may be added before it thickens. Spread on Cardamom Buns while they are still slightly warm. Serve with herb tea. One author prefers Rose Geranium leaves with china tea.

Rosemary's Rose Geranium Tea
Use two bags of your favorite orange pekoe or china tea; then add four fresh Rose Geranium leaves to the pot. Brew the tea as usual. A slice of orange may be added, but then serve without milk.

HARVEST: When it is time to bring the tender Pelargoniums in from the garden before frost, it is generally too late to harvest the best of them. The leaves to be dried for scented potpourri should be taken often to increase dehydration of the furry leaves. Scented Geraniums, as they are called, do not keep a deep green color, but when they are to be put in sachets or mixtures of Rose petals and leaf herbs it doesn't matter. Cuttings should be taken in August to be potted for indoor growing. Hormone powder does not seem needed. A one-step process of placing slips in soil right from the garden often avoids black-leg which occurs in wet sand or other rooting media. Indoors, pinching back tops or cutting them down several inches yields another harvest. The weaker growth is still fragrant and may be used fresh or dried.

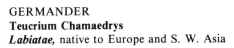
Germander/Teucrium Chamaedrys   Germander Edging

GERMANDER   PERENNIAL
Teucrium Chamaedrys   Zone 5
Labiatae, native to Europe and S. W. Asia

HABIT There are two forms of Germander grown in the herb garden. One is named for the Oak-leaf shaped leaves which are glossy and dark green. It grows upright to 12 inches until the flowers on one-sided spikes appear in late summer to add another 4 to 6 inches in height. It is a hard choice to make whether to cut them off, losing the pretty pink two-lipped blooms, to keep the miniature hedge effect of the clipped plants. For formal use in a knot garden (where the design of the green and gray herbs may emulate a ribbon's bow), the flowers have to be sacrificed to keep the pattern. In an informal setting the blossoms may be welcomed. The inflorescence must be left over winter to increase the hardiness of the roots. If clipped after a long flowering period, the Germander makes new growth which will die back. The prostrate form, which has leaves of similar pattern and size but dull in finish, is *Teucrium Chamaedrys, var. prostratum,* is lower growing and spreads over considerable space in a few years. It is good on a bank or rough place that needs a ground cover. But it has to be weeded however hard it clings to a slope. The upright Germander was called "Wall Germander" in 17th century England because it needed the protection of a wind-break. Both forms are fragrant, bearing similar pink flowers. It is hard to tell them apart until you discover the invasive potential of the prostrate form. Unfortunately, this was sold for a time as *Teucrium canadense.*

CULTURE: Germander can be grown from seed started in a flat at 70° F. temperature. Two to three weeks for germination will produce small plants that take all summer to grow to a size to put out in the garden. Propagation by divisions of 2nd year clumps or by cuttings is more satisfactory. They will stand partial shade but thicken up and are hardier where they get full sun. In areas where snow is heavy and the ground is frozen for long periods, some protective cover such as salt marsh hay, pine boughs or other evergreen branches will help the woody bases of the plants to remain evergreen. Drainage is important, as is seeing that the herb is not crowded out by other plants.

USE: Decorative qualities in the garden are the main modern use for Germander. It serves where Boxwood is not hardy as a neat edging or divider for knot patterns. The fragrance isn't evident except to the weeder or person splitting up clumps to make more in early spring. Still it is there, perhaps keeping the plant free of insects and slugs. As a medicinal herb, it was once used to treat symptoms of gout.

GINSENG   PERENNIAL
Panax quinquefolius   Zones 4-5
Araliaceae, native to North America, E. Asia

HABIT: A small plant with a big reputation, Ginseng grows in the Appalachians. It is a forest plant, under growth of hardwoods. The leaves are parted into five broad but pointed leaflets arising from a single basal stem. They center round an umbel of 6 to 20 stemmed flowers of greenish hue. The most striking feature is the fruit, bright red berries, each on its own stem. The whole plant is a foot to a foot and a half in height. Aside from collecting the seeds for propagation, the 'seng' hunters are interested in the oldest roots they can find. The age is determined by the scale on the top of the root. It is left when the previous year's stem dies down. Some prize roots fifty years in age were discovered in this way. Fortunately Ginseng is now in cultivation. It has been collected in the wild, with ever increasing value of the deep tap roots, for hundreds of years. Before the World Wars most of the crop went to China. Since then Korean Ginseng has been imported into the U. S. All the plant's supposed effects of revitalization of the body of humans, were probably conferred upon it by mystics, in much the same way as the true Mandrake. Studies are being made of the herb's medicinal properties in the U. S. and China, now that information can be exchanged by suppliers and users. Garden cultivation is for specialists who like finicky plants.

CULTURE: Seeds must be fresh for good germination. They are planted in the special soil as a berry as soon as ripe. It takes up to four years for a plant to flower and seed. The first year seedling produces a tri-parted true leaf. Second year stem forks at the top with each stemlet bearing two leaves, five parted. It is said that Ginseng is the slowest growing plant in cultivation. The leaves increase in size to 3 to 5 inches long at fruiting age. Thus the seed offered by some Ginseng dealers who promise to buy back the crop are suspect. There are many hazards to the plants in soil diseases, weather vagaries and other disappointments to the grower. Some screen the beds and have to shade them where there is no forest cover that permits half-sunlight to reach plants. Roots are not dug until at least 3 years old. They must have porous loam which is well-drained. Fashions in root appearance have changed with the widening of the oriental market. Deep roots were desired before World War One. After it the Chinese wished to have broader but shorter roots. As each one was sold in a silk-lined box, some of which are displayed in Chinatowns in the U. S., the appearance was important. The marketing of Ginseng is even more dicey than the growing. Sometimes it is necessary for the grower to take up the whole plantation and replant in sterile soil to produce attractive roots.

GOOD KING HENRY   PERENNIAL
Chenopodium Bonus-Henricus   Zone 4
Chonopodiaceae, native to Europe

HABIT: A perennial pot-herb, cooked like spinach or Lamb's Quarters, Good King Henry has a more attractive name than the plant has looks. It grows from a deep root which sends up a clump of triangular leaves with what the herbalists called "ears" at the base, botanists call "hastate". The surface of the leaves is dark green and underside lighter with a mealy feeling. There lies the resemblance to the wild pot-herb, Lamb's Quarters. They are both in the same family, also, as are beets. The herbage permits frequent cutting. This helps to keep down the panicles of flowers which are not decorative if allowed to go to seed. The clump falls apart when the inflorescenses develop. If it produces seed, the herb self-sows also. With such unprepossessing garden value, how did it get such a delightful name?

CULTURE: As a perennial spinach, Good King Henry is grown from seed planted in the garden and covered with twice its depth of soil. Seeds germinate at 55° F. so may be sown in the fall as well as early spring. Space seedlings 12 inches apart. If they have been started in a flat under cool condidtions, set them out while still in the first true leaf stage. When larger, the tap root makes moving difficult. Give full sun and good garden soil. Harvest often to keep it trim.

Good King Henry/Chenopodium Bonus—Henricus

Honeywort/Cerinthe minor

USE: Flavor of all the Chenopodium family is bland. Lamb's Quarters, the garden weed, Good King Henry and evan Orach used as greens, benefit by addition of a few Sorrel leaves for a lemony savor. 'Shoemaker's Heels', 'English Mercury' and 'Blite' are names given to Good King Henry in the 17th century. 'Blite' means bland in this sense. When most winter vegetables were of the cabbage family or root crops, the greens of the herb were welcomed from early spring to midwinter in the garden.

HONEYWORT	BIENNIAL
Cerinthe major	Zone 4
Boraginaceae, native to Europe	

HABIT: The smooth spotted leaves and yellow flowers make this sun-loving member of the Borage family eye-catching. Usually, the plants of that group have blue and pink blossoms and rough leaves and stems. Honeywort is less known than other members but a useful plant for its continuous bloom from May to September. Leaves are rounded at the tip, with white spots. Flower stalks of 2½ feet bear the scorpioid blossoms ranked in pairs on either side of the petiole. Upper leaves almost surround the stems with their rounded bases.

¯ULTURE: Seeds sown in the garden in April or in a flat with light sandy soil, temperature 55°-65° F. are spaced, in May, 4 to 6 inches apart. Plants may flower the first season and self-sow thereafter. There is a violet-flowered form, known in Europe.

USE: Honeywort is also called "Wax-plant" because bees gather material from it for making honey comb. It was introduced to England in the 16th century and to gardens here in the last 20 years by the authors.

HONEYWORT	BIENNIAL
Cerinthe minor	Zone 4
Boraginaceae, native to Europe and the Alps	

HABIT: Yellow flowers usually are not found in the Borage family. It is noted for its pink and blue blossoms or pink turning to blue as in Comfrey and Borage. The biennial *Cerinthe minor* is different in another way. The leaves are smooth and almost waxy in texture, where other genera and species of this family are hairy and almost bristly on stems and foliage. Plants are 18 inches tall when in bloom. Flowers are yellow in scorpioid heads; that is curled over like a shepherd's crook. They produce oval black seeds which fall out as soon as ripe. The basal foliage is quite ornamental because of white spots on the blue-green, round tipped, clasping leaves. A purple flowered form, (seed of which came to use from New Zealand), is not hardy, being native to Greece. The typical Honeywort with yellow flowers was grown in our garden 20 years ago from

Horehound/Marrubium incanum   Horehound/Marrubium vulgare

seed from Portugal. We have never replanted it since, as the biennial volunteers readily every year.

CULTURE: Seeds may be sown 1/16 inch deep in the garden, where plants are to grow. They may be planted in April or October. If spring is chosen, flowers may not develop until late summer. Autumn sown seed will begin flowering in May and June of the following year. To start plants indoors, sow seed in soil substitute, uncovered, keeping temperature at 72° F. or less for germination in 14 days. Seed does not keep well. Seedlings may be transplanted outdoors, after pricking out to 2 inches apart in flats and hardening off. In the garden, Honeywort plants need at least 10 to 12 inches between plants. They cannot be moved once flower stalks begin to develop. Thinning of those drilled in the garden is necessary as soon as they develop 4 true leaves. The plant stands partial shade but looks best in full sun. It needs good drainage but is not particular about soil.

USE: Honeywort was first introduced to England in the mid-sixteenth century. In the Johnson edition (1633) of Gerard's *The Herball* we discovered that our species is the 'minor' or smaller Honeywort. *Cerinthe major* is described as hairy leaved with flowers of purple at the base, yellow at the tip. Gerard spoke of their being like 'little boxes' in that the petals do not seem to open. He noted that the plants did not grow in England, "yet I have them in my garden". Under "Vertues" he commented - "There is not any experiment of their vertues worth the writing". But in 1731, Philip Miller told how bees are great lovers of the herb from which they extract a juice 'wherewith they make their wax'. In our garden they are mainly visited by bumble bees who push open the flower petals as they do those of closed Gentians and provide pollination. Miller felt that the plant was ornamental and worth starting from seed for constant volunteers. He described 7 kinds, which do not seem to be around today.

HOREHOUND, SILVER   PERENNIAL
Marrubium incanum   Zone 4
Labiatae, native to Crete

HABIT: Silver Horehound is one of the elegant herbs introduced to gardens in this country by the late Helen M. Fox. It is taller than other species and has silvery leaves with felty texture. The flowering stems are of a white, cottony appearance, upright and studded with whorls of small whitish flowers in conspicuous green calyces. They are quite upright until weight of seeds causes them to arch over from their 2½ foot height. The inflorescence is so attractive when green or dried that the herb is much used in line arrangements. Leaves have a typical Horehound aroma and less bitterness in their taste. The plant enjoys immunity from insects because of its quality of being 'hot and dry' according to the herbalists.

CULTURE: There is no finer plant for a sunny, dry situation or rocky area. It may be grown from seed and when established will seed itself. Every chance plant is worth rescuing for its beauty. Horehounds are species for hot, dry soils. Sow seed in a flat, with sandy mixture of soil, peat and sand or perlite. It germinates best at 72° F. and may be set out in early spring 12 inches apart in full sun.

USE: By chance we learned that Silver Horehound is quite as useful for making Horehound drops or candy as the typical White Horehound herb. The arching flowering tops are cut before or after seeds set in the prickly whorls to be placed in fresh or dry bouquets.

HOREHOUND, WHITE   PERENNIAL
Marrubium vulgare   Zone 4
Labiatae, Native to the Mediterranean but naturalized in California and dry northwestern states.

HABIT: White Horehound is more of a spreading plant, not exceeding 2 feet in height. Leaves are wrinkled and hoary, which gave the plant its common name. It grows more densely as a young plant than the Silver Horehound - thus is likely to winter-kill if subject to soil that is poorly drained or snow covered. Flowers are smaller in less showy whorls. Dried seed heads are prickly as the calyces are sharply pointed.

CULTURE: Seeds may be planted in very shallow drills where plants are to grow. Little plantlets started in flats transplant easily to be set out 12 inches apart. Soil substitute should have a gritty quality rather than the moisture holding peat mixtures. Large plants are difficult to lift and move about as the root system is slight but deep. This enables the plant to reach moisture in arid situations. The gray hairiness conserves it. In California and desert areas, the typical Horehound is quite a weed.

USE: Use both Horehounds to make the candy which is soothing to coughs and pleasant to taste. The Silver Horehound is lighter in flavor and can be substituted where Horehound is not grown because it is considered a weedy pest to agriculture.

NEW ENGLAND HOREHOUND CANDY

Make a strong infusion of ½ cup dried Horehound leaves or 1½ cups fresh leaves by steeping them in 2 cups boiling water. Strain after 10 minutes into a 6 quart saucepan. Add 3 cups granulated sugar and ½ teaspoon cream of tartar. Boil to the hard crack stage of 300° F. on a candy thermometer. Pour quickly into a buttered pan. A jellyroll pan already buttered works well. Also 1 tablespoon fresh lemon juice added just before pouring the slightly browning sugar candy into the pan adds a nice zest. This is not an undertaking for humid or wet weather. The candy will remain tacky under such conditions unless cooked to 320° F. to 322° F. Mark off into squares as soon as the candy begins to harden. Move the pan to cooler surface as it heats the space upon which it is set. Do not let stand for long. When it shrinks enough to turn out of the pan, sprinkle with powdered sugar or a mixture of fine granulated and confectioners' sugar. Turn it out inside a large pliofilm bag. Break it up by gently tapping the handle of a knife along the bottom side. The candy remains in the bag so that it will not absorb moisture from the air while cooling. Package candy while still warm or seal large bag until candy is thoroughly cool. Too much sugar left on cooked candy absorbs moisture. Move it around in the bag to cover and then strain it out. It handles more easily with a little sugar. The improvements on Helen N. Webster's recipe in one of the author's books are kindness of her daughter.

Hyssop/Hyssopus officinalis

Hyssop/Hyssopus officinalis

HYSSOP   PERENNIAL
Hyssopus officinalis   Zone 4
Labiatae, native to Europe

HABIT: The description of the habit of Hyssop is 'neat'. The two foot tall plant with narrowly ovate leaves makes a fine edging to a perennial border or miniature hedge between herbs and pot-herbs in the vegetable garden. It is aromatic, with a slightly skunky, musky scent. What is most pleasing about it, besides its ability to be clipped often for even tops, is the long lasting flowers if you don't exercise that option. The blossoms, on spikes about 6 inches taller than the foliage, are showy and may be deep blue, pink or white. Flowering goes on for most of the summer. Hyssop is a simulated hedge which is grown from seed. It can be used in a knot garden by trimming to prevent bloom. Plants are hardy and thrifty.

CULTURE: Seed started indoors in a flat at 60° to 70° F. will bloom the first year after one transplanting before setting out. Allow a foot between plants as the second year those slender plants, that look so much like French Tarragon, will have become small shrubs almost a foot across. They may be divided in later years as soon as the first spring growth starts. Hyssop is economical to grow as a long-lived perennial. Cut back the dry stems as early in the spring as possible.

USE: The herb is not culinary. The fragrance is not sweet. It might be employed in potpourri as a fixative of other perfumes from sweet-scented plants. Civet, a strong oil used for that purpose, comes from a skunk-like animal. The flowers are pretty enough for cutting, but Hyssop is not usually dried for any purpose. The name as used in the Bible probably does not refer to the European plant we grow in gardens. It has had scholars mystified for hundreds of years, ever since English translations of the Bible. Parkinson wrote about a Golden Hyssop that ladies wove into wreaths and garlands. In 40 years of growing the herb, this form has not been seen. But seed of Blue Hyssop may produce an occasional white or pink-flowered plant. If separated from the others, or propagated by division, the color form will keep. These lighter hues seem to be products of somewhat weaker plants. Hyssop's strong aroma is considered protective against the cabbage butterfly in the vegetable garden. They do hover over the blossoms in preference to other plants but their larvae do not appear on them. It is a plant for partial shade if no sunny spot is available. The shrubby look is lost somewhat without full sun, but rather than having no Hyssop at all it is worth planting even there.

Job's Tears/Coix Lacryma

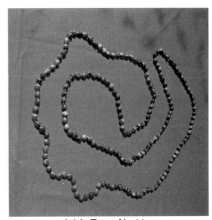

Job's Tears Necklace

JOB'S TEARS   PERENNIAL

Coix Lacryma-Jobi   Zone 9

Gramineae, native to East Indies and Asia

HABIT: It took a Californian to introduce us to Job's Tears. Of course, it is not perennial in New England or many other cold states. But it is worth growing for its fascinating fruits. The herb looks so much like miniature Maize when starting from seed and yet it grows into a fairly thick clump in one season. The leaves are ribbed, not so broad as those of corn but bright green and glossy. In cold climates the plants may not attain their full 3 to 4 feet but they do flower and produce their interesting beads. If there were no curious fruits, the foliage of the Grass family would still be ornamental in the garden. The name indicates the ancient heritage of the herb. It has been used for rosaries, necklaces, teething strings, worry beads and many other things for centuries in many parts of the world.

CULTURE: To get a head start on the season, plant one or two seeds in a pellet pot indoors. Keep the peat contents as warm as possible. Germination won't begin lower than 68° to 86° F. The variation in temperature is possible in a light garden where the temperature drops during the off hours according to a timer. If seed is soaked in warm water overnight, sprouting may occur in less than the usual three weeks. Job's Tears quickly sends roots out to the nylon netting of the pellet pot, so a 'one-step' cube of the same soil substitute is better. If the pellet is used. remove the netting gently before setting the plant in warm garden soil after the last frost. Plants require 1 foot to 2 feet distance. In the North, the richer the soil the better. In warm climates, too much encouragement may produce lush clumps that become weedy. It is the seeds that are wanted; full sun speeds fruiting. It will grow in partial shade but more sparsely.

USE: About two months after planting, Job's Tears will begin to develop what is to them 'flower' structures. Round stalks will come up among the 'corn-like' leaves with green, pointed spikelets from which hang single beads ¼ inch across and ½ inch long. They remain green to golden colored for many weeks, finally taking on a dark blackish color. This lightens to pearly gray showing ripeness for picking. If frost takes the clump before this metamorphosis, the fruits turn pure white. They will have the same small hole through them that makes each 'tear' a bead to string, but they will not keep. The color change from black to shimmering gray hardens the pith within the bead. These are the ones to use for necklaces as natural as man can make. All is not lost with the frosted plants. The dry, corn-shock look is attractive for arrangements and the non-shiny white beads hang on till spring.

Kochia/Kochia scoparia

Kochia/Kochia scoparia

KOCHIA   ANNUAL
Kochia scoparia
Chenopodiaceae, native to Eurasia

HABIT: Kochia may be better known as 'Burning Bush' or 'Summer Cypress'. In the 16th century it was considered a form of Toadflax. We had not thought of the bedding plant which looks so much like a soft-evergreen for its multiplicity of narrow green leaves, as a herb. But it was in the Queen's Garden, at Kew, used to outline some of the parterre. The garden consists of 16th and 17th century plants labelled with quotations from the Herbals. Kochia was called "Scoparia", or "Broome Tode Flaxe" in those days. It is a delightful addition to the herb garden, for its bushy growth of 2½-3 feet, bright green in summer and then turning flaming red in the fall. Flowers are inconspicuous, leaves somewhat hairy, plants globe-shaped. It needs warmth to complete its season and autumn color. The plants may be perennial in southern Europe but perish with frost in the north. They used to be popular in Victorian gardens. The amusing use in the 16th century warrants a revival of interest in growing Kochia.

CULTURE: Seed started in soil substitute need no covering. Light improves germination. Temperature of 70°-75° F. brings on sprouting in about 2 weeks. Seedlings are small and show no signs of the fat little bushes they will become. Set them at least 1½ to 2 feet apart after the ground is warm. They love hot weather but need excellent drainage and full sun. If plants have a chance to mature they may self-sow from flowers that bloom and seed without being noticed. The seeds do not keep from year to year, but may grow on their own as volunteers where there is no deep freezing.

USE: There are explanations for the names of 'Scoparia' and 'Belvedere' given by the herbalists. John Gerard, 1597, has an even more intriguing appellation—"The plant called Scoparia, is named *Herba Studioforum,* because it is a fit thing to make Broomes of, wherewith schollars and students may sweepe their own studies and closets." Thomas Johnson, after Gerard's death, revised Gerard's *The Herball.* His is called the *Johnson Edition,* 1633. He chose to leave out that charming remark by the original author. He changed the name to "Bushie or Besome Tode-flax". He said that in some places where it grew wild it was called Belvidere. They made "besomes of it" whereof it tooke the name Scoparia". John Parkinson, writing in 1629, mentioned that it had no beautiful flowers but because it was so delightful to behold, being in Italy not only planted in their gardens but set in pots to "furnish their windows" he thought it worthy to be among the delights of his garden.

Lady's Mantle/Alchemilla vulgaris

LADY'S MANTLE   PERENNIAL

Alchemilla vulgaris   Zones 3-8

Rosaceae, native to northern Europe, Greenland, England

HABIT: One of the most trouble-free, hardy perennial beauties of a herb garden or any other planting that needs an 18 inch tall plant for sun or partial shade, is Lady's Mantle. It is a member of the Rose family but has none of the vanities of hybrid teas. The leaves are felty in texture, evenly scalloped into nine slightly rounded, tooth-edge lobes, measuring 4 inches across on some plants. Before opening to full dimensions, they are delightfully pleated into soft folds which give rise to the popular name. The basal clump is so handsome and it appears almost evergreen. This would be enough to ask of a plant that never goes off its looks but there are corymbs of small chartreuse flowers that are ideal for picking as they last so long in a bouquet and also dry beautifully. It seems to have no insect enemies except for early season deposits of spittle bugs in dry seasons. The leaves collect or exude drops of sparkling dew (or make distillation from the air) which remain perfectly round, poised on tips of folded leaves during most of the day. This feature intrigued the herbalists who named it for their colleagues, the alchemists, always searching for ways to transmute something into gold. Lady's Mantle seems to have done it better, with diamonds. It is listed in *Ladies Companion To The Flower Garden,* U. S. edition, 1845.

CULTURE: Once established in the garden, the herb self-sows freely. But to catch the seed in the still attractive flower heads is quite a trick. It must be there because the volunteers prove it. Divisions of roots are the main means of propagation. It is a plant of the Far North so needs no coddling and prefers no covering to pin down its soft, down-covered leaves. The roots spread out but also anchor deeply. Large plants are hard to lift. They last for years without resetting and permit few weeds to invade their clumps. Drainage is important to the plant as is side dressing of compost in autumn. Flowering does not begin until the second year from seed. Germination is aided by freezing over the winter. Bloom period lasts up to two months in dry weather. Neither leaves nor flowers are scented.

USE: The herb is astringent with styptic properties. It shares that medicinal quality with its close relative Salad Burnet. It has all sorts of legendary uses connected with women, partly because of its name. If placed under the pillow, one says, the herb will promote quiet sleep. No men being about, perhaps. Philip Miller described its cultivation at the Chelsea Physic Garden in London, in 1731. As with many medicinal plants from England, Lady's Mantle probably came with the Pilgrims (or slightly later) to this country. It may be planted in Colonial garden restorations though it is not listed in current books on the subject. Nice, because it takes care of itself which is a necessity in most public gardens.

Lamium Species/Lamium maculatum

LAMIUM SPECIES   PERENNIAL
Lamium maculatum   Zone 4
Labiatae, native to Europe and Great Britain

HABIT: The name 'Dead Nettle' doesn't conjure up pleasant pictures but 'Archangel' suggests something promising in a plant. *Lamium maculatum* is most useful as a ground cover that flowers much of the summer. It tolerates shade and yet will grow in the sun. The attractive form with silvery stripes down the middle of the leaf, has almost heart shaped leaves and grows not over 12 inches tall. There is a taller species, all green with white flowers, known as "Archangel". When it has rose colored two lipped blooms it is usualy called "Dead Nettle". This term is more appropriate for the all-green variety as its pointed leaves are rather like miniatures of those of true Stinging Nettle but without needle-like hairs that do the irritating. Sometimes we think it possible to pick out the white flowered Dead Nettle before it has its showy blossoms. The foliage is lighter green than the colored bloomer. But actually they both look much alike in foliage when flowering. The golden leaf form is less vigorous in growth and may not be quite as hardy as the type but it is very pretty. Ask for *L. maculatum 'Aureum'* to secure it.

CULTURE: If seed were available, Dead Nettle would be easy to grow from seed. Each spring any plants which have died off during the winter are quickly replaced by volunteer seedlings. Though it is a ground cover, each plant has its own root system and it does not send out runners. The foliage and flowers reach quite far from the root stock to fill out space gracefully. If crowded by other plants they will reach upward for light and be less mat-like. A few plants will give a start of a sizeable plantation if you want to let them go. If not, Dead Nettle is easy to extirpate and almost always easy to share. It has no particular fragrance but serves as a filler where bulbs die down in midsummer. To provide foliage for fall-blooming Colchicum, there is nothing better, in our experience. The yellowing leaves that *Colchicum autumnale* has put up early are quickly obscured by the Lamiums. Then when the blossoms follow in September the lavender cups of this Autumn Crocus, which is not a Crocus, have a nice foil of silver striped foliage.

USE: It is an old medicinal plant used to stop bleeding, which is what a styptic means. The modern horticultural values are more important to the gardener.

Lavender/Lavandula angustifolia   Lavender/Lavandula angustifolia

LAVENDER, ENGLISH   PERENNIAL
Lavandula angustifolia and Cultivars   Zone 5
Labiatae, native to the Mediterranean Area

HABIT: The garden Lavenders which live through the winter where soil is
light and on the alkaline side are mostly shrubby and have narrow gray
leaves. New growth is greener than gray but the old plants look attractive
all through the winter with their woody stems and typically lavender-
scented leaves. The earliest to bloom, in the second year from seed, is the
cultivar called "Munstead" after Gertrude Jekyll's home. Its flower spikes
are true lavender color and each two-lipped flower of familiar perfume is
closely packed to the one above it at the end of the stem. It is not as tall as other forms or as the
type, as *Lavandula angustifolia* is called. The flowering parts of this species have square stems,
held above the foliage, which harden after the plant goes to seed. French Lavenders have softer
and less erect inflorescences. Other named culivars are 'Alba' which has white blossoms; 'Jean
Davis', similar but pink; 'Dutch' which is said to be deep blue; 'Hidcote' with dark purple spikes;
and 'Twickel Purple' with spikes in fan formation. Most of the variants are available in the trade
in this country. Many more are grown in England and New Zealand. A tall one that reaches the
full 3 feet in height is called 'Seal' it was developed at The Herb Farm, formerly in a place called
Seal, Sevenoaks, Kent, England. The climate contributes to size of Lavender and hardiness. In
California, where soil is alkaline and winters free of frost, we have seen a beautiful collection of
Lavenders grown by Miss Edna Neugebauer.She gave them to the Herb Garden at the Los
Angeles Arboretum in Arcadia. Among the plants are French Lavender and many tender
species from different parts of the world which the keen gardener grew from seed.

CULTURE: It is challenging to grow the garden Lavenders from seed. *Lavandula angustifolia,*
formerly called *L. vera or L. officinalis* is available. Seed may be started in a sterile medium at
70° F. and may take up to a month to germinate. Gardeners who have flowering plants that
produce seed sometimes plant it in a seed bed outdoors in late autumn. Then seeds are ready to
sprout in early spring. Any aid to growth the first summer is valuable, as Lavender plants are
small and subject to winterkill the first year, if not protected. Once established, 12 inches apart,
in a suitable sandy, limy soil, the herb can winter well, even in Zone 4, if it has perfect drainage.
The tops lose some of their evergreen nature where snow cover is heavy but quickly make up for
it with new green leaves in the spring. English Lavender as described above is usually 2 feet tall in
Zones 4-5. "Munstead" is a little shorter and sometimes hardier than the type. Both should have
seed heads cut back after flowering to improve their looks and yet not be pruned heavily. Plants
may be increased by cuttings (slow to root) or root divisions of very old ones.

Lavender/Lavandula dentata

Lavender/Lavandula lanata

LAVENDER, FRENCH   PERENNIAL
Lavandula dentata   Zone 7-10
Labiatae, native to Spain and southern France

HABIT: These tender Lavenders with indented leaves, which are stemless, may grow up to three feet in California and frost free areas. They need full sun and a richer soil than do the English Lavenders. The foliage is greener than that of *L. angustofolia* cultivars except in *L. dentata var. 'Candicans'* which has larger leaves which are quite gray when young. Flower stems are weaker and more arching than those of the hardy types but produce hop-like heads of light purple flowers that have a rich fragrance. The herb is a beautiful hanging basket plant which will keep on blooming all winter indoors. In a plastic basket, it requires more watering and feeding than other tender Lavenders. In the garden of Mrs. Lockwood de Forest in Santa Barbara, California, this species, in green and gray forms, makes an allee through the herb garden, as it grows beyond the usual 3 feet in height. During the rainy winter of 1978, the French Lavender stood up to all the wet in February and March, blooming constantly. Other tender herbs in the spectacular garden were somewhat dimmed by excess moisture but not *Lavandula dentata.*

CULTURE: French Lavender may be grown from seed planted in sterile soil substitute at 70° F. constant temperature. Seedlings are potted up in a lean soil mix to which horticultural lime has been added. If they are to be kept as patio plants or need house warmth in winter, they should have feeding every month to maintain their flowering. A balanced liquid fertilizer in the watering program keeps the plant in health. It is not bothered by white flies or spider mites, possibly because of its strong essential oils. Cuttings root at all times of year in a mixture of perlite and peat. The plants need warmth and water to give a continuous display. Tender Lavender, such as *Lavandula Stoechas,* which is grown in the south of France for oil of Lavender, as *L. angustifolia* is grown in England, is a more difficult house plant than French Lavender. It is called "Spanish Lavender" because it is native to Spain and Portugal. The spikes are almost square on short stems above gray foliage that is without indentations. The individual blossoms have curious bracts above the purple, two lipped blooms. Plants need good drainage indoors and out. If the roots are soggy for any length of time a root rot quickly takes the whole plant. *Lavandula lanata* is almost white because the hairs on the narrow leaves are so dense. Its hoary effect continues right up the inflorescence so that dark rosy purple blossoms peek out from floral leaves that are intensely woolly. It is tender in the North. There are several Lavenders, also not hardy, which have greenish foliage, finely cut, called *L. pubescens* (properly L. multifida) which have more of a turpentine aroma, and one with all green smooth leaves and lemony scent. But they are collectors' plants to be grown from seed.

Lavandula lanata

Lavender Fan

USE: Aside from their garden beauty, Lavenders are the traditional herbs best known for fragrance. The scent is better known than the plants. Unfortunately, the spent flowers, left from distillation of the oil, are sometimes jazzed up with synthetic lavender oil and sold as sachet material. The fresh, clean perfume of Lavender which has been grown in the sun and dried in the shade may be unknown to people who associate the name with purple colored soap and drug store sachets. It is a delight to grow the herb in variety to collect the spikes of bloom for one's self. It won't be enough to keep them that way as the temptation to make gifts of them is great. In the Northwest and California, English Lavenders grow such long stems that they are worked into covers for coat hangers by weaving the stems with satin ribbon. The fragrance remains for years, increasing with damp weather.

LAVENDER FANS

Lavender fans are what the early writers called a 'conceit'. Something to make for a friend in hospital or a daughter who loves the elegance of Victorian costume. The longest sprigs of blossoms are laid upon a semi-circle of pastel material that has some stiffness but is 'see-through'. The heads are fanned out at the top, with their stems bunched together to make the handle. The material is pleated slightly to allow for the bulk of the flower heads between two layers, yet to have it so that it will meet at the center to close over the stems. The edges are stitched together by hand to secure them. The lower layer may be scalloped at the top and the upper edged with embroidery. A few fine stitches tacking it together between the spikes of fresh Lavender will keep the stems from slipping aside. The stems may be held together by lacing a ribbon through their layers to stiffen them and add color. Many loops of a bow of satin ribbon used to secure the stems may be added. The perfume of the Lavender remains for years, as the fan is waved it floats upon the air. The late Beverley Nichols suggested that Lavender fans be given to members of Parliament to clear the air in the stuffy old chambers and calm the tempers and tone of debate. Just smelling fresh Lavender is said to relieve headache, though a whole field of it in bloom may cause the same. Oil of Lavender will chase the odor of mildew from cloth and boxes lined with it, as old trunks.

HARVEST: It's a hard thing to sacrifice the mauve haze of a row of Lavender in bloom to preserve the aroma for future use. But the strongest scent occurs just as the plants are opening their pretty two-lipped flowers. They dry easily either in bunches, on the stem, or spread on screen. The blossoms are not stripped off until the stems are dry. Then the decision may be made as to their use. For tiny sachets and potpourri mixtures, the florets without stems are desired. For dried bouquets, or future tussie-mussies out of season, the stiff stalked, sweet spikes may take the place of fresh ones. If Lavender flowers are removed from the stems, don't throw the sticks away. They may be bundled for fragrant faggots for the fireplace, a scented kindling!

Lemon Balm/Melissa officinalis

Lemon Balm/Melissa officinalis

LEMON BALM PERENNIAL
Melissa officinalis Zone 4
Labiatae

HABIT: Many years ago a friend wrote of the way in which Lemon Verbena persisted in his northern garden. It roused a strong suspicion that he must be growing the deliciously scented member of the Mint family rather than the tender herb from Mexico. He remarked on the way his plants self-sowed and he had such an abundance. We asked him, as we often do our readers, to send a leaf or two for confirmation of genus and species. It's one way we learn about regional cultivation of herbs. He sent some fine, heart-shaped leaves of dark green with evenly scalloped edges. They could come only from Lemon Balm. That is why we have listed it here, instead of following Bee Balm. The scents of the two plants, Lemon Balm and Lemon Verbena are so similar as to cause confusion. But the habit of growth is different and Lemon Balm is the one for cooler climates. It makes a thick clump of stout roots, above which rise mint-like 2½ foot tall stalks with smooth green leaves that almost hide yellow buds, which open to white flowers, peeping out from between them at the end of summer. The stems turn woody and reddish in color as the plant goes to seed.

CULTURE: Seed may be sown in the garden, either broadcast in one spot or in rows, as soon as the ground can be worked in the spring. It will germinate rapidly in light in a flat at temperature of 70° F. in the medium. Seedlings should be transplanted, when they have 4 true leaves, to a deeper flat or small pots and hardened off before setting out. Lemon Balm will grow well in partial shade or full sun. It probably exhausts the soil after two or three years because it makes such a large clump. The old plants may die off in a wet winter, especially where they do not have adequate drainage, but seedlings volunteer from any plant that is not cut down completely at the time of flowering. The roots do not seem to put out runners as do Mints, but they increase into a hard-to-divide clump. There is a variegated form, called "Golden Lemon Balm" which was a gift to our garden in 1961 from the late Margaret Brownlow, of The Herb Farm, in Kent, England. It is now available in the trade in this country. Some strains of this pretty plant go quite green in summer unless the plants are grown in shade.

USE: Lemon Balm has more citrus quality in its fragrance than in its flavor. But the look of a sprig of the Golden Lemon Balm topping a fruit drink can quite make up for a lack of expensive fresh lemon juice. The herb dries well and gives a tea-like color to herb tisanes, as the French call the bedtime beverage. It should not be steeped too long or boiled in the water to be used for tea as it can cause headache if the infusion is too strong. To dry Lemon Balm, simply cut the stems down to the base as they come into bloom. Hang in small bunches in a large brown bag. In two weeks leaves may be stripped from stems, finished off and packaged.

Lemon Verbena/Aloysia triphylla

Lemon Verbena/Aloysia triphylla

LEMON VERBENA   TENDER PERENNIAL-POT PLANT
Aloysia triphylla
Verbenaceae, native to Argentina and Chile

HABIT: Formerly known as *"Lippia citriodora"*, Lemon Verbena is a somewhat deciduous shrub growing to 10 feet high in Zones 8-10. That means that the narrow leaves, to 3 inches long will drop off in winter. This will happen even in California, Mexico and the deep South where the plant survives the winter in the garden. They may do so in a pot if moved indoors from the garden or subject to a drastic change of temperature. It seems to be a device to enable the plant to rest after a period of tremendous growth from ground to over head-height in one season. In a pot, sunk in the earth, in the garden, it may put on 2 to 3 feet of new stem. It has panicles of lavenderish white delicate blossoms which seldom set seed. One of the charms of the lemon-scented plant is the subtle manner in which its scent perfumes the air only when it is brushed against or the sun-kissed leaves are stirred by a breeze to actuate the ambience.

CULTURE: Cuttings are the means of propagation of the favorite greenhouse herb. As green stems begin to harden in July and August, cuttings will strike best. Take slips of 4 inches. Strip lower leaves and dip ends of stems in hormone powder. Place in sterile soil substitute in a small pot in which the plant may grow for a least four months after rooting. This saves disturbing new roots by potting up as soon as they appear. Young plants do not drop their leaves or make much growth even in a greenhouse, in winter. Older ones brought in from the garden may be allowed to go dormant by withholding water, but not drying the root ball out completely. They must be kept warm, but do not need full light when in a dormant state. Temperatures should not fall below 55° F. Water freely again in March as the days lengthen. Cuttings need 65° F. temper-ature to root which is why they do better in mid-summer than during the winter. Also the stems are sufficiently hardened by outdoor growing. Cool conditions in winter help to curb the one great pest on the glandular leaves, spider mites. These have been treated with success by spraying plants with a hard jet of cold water.

USE: Fresh sprigs of Lemon Verbena are mixed in fruit compote with care to remove them before serving. Leaves are difficult to chew as one may find out by trying to nibble a sprig placed at the tip of a honeydew melon boat or in a beverage glass. Victorians floated the leaves in finger bowls. We save every leaf, plucking some off the stems towards the end of summer but leaving the tops for cuttings. The leaves are dried by spreading on a screen or nylon netting, after stripping them from the stems. Some branches are cut back when the herb is repotted several weeks before frost. Lemon Verbena tea of the dried foliage is called "Vervein" in France. Dried leaves make a base for lemon-scented potpourri.

101

Lovage/Levisticum officinale

Lovage/Levisticum officinale

LOVAGE
Levisticum officinale
Umbelliferae, native to southern Europe

PERENNIAL
Zone 3

HABIT: Lovage is compared to celery, not only because it has a similar flavor in stems, leaves and seeds but because it needs the same cultivation. Deep, rich loam and ample moisture are vital for it to produce full clumps. In the sun, in the right situation, they may reach two feet across. Flower stems run up to 6 feet or more in height, unless cut back to prevent seeding. At blossoming time the foliage is apt to fade and yellow as all nourishment goes toward seed formation. Roots are deep, thick and very hardy except where conditions are arid and the plant has no chance to go dormant in cold weather. In the South, plants require shading, watering and may be treated as annuals. There is no great loss in removing the hollow flower stems which produce small umbels of yellow blooms, followed by light brown seeds. New basal leaves will fill in where these stalks are cut back to the root. The greatest use of the plant is the celery-like leaves which are broadly indented at the top and darker green than celery's. Seeds are savory but should be crushed before use in cooking. They must be dried first.

CULTURE: Lovage is grown from seed in a flat at temperature of 60°-70° F. which produces germination in 10-14 days. It may be sown in a special seed bed in late summer or early fall outdoors. The seeds may not germinate until spring but will get an early start as the ground warms up. As it is a long-lived perennial, seeding in a vegetable garden is not advisable. One or two clumps of Lovage are enough for family use if it is well grown. Divisions of roots may be made in early spring as the first russet colored leaf tips appear. They produce bigger plants the first year. Those from seed remain in a juvenile state with small leaves for the first season unless started indoors very early and fed and watered as for celery. Seed harvest is dicey because of aphids.

USE: Fresh leaves and peeled stems are used in salads, especially chicken or fish salads. They may be put in soup, stew and sauces and removed before serving. The flavor is stronger than that of celery with an overtone of curry. Leaves chopped in the blender with half again the quantity of water make a green puree to freeze in ice cube trays. They are then packed for storage in the freezer. One cube is enough to flavor a pint of soup. Drying Lovage leaves requires special care. They quickly yellow if not cut off the stems. It is difficult to get a good green dried herbage if Lovage is hung in bunches. The dehydration must be rapid and out of bright light. Second year clumps are the best source of leaves for drying. In early summer, stems are cut and leaflets snipped away as rapidly as possible before spreading on screens in a single leaf layer. As with Parsley, Lovage leaves will 'heat up' within 24 hours if laid one on top of another or left unturned. Finishing off in a warm oven not over 100° F. is essential before cooling for bottling.

102

Tuna Ingredients   Tuna Sandwich

Lovage is used in place of salt in flavoring diets which call for low-sodium foods. It probably rates with celery in amount of sodium. Its pervasive flavor, added to salt-free herb mixes in small quantities, will satisfy the dieter who is try to break the habit. In a Tuna Salad with Horseradish it is better than celery and at hand all summer in the garden—

TUNA SALAD

1 can (9 ounces) tuna packed in water
Drain tuna and flake with a fork.
Put in a bowl with
½ cup cottage cheese
2 Tablespoons grated Horseradish
2 Tablespoons fresh Lovage leaves finely chopped
Mix the above completely and serve on individual lettuce leaves. A sprinkling of chopped Chervil makes a fine garnish.

SODIUM CONTENT OF HERBS AND SPICES

Allspice - ground	0.12%	Garlic - whole	0.016%	Pepper, black - ground	0.019%
Anise seed	0.013%	Garlic - powder	0.022%	Pepper, black - whole	0.014%
Basil leaves	0.016%	Ginger - whole	0.016%	Pepper, red - ground	0.028%
Bay, Laurel leaves	0.027%	Ginger - ground	0.041%	Pepper, red - whole	0.014%
Caraway Seed	0.027%	Mace - whole	0.15%	Pepper, white - ground	0.009%
Cardamon seed	0.022%	Mace - ground	0.082%	Pepper, white - whole	0.007%
Celery seed	0.14%	Marjoram - powdered	0.032%	Poppy - seed	0.011%
Celery flakes, dried	2.3%	Marjoram - leaf	0.049%	Rosemary - leaves	0.048%
Cinnamon - ground	0.021%	Marjoram - rubbed	0.083%	Saffron, Spanish	0.024%
Cloves - ground	0.021%	Mint - flakes, dried	0.043%	Sage - rubbed	0.014%
Cloves - whole	0.023%	Mustard - ground	0.010%	Savory - powdered	0.017%
Coriander seed	0.040%	Mustard - seed	0.009%	Savory - rubbed	0.054%
Cumin - ground	0.014%	Nutmeg - whole	0.011%	Sesame - seed	0.060%
Curry powder	0.064%	Nutmeg - ground	0.024%	Thyme - powdered	0.043%
Dill - seed	0.018%	Onion - powdered	0.093%	Thyme - ground	0.024%
Fennel - seed	0.052%	Oregano - leaf	0.031%	Thyme - rubbed	0.040%
Fenugreek - seed	0.086%	Paprika - ground	0.071%		
Fenugreek - ground	0.089%	Parsley - flakes	0.49%		

Prepared by Dr. C. A. Elvehjem and C. H. Burns, University of Wisconsin

Love-In-A-Mist/Nigella damascena   *Love-In-A-Mist/Nigella damascena*

LOVE-IN-A-MIST   ANNUAL
Nigella damascena
Ranunculaceae, native to Mediterannean region

HABIT: There is no prettier flower in late summer in the herb garden than *Nigella damascena.* The 'mist' in the common name refers to the green, twisted thread-like bracts which surround the petals, and conspicuous pointed anthers in midst of the 1-1½ inch flower. Flowers are either sky-blue or white, and sometimes red or multicolored blue and white. Plants stand 18 inches tall with branching stems and linear leaves above the seedling leaves which closely resemble those of Caraway. It is a graceful annual in all stages. The fruiting bodies are little inflated green ballons which hold pockets of curved black seeds. Though not fragrant, the Nigella species were highly regarded in the 17th centruy as protectors of the garden against flea beetles. They are to be encouraged to self-sow because even mixed with other plants, the suddenly-appearing flowers cannot be regarded as "Devil-in-the-Bush", which is another name for the annual. Excess volunteers are easily pulled but don't be ruthless about it as someone always wants the pods. The plain sister of this little princess, is *Nigella sativa.* It lacks the showy blooms and the tasty black seeds are formed in horned pods. The whole plant is much slighter and less ornamental. Its many familiar names attest to the long centuries of usefulness - 'Fennel Flower', 'Bitter Fitch' (of the Bible, Isaiah 28: 25-27), 'Black Cumin', 'Nutmeg Flower', 'Black Caraway' and 'Roman Coriander'. The similarity to Caraway is in the basal leaves and usage of seeds to top Russian rye bread and other baked goods.

CULTURE: Seed of Love-in-a-Mist may be planted from early spring to summer in drills or just broadcast and lightly covered in a spot where they are to grow. It is possible to start seeds in pellet pots at 65°-70° F. indoors with germination in 10-15 days. Set out while the ground is still cool, but remove nylon netting as you plant them. The herb is a hardy annual once started in the garden. Fitches, *Nigella sativa*, were suggested for interplanting with pot-herbs (vegetables) by Thomas Hyll, 1652. As seed of them is available in stores that sell Middle Eastern specialities of grains and beans by the pound, it might be possible to try such companion growing.

USE: We have found that Love-in-a-Mist calls attention to itself in flower and in seed pod. They dry on the stem for stunning effect in arrangements. The black seeds do not drop until the ballon-like receptacles are shattered, if they are picked just before the slits appear in the top. Harvest of *Nigella sativa's* culinary seeds is disappointing unless the plant has rich soil. It is a plant for a collection of Bible plants rather than for its beauty.

Marigold/Tagetes species

Marigold/Tagetes lucida

MARIGOLD, ANISE-FLAVORED   PERENNIAL
Tagetes species   Zone 10
Compositae, native to Mexico

HABIT: The perennial Marigold, *Tagetes lucida*, is a substitute for French Tarragon in climates where the Artemisias do not winter well because it is too warm for them. The Anise flavor of the 'Sweet-Scented Marigold' is not as subtle as Tarragon's but the plant is worth growing even where it has to be a houseplant in winter. The flowers are single on 1-1½ foot tall plants which have sessile, oblong-lanceolate leaves, fine-toothed on the edges. 'Cloud Plant' is a popular name for the herb in its native mountains of Mexico. The use of the foliage for flavoring and herb tea may be as old as the Aztec culture. In the North, it is grown in the garden in summer and potted for the window garden when frost is imminent. It is not as tender as the larger flowering Marigolds. A touch of frost does not blacken the glandular leaves.

CULTURE: Sow seed in sterile soil substitue indoors 6 weeks before planting-out time. Germination is rapid; 5-7 days at temperatures of 70°-75° F. Seedlings started in peat or pellet pots need no transplanting before placing in the garden after a hardening-off period. This means moving the plantlets into the sun for a few hours a day, sheltering them from wind. If in peat or pellet pots, they must not be allowed to dry out. Setting the starting pots in compost or sphagnum in a flat will help to keep the peat from hardening as it looses moisture. 'Cloud Plant' slips will root in water (if it is untreated with chemicals) more easily than in sand and peat. The cuttings wilt badly the first week in the usual rooting medium. Those placed in a green glass bottle in spring water do not suffer such delay.

USE: The cut-leaf bushy Marigolds are used, by one chicken raiser, to color the flesh and fat of his bird. He couldn't tell us which species as his Marigold petals came from South America. Another Tagetes group is planted, not for flowers or even for fragrance or flavor but for the way in which the roots deposit a substance in the soil where they are grown that deters nematodes. It is a pleasure to grow flowering and scented Marigolds in and around the herb garden. They should be spaced 1-1½ feet apart as the foliage is so thick on the annual species that it overwhelms some smaller annual herbs. Experiments with the Marigolds against nematodes were conducted at the Connecticut Agricultural Experiment Station some years ago. Not all kinds work as well as those used there. They were varieties of tall *Tagetes erecta* and small *Tagetes patula*, commonly grown for their double or single flowers.

Marjoram/Origanum Onites   *Herbs in a Window Garden*

MARJORAM, POT   TENDER PERENNIAL-POT PLANT
Origanum Onites
Labiatae, native to Greece and Crete

HISTORY: Herbs make friends for gardeners! You never know what such contacts may lead to in the way of plant discoveries. When Dr. and Mrs. Robert Whallon were living on the Island of Crete they were taken with the flavor and fine appearance of the plant known in literature as "Pot Marjoram". It was called by the natives "Rigani" and proved to a distinctly different plant from Sweet Marjoram, Oregano or Dittany of Crete, all of which they had known in their garden in the United States. *Origanum Onites* had been discussed in books and was thought to be growing in gardens here but no one seemed to have it, in fact. This inspired the scholarly couple to set about collecting seed of the herb which grew wild on Crete. They made herbarium specimens for botanical institutions in the U. S. and England so that the herb could be studied. We had the unique opportunity of distributing, through our magazine, a small quantity of seed, carefully cleaned and packeted by the Whallons and sent to us. Over 200 gardeners had a chance to try it, as a result of their work. It was a labor of love all the way around, but it established that there was really a Pot Marjoram still in existence and used for cooking and herb teas.

CULTURE & HABIT: *Origanum Onites* was grown from seed in different parts of the country. Some of the precious grains were started in sterile soil substitue at 70° F. temperature just as for Sweet Marjoram. In California, gardeners planted some directly in gardens. A file of letters from these people was passed on to the plant and seed finders. The leaves of the plant are somewhat more pointed than those of Sweet Marjoram. Flowers resembled those of Oregano, with calyx one-lipped, known mainly for the slit down one side as in Sweet Marjoran and Dittany of Crete. This has to be observed through a hand-glass, which is available now in a seed catalog. The fragrance of Pot Marjoram and its flavor are sharper and brighter than the more cloying aroma of Sweet Marjoram. The sea-shell effect of the calyx is the real clue to the herb's distinctive identity. Flowers are white, ¼ inch or less on stems 1½ to 2 feet tall, arranged in round or broadly flat-topped heads.

USE: Mrs. Whallon followd the natives in using "Rigani" in tomato, eggplant and zucchini dishes and especially on grilled meat and fish. In Greece and Crete it grows wild so it is not found in gardens. However, the herb is exported from collections made on the hillsides and dried; the dried leaves may be used as a home remedy for an upset stomach, she recalls. It is the same plant which was grown in England in the 16th century as a pot plant because the climate there did not permit having it become perennial in gardens.

Marjoram/Origanum Majorana

Marjoram/Origanum Majorana

MARJORAM, SWEET   TENDER PERENNIAL
Origanum Majorana   Zone 10
Labiatae, native to the Mediterranean

HABIT: This tender perennial herb is grown as an annual in most areas of the country. In Florida it looks such a different plant beause its rounded, soft-textured leaves are much greener than where it is treated as an annual. The foliage is frost hardy and stays gray-green far into the winter but the roots need protecting from freezing. They are shallow and tightly clumped. The young foot-tall stems are soft. They harden to woody when the plant starts to produce its knotted buds of overlapping bracts that have small white flowers peeping out between them. It is a pity that Sweet Marjoram is confused so often with Oregano, as that may be hardy while _O. Majorana_ is not. The scent and flavor as well as looks of both plants are quite different when they come into bloom. This is where a hand glass would be a great aid to growers. The glandular dots on the leaves and amount of hairs and their density have a lot to do with the identity of species in the popular _Origanum_ genus. Sweet Marjoram has the rather sweet pungency that is its special flavoring adjunct. To know it you have to grow it.

CULTURE: Sweet Marjoram is not the easiest herb to start from seed. Germination happens rapidly in a sterile soil substitute at 70° F. It may come up in a week but the trick from that point on is to keep the seedlings from becoming weak. They damp-off very easily if overwatered. Sprinkling from above may knock them down. Put a layer of sterile sand over the soil medium before sowing to give support to plantlets and deter soil-line fungus. Seed may be sown in the garden when earth is warm night and day. Keep moist but not too wet and sturdy seedlings may result if the tiny grains of seed are barely covered with finely sifted compost or sand. Space 6 to 8 inches apart, upon setting out or thin seedlings to 4 inches and then a wider distance. Use the little plantlets for flavoring. The fun of growing herbs from seed is that the characteristic aroma is there however young. Sweet Marjoram is propagated by cuttings where the plant becomes woody and winters outdoors. Or root divisions are made by pulling the clump apart. In the house a hanging planter is decorative when planted with the herb. It tends to sprawl in winter and will cover the rim of the basket and curl upwards.

USE: Sweet Marjoram is used fresh in omelettes, cheese casseroles, with string beans, and in other bean pots. It may be dried in small quantities through the season, or left until a real freeze is imminent. All parts of the herb dry quickly when spread on screens. The leaves rub off the stems after a heat treatment to crisp the Sweet Marjoram. Temperature not over 100° F. is sufficient to dry to storing quality in the oven after all moisture has been evaporated by air drying out of bright light. Plants that would otherwise die from frozen ground may be dug and potted to enjoy for a few months in the house. They will need a soil mixture with 1/3 sand and occasional feeding with liquid fertilizer diluted to ¼ strength. Pick a few leaves at a time from different sides of the plant rather than shearing the growing tips all at once. Sweet Marjoram makes a good light garden plant if it is not over-watered. The herb plays a part in a wonderful garden soup which may be frozen for winter use—

HERB AND GARDEN SOUP

7 lbs. tomatoes, skinned and quartered
1 twelve ounce can tomato paste
4 cloves Garlic minced
3 chicken bouillon cubes (or jelly of one boiled chicken)
1 Tablespoon sugar
½ teaspoon cracked pepper
4 small Bay leaves
¼ cup butter
Simmer the above for a ½ hour; then add these fresh herbs and cook 10 minutes more—
4 sprigs Sweet Basil, 4 to 6 inches
2 sprigs of Sweet Marjoram, 6 inches
10 sprigs of Parsley - without stem
10 strands of Chives, snipped

Cool the mixture, remove Bay leaves. *Then and only then*, blend 2 cups at a time in the blender until pureed. To serve as soup, heat until bubbly and stir in a little milk or light cream. If you are fancy, float one teaspoon sour cream and a sprig of Parsley in the middle of each soup bowl.

Addendum - For a second use, add browned hamburger or sausage; making it a spaghetti sauce. Do not cook it more than 20 minutes additional time or all herb flavor will be lost. If you like aspic, heat a quart of the mixture made for soup, adding 2 envelopes of unflavored gelatin. Pour into a mold and chill. Some like it hot, some like it cold, some like it out of the freezer to make a quick meal.

MARJORAM, WILD   PERENNIAL
Origanum vulgare   Zone 4
Labiatee, native to England, Europe

HABIT: It might be better to call the Marjorams of this species "hardy" rather than "wild". Only one is an escapee from gardens in the Northeast. It is the tallest of the genus. Its pink flowers have overlapping purplish bracts on stems 3 feet tall at times. On abandoned pastures in eastern New York State, Wild Marjoram and Wild Bergamot romp about together. In midsummer the combination of pink and lavender flowers is beautiful.

Leaves of Wild Marjoram are ovate, up to 1 inch long. Roots spread to a dense clump in a few years. Foliage resembles a ground cover early in its first year and again after the plants bloom. It can be mowed to prevent flowering if used in that way. Origanum species thrive on the limestone soils in certain valleys in New England. Certain cultivars are choice plants for the herb garden. Wild Marjoram is too rampant to include among the culinary herbs and its scent and flavor are minimal here. On the rocky slopes of Greece it develops the rich scent that is known as Oregano in certain varieties that are indigenous there. They are quite hardy in this country and several are available here. Most surprising is the cultivar *O. vulgare cv. 'Aureum'*. It forms a ground-hugging mat of round, rather hairless golden leaves with sweet aroma. When it first came to the U. S. it was treated as a tender Marjoram. In time we realized it was hardy and better left out in winter.

Dittany of Crete/Origanum Dictamnus

Dittany of Crete in Strawberry Jar

While this golden form is not productive of foliage to use in cooking, several other variegated forms have the 2 foot tall flower stems and thick clumps of the species. They are more fruit-scented than Oregano. Madge Hooper of Stoke Lacy Herb Farm in Herefordshire, England introduced one with lemon-colored leaves in spring and fall, sometimes green during the heat of U. S. summers. It has pink flowers which are nice for bouquets and perfumed leaves to dry for potpourri. In her own garden a special variant has green leaves with golden tips. That has not proved hardy in our gardens. The all lemon or light gold-colored one is long-lived. Two varieties of Oregano also live in Zone 4. *O. vulgare var. 'Viride'* has green foliage and white blossoms with light green bracts. Its introduction to the herb trade began in the 1940's at our Laurel Hill Herb Farm with seed shaken out of a bundle of Oregano imported from Greece. We found it in a market in New York City and curiosity as to what the pizza herb looked like led to planting it. Flowers are white, the overlapping bracts of the spikelets light green. Leaves have a good Oregano smell and flavor, which increases with drying. Another from Greece is *O. vulgare var. 'Prismaticum'* also with white blossoms on hardy plant. The names for Marjorams have been in confusion since the 16th century when species from the Mediterranean region were first grown in England. The charming round-leaved, gray felty *Origanum Dictamnus*, which grows wild on Crete, was also known at that time in England. It is of the tender group, needing pot plant culture. But it is collected in the wild on the island for which it is named 'Dittany of Crete'. Flowers look almost hop-like because of light green bracts that surround the pink tubular blossoms. The calyx is the key to its close relation to Pot Marjoram and Sweet Marjoram.

CULTURE: The common Wild Marjoram grows from seed and root divisions. It is easily started in a flat in potting soil Temperature of 70° F. brings on germination in 10 days. Seedsmen have had a great deal of trouble distinguishing this spreading, vigorous plant from the less rambunctious but more flavorful herb of the same botanical name with Oregano flavor. The seeds look identical. Now, there is confusion in the nurseries between *Origanum vulgare* and *Origanum Majorana*. It really should not be too difficult to tell the more hairy leaves of the first from the soft-velvety texture of the other. When in flower it is obvious why the latter is called "Knotted Marjoram" by the herbalists. The flower buds are like green knots or knobs and white flowers barely protrude from them. The herbs may be used interchangeably but for the purist, it is annoying to buy one for the other. Naturalized Wild Marjoram will grow in sun or shade. Oregano varieties need all the warmth and sun they can get. They also need calcareous soil and excellent drainage. They reach only 1½ feet in bloom and are more upright as young plants than the wild plants. The golden forms do not set seed readily and seldom self-sow, especially little variety "Aureum" which produces hardy any flowers.

Apple Mint/Mentha suaveolens

Pineapple Mint/M.suaveolens cv. 'Variegata'

MINT, APPLE   PERENNIAL
Mentha suaveolens   Zone 4
Labiatae, native to Europe

HABIT: Sometimes called "Dry Land Mint" because it stands full sun and dry conditions better than other species, Apple Mint grows to 3 feet tall. Leaves are an inch or more in diameter, rounded in shape, attached directly to the stem. They are woolly and pleasantly scented of apple. The flowers are white on hairy stems that branch at right angles atop the plants in late summer. The runners are thick and white in color. There is a variety called 'Bowles Mint' in Britain which is used for Mint sauce and jelly. Leaves are larger and more rounded and whole plant grows taller than the species. Pineapple Mint is a cultivar of Apple Mint. It has charming multicolor leaves *(M. suaveolens cv. 'Variegata')* of cream color and green. Sometimes the markings are all around the leaf leaving green centers. Other forms have one leaf all cream color, other partly. Both varieties are useful fresh and dried for cooking, nosegays, sachets and candied Mint leaves. Apple Mint is especially good for the latter purpose as the leaves are large and do not wilt readily. Pineapple Mint is lower growing with fewer blooms.

CULTURE: Seed of Apple Mint is not often available. If found, it should be started in soil substitute indoors early in the spring. Germinates well at 70° F. in about 10 days. For Mint in winter indoors, seed grown plants are easier than digging roots from the garden. The latter have to go dormant and freeze before they produce healthy growth again after maturing outdoors. Mint plants should have 18 inches between them which will quickly fill in when they put out stolons in late summer. If Pineapple Mint is given a mulch of compost at the end of the season it will be less subject to winter kill. Attempts to confine Mint roots with barriers are usually unsuccessful. They search for new ground even when planted in large cans sunk in the ground. Far better is the simple expedient of cutting off the spreading runners with a spade. Mints should be lifted after three years; old roots without new growth discarded and small amounts of live ones reset in new soil.

USE: Apple Mint loses its fuzzy feeling when chopped fine for adding to fruit compote, salads or Mint sauce. Whole leaves may be brushed with the white of an egg, slightly frothed with water and painted on both sides of leaf. Dust with powdered sugar and lay on wax paper. They will dry with a frosted crystalized covering to make pleasant tasting candied Mint leaves. The large downy leaves take up the egg white and sugar better than smooth varieties. Pineapple Mint may be used for the same confection. Little boxes with clear plastic top make attractive containers for the leaves for gifts or selling.

Iced Drinks   *Bergamot, Orange Mint/Mentha aquatica*

PINEAPPLE (MINT) CREME

1 cup heavy cream whipped
2/3 cup granulated sugar
1 Eight-ounce can Dole's crushed pineapple,
    in its own juice, unsweetened
1 Tablespoon unflavored gelatin
1/3 cup lukewarm water
2 six-inch sprigs Pineapple Mint

Place pineapple fruit, sugar and (stripped from the stem) leaves of Mint in the top of a blender. Blend for 1 minute. Add softened gelatin which has been soaked in lukewarm water. Whirl again until Mint is just small flecks.
Beat cream till thick in a large bowl. Fold in fruit puree from blender. Pour into six individual molds or 1 large one that has been rinsed in cold water. Chill till firm. Raw sugar that has had a Vanilla bean flavoring in it is nice to use in this.

MINT, BERGAMOT   PERENNIAL
Mentha aquatica var. crispa   Zone 4
Labiatae, native to Europe

HABIT: Bergamot or Orange Mint has dark, somewhat crisped leaves. They are more ovate at the bottom, rounded at the top. The smooth surface and darker color of the foliage is a distinguishing feature. The scent is strongly fruit-like, quite different from other Mints. A variety with mostly rounded leaves is called "Eau-de-Cologne Mint" in Great Britain and New Zealand. It has a real perfume, suggestive of the toilet water for which it is named. This variety is dried for adding to sachet and potpourri material. The species has a place in herb teas to add authority, as well as piquancy. The Lavender flowers are pretty.

CULTURE: Set out plants in semi-shade in moist soil as early in the spring as possible. Keep separate from other Mints so that the whorls of purple flowers are not crossed with other species by the bees. They grow 2½ feet tall and as wide.

Spearmint/Mentha spicata

Ginger Mint/Mentha x gentilis

MINT, SPEARMINT   PERENNIAL
Mentha spicata   Zone 4
Labiatae, native to Europe

HABIT: One of the greenest of the Mints, Spearmint is the old favorite for iced tea, Mint julep and Mint sauce. It grows to 3 feet, with narrow pointed leaves of bright green with conspicuous veins. Stems are green and spikes of flowers pinkish in close-set whorls. Many hybrids of Spearmint have developed in its long association with man. There are curly leaved types called *var. 'Crispi',* which are attractive in the garden. Wild Mint, *M. arvensis* is found along streams in New England. The flavor is weaker than Spearmint's and leaves are hairy. If you have no other Mint, it can be used similarly. Spearmint is offered as seed in catalogs.

CULTUE: Start seed in flats, temperature 70° F. for germination in two weeks. The seedlings should be set out after all danger of frost is past. Seed can be started in the ground in early spring or fall for a head start. It is a very hardy plant which will find its own route to new ground after a year or so. Plants from seed are better for growing indoors than clumps taken from the garden. The latter need a resting period to grow well. Pot roots, leave out to freeze for 2 months and then bring in if you have no seedlings.

USE: It has never been said what Mint is used for tea in Morocco and Arabia but the herb has travelled round the world. When American Field Service students were guests in our home one summer, Spearmint was the plant which all of the group from 7 different parts of the world knew when it was growing in our garden. We made a tussie-mussie of Mint, Sage, Thyme flowers and Marjoram for 'joy of the mountain' (Canaan Mountain) for the girls to carry away on a hot bus trip back to the port of departure.

MINT, GINGER   PERENNIAL
Mentha x gentilis   Zone 4
Labiatae, native to Great Britain and U. S.

HABIT: As long ago as 1938, the striped Mint hybrid *M. x gentilis, 'Variegata'* was known as Scotch Mint and American Apple Mint. *M. gentilis* is now recognized as a cross between the wild Corn Mint, *M. arvensis* and Spearmint, *M. spicata.* It was grown in herb gardens in the United States and England for its spicy scent and golden lines along the midrib and main side veins. The stems are hairless, often reddish, smooth leaves are pointed at both ends, on short stems. The stalks grow 1 to 2 feet tall with violet colored flowers in clusters in the axils of the leaves. Names such as 'Emerald' and 'Gold' and 'Ginger Mint' have been attached to it by nurseries here and abroad. Whatever it is called, the plant must be started from root divisions to

Honey and Mint Ice

hold its variegation. Mints hybridize readily but garden volunteers often are less attractive and aromatic than the true divisions of plants. That is why it is suggested that you grow Mints in separate parts of the garden so the creeping rootstocks will not become intertwined.

CULTURE: Where Mints are grown for distillation of the oil, the roots are plowed up and replanted every few years. New soil helps to maintain healthy stock. This means that a large Mint bed may run out if the spreading stolons are not lifted and planted elsewhere. The idea that Mint can be confined by placing plants in bottomless tins or basins has its drawbacks. The centers of the plants will die out and yet the adventurous autumnal growth may climb right over the edges of the confining metals. In a wooden barrel, the Ginger Mint has found a way to creep down inside and push its green and golden shoots out under the bottom in the spring. It is a vigorous but popular Mint for flavoring and for its golden gleam in a shady part of the garden. As with many variegated herbs, full sun seems to reduce the whole plant to green in mid-summer. The scent is sufficiently different to make it recognizable even when not striped. The smooth leaves and stems are quite noticeable.

USE: Ginger Mint offers the coolness of Creme de Menthe with the spice of Ginger root in its flavor. Try some in—

HONEY AND MINT ICE

1½ cup cold water
½ cup honey
1 cup orange juice
2 Tablespoons lemon juice

1 teaspoon grated
orange peel
½ cup Ginger Mint leaves

½ teaspoon cinnamon
pinch of salt
1 cup whipped cream
6 Tablespoons Grand
Marnier or Cointreau
3 Tablespoons chopped
walnuts for garnish

Put water, Mint and honey in saucepan. Place over heat and boil. Let bubble for 2 minutes without stirring. Remove from heat and add orange juice, lemon juice, grated orange peel, cinnamon and salt. Strain and freeze in ice tray or shallow dish. When ready to serve, scoop ice into bowls. Pour liqueur over ice. Top with the already whipped cream and sprinkle nuts on top.

Peppermint/Mentha x piperita

Corsican Mint/Mentha Requiennii

PEPPERMINT   PERENNIAL

Mentha x piperita   Zone 4

Labiatae, native to Europe

HABIT: The Peppermints bring to mind candies when you smell the smooth leaves. The plant is grown in parts of the United States for its oil, as is Spearmint. The familiar flavor, judiciously used, is refreshing on a hot day. But too much oil of Peppermint can be harmful, so make tea of the herb leaves not too strong. The Mint is a fine example of a little being good but a lot being deleterious. The same thing can be said of it in the garden.

The roots spread faster than they can be pulled if the ground is rich and moist. We keep them along the bank of a stream where we will be sure to recognize the black stems and smooth green leaves. There is a white, or green-stemmed variety which is milder. All of the Mints, except the tiniest Corsican Mint, *Mentha Requienii,* which has round leaves less than ¼ inch in diameter and creeps along, dry well for potpourri and herb tea. But here again, do not let Peppermint steal the show. It's aroma is so pervasive that it can overpower other scents. This is good when it's mildew odors that are to be chased with oil of Peppermint, but would make for a restless night if the herbage was predominate in a sleep pillow. The flowers of Peppermint are lavender whorls around the square stem. The scent of its tiniest relative, Corsican Mint is like that of Creme de Menthe. It has minute purple flowers among the flat foliage. They set seed somehow to volunteer around the wet stones beside a pool or on sphagnum moss growing on rocky steps. Visitors are surprised when you say, "press here" about the green mossy looking plant, that looks like Baby Tears. They find it has a powerful perfume which that Corsican plant lacks. *Mentha Requienii* is not perfectly hardy but will winter in Zone 4 in a protected spot if covered with a mulch after the ground freezes.

CULTURE: Peppermint can be tucked in the ground and watered any time of the growing year. It should be curbed by spading the spreading stolons early in the spring if you don't want it to run over other plants. It is not a good idea to put all your Mint varieties in the same bed or even closely associated in a garden. The bees will visit one after the other and they hybridize naturally. Not all crosses are as good in flavor as the originals. This will not be noticed until seedlings volunteer the next season. Keep manure out of a garden where Mints are growing. It may contain fungus which is harmful to the plants, though Mint rust is not a garden problem in most gardens. The striped beetles which visit members of the Mint family, scraping off chlorophyll and leaving brown spots have given the illusion of Mint rust. Their disfiguring traces on Oregano, Mint and Sage do not harm plant or people. If those leaves are cut off, new ones will soon grow out fresh and green.

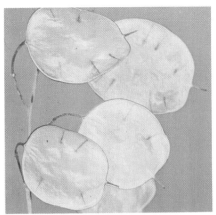

Money Plant/Lunaria annua   Money Plant/Lunaria annua

MONEY PLANT   BIENNIAL
Lunaria annua   Zone 4
Cruciferae, native to southern Europe

HABIT: Money doesn't grow on trees but the fragile, inner portions of the pods of 'Money Plant' are much coveted by flower arrangers in the autumn. This Mustard family herb has heart-shaped ovate leaves with toothed margins. If seed is planted in late summer, the biennial plants are ready to produce flowers in April and May. It has an attractive pinkish lavender four-petaled flower, similar to Sweet Rocket but in smaller panicles. There is a white flowered form with lighter green, smaller leaves. It is only half the 2½-3 feet tall that the usual Money Plant attains. In England, we have seen a variegated *Lunaria annua,* with creamy white markings on the leaves. They are less conspicuous when the plant is in flower than when it is just basal foliage. Not all seeds of the two varieties come true, the white-flowered reverts to lavender blooms; the variegated to all green.

CULTURE: *Lunaria* may be started in peat pots for planting out in early spring. Grow at 70° F. It is a hardy biennial except where it is wet with poor drainage. Partial shade is acceptable but wet feet are not. Transplanting, except out of pots, sets back growth. Sowing directly in the garden is best and very easy. Seeds from plants that have been shelled of their sooty looking pods to reveal the lovely fragile placentas, often self-sow. The plant deserves far more attention than it gets until these disks are ripe. When it begins to set the seed pods that have been described as looking like cucumber slices, it attracts notice. If they are left on the plant without shucking, it invites derision. But it is amusing to show people what's hidden by the covers accounts for the old name "White Satin" given to the plant by the herbalists.

USE: 'Honesty' is another name for Money Plant. It's quite a game of chance, to shell the pods. If grasped at the top and gently rubbed, the covers slip away from the silvery centers without damage. This can be done on the plant before cutting the stems for bouquets. If the inflorescences are cut and bunched, it is honestly a chore to untangle them without tearing the 'money'. Left too long, all shelled in the garden, the wind will tatter it, too. A lady who was gifted with patience used her hours waiting on jury duty to make flowers out of the 'money'. She took centers of dried coneflowers or black-eyed-susans and glued the silvery papery *Lunaria* around them to make charming floral dried bouquets. John Gerard, 1597, said the roots were used in salads. We tried peeling roots of surplus plants in their second spring. They tasted like mild, large radishes.

Nasturtium/Tropaeolum majus　　　　　　　　*Nasturtium/Tropaeolum majus*

NASTURTIUM　　　　　　　　　　　　　　　　　　ANNUAL

Tropaeolum majus

Tropaeolaceae, native to South America

HABIT: There is only one genus with some 50 species in the Tropaeolum family. The name comes from a greek word for 'trophy', referring to the shield-like leaves. You seldom meet anyone who calls Nasturtium by its botanical name; even less often talk to a person who knows that the common name 'Nasturtium' is the Latin name for Watercress. The yellow, red and orange blooms of Nasturtium are held on their own hollow stems above the roundish leaves. They have 'spurs' as tails for the funnel-shape corollas that sometimes reach 2 inches in width. There are sprawling and vining types, the latter being perennial in gardens in England. Perhaps the cooler summers there extend their growing capacity. Dwarf, bushy types make colorful edging for herb garden beds.

CULTURE: Where summers are hot, Nasturtiums are avoided because of their susceptibility to black aphids. They also flower less and produce mostly leaves if soil is moist and rich. But they deserve a fair trial for the joy of their piquant flowers and leaves which can be used in sandwiches and salads. Sow seed where plants are to grow. The big wrinkled seeds are perfect for the beginner because they can be planted individually and if soaked overnight before planting, will come along in 7 to 10 days if the soil temperature is at least 65° F. In the North, Nasturtiums are planted in full sun, in the South, shade would be preferred. A native of the Andes, the 'Indian Cress', as the herbalists called it when first introduced to Europe and England about 1629, flowers best in cool conditions. The vining types are choice for a cool greenhouse or sun-porch where the soil will not freeze. The seeds for winter growing should be started in deep clay or plastic pots in August when germination is easy because of warm weather. Cover seed with soil to a depth of twice the diameter of the seed. Keep watered but not really wet when growing on. Watch for aphids, both indoors and outdoors, because when the plants are under stress aphids are something of a pest on the flower stems. A hard spray of cold water will dislodge them and wash them off. The feeding nymphs do not fly so they will not climb back on the plants. Ants, which like loose, sandy soil, that is also good for Nasturtium, place the aphids on the stems as a source of honeydew for themselves. If you can get rid of the ants' nests, the problem may be solved. Here, again, the herbalists had a word for it. Pour olive oil into the nest and the ants will leave. A bit luxurious for our time, but an oil based, natural insecticide, such as Cedo-Flora, which is made of cedar and hemlock tree oils, will work as well.

USE: In John Parkinson's first garden book, in 1629, he called Nasturtium "Yellow Lark's Heel". He suggested that the 'sent' was fine enough to qualify the red flowers for placement in the middle of some Carnations and Gillowflowers (Clove Pinks), "to make a delicate tussie-mussie, as they call it, or Nosegay, both for sight and sent." He mentioned that the Spaniards and others use the leaves instead of ordinary Cresses, because the taste was similar, but he had

116

Herb Garden

Orach/Atriplex hortensis

heard of no medicinal properties attributed to the herb. A modern doctor told us that the seeds contain oxalic acid in sufficient quantity, considering their volume, to make it inadvisable to pickle them for a caper substitute or eat them raw. However, the flowers and leaves do not have even a microscopic quantity of it. The bright blooms are added to green salad in season and may be the basis of a Worcestershire type sauce, according to Jo Ann Gardner of Nova Scotia,

NASTURTIUM FLOWER SAUCE

1 pint malt vinegar
3 cloves Garlic
6 whole Cloves
½ teaspoon Cayenne pepper
½ teaspoon salt
4 Shallots or an Onion

Chop the Shallots or Onion and Garlic and boil up with the vinegar, salt and spices for 10 minutes. Pour over ½ pint loosely packed fresh Nasturtium flowers. Cover and leave this for 2 months in a glass-top canning jar. Strain it and add Soy sauce to taste (about 1 cup). Then bottle for later use.

ORACH   ANNUAL
Atriplex hortensis, cv. 'Rubra'
Chenopodiaceae, native to Asia

HABIT: An antique plant which was grown originally for its cooked greens, which turn from the purple color of the leaves to spinach shade, Orach is used for ornament in the garden. Sometimes known as 'Arrach', in Medieval times, it was originally found as a wild pot-herb. Lamb's Quarters, *Chenopodium album,* is the member of the family of Goosefoots better known in this country. Both plants have the same triangular-ovate leaves with halberd shape. *Atriplex hortensis, cv. 'Rubra'* is an excellent example of a plant which adjusts itself to the fertility of the soil. In rich loam, such as in a vegetable garden, it may grow 6 to 7 feet tall. Sandy, lean soil may produce a flowering plant only 6 to 10 inches. Both will begin to flower in the heat of summer, whatever the height may be. The stems are reddish and leaves that are seen with sunlight shining through are almost ruby colored, though this cultivated plant is called Purple Orach. The inflorescence has similar color until the purplish bracts, which cover the inconspicuous flowers, dry up as the seeds ripen. They enlarge to cover the flat seeds in the process. A green or yellowish green form is grown in England and Australia for the dried plant which is used in arrangements in winter.

CULTURE: Orach is started from seed where the plants are to remain. They are thinned to at least a foot apart because at maturity the flowering, branching plants may be several feet wide at the top. Stems are strong enough to hold the lush panicles of flowers erect without needing staking. Seeds have a long life. As with Lamb's Quarters they seem to germinate year after year even if none are planted where seeding plants were cut for drying upside down. Temperatures of 65° to 72° F. in soil or soil substitute in peat pots for later planting out will give easy germination. The container grown plants are handsome and seem to stand dwarfing very well. In the garden, Orach plants may be pinched back to induce branching if wider plants are desired. It is not an herb of any fragrance but attracts attention by its color.

USE: To discover the antiquity of the herb, it must be found in herbals under curious names and spellings. Gerard, 1597, "Garden Oraches grow in most gardens, the Wilde Oraches grow near pathways, and ditche-sides, but most commonly about dunghills and such fat places." That is why Lamb's Quarters is called "Fat Hen". Parkinson liked Orach for "colour of the leaf-stalks and seed of a mealy dusty, purpleish colour." He added that "it was boyled and buttered, or put among other herbes into the pot to make pottage. There are many dishes of meat made with them while they are young, for being almost without savour themselves, they are more convertible into what relish anyone will make with them . . . " Lamb's Quarters are made into soup, today, in the same way.

OREGANO   PERENNIAL
Origanum vulgare and cultivars   Zone 5
Labiatae, native to Greece, Spain, and Southern Europe

HABIT: Oregano was not found in herb seed lists in the 1930's. Wild Marjoram, *Origanum vulgare,* was mentioned in *Herbs Their Culture and Uses* by Rosetta Clarkson, in 1942 but with no specific culinary use. She knew the plants which grew wild in New York State along roadsides. The reddish bracts and small pink flowers were added to bouquets and used for dyes. It took World War II and returning soldiers from the Italian and other campaigns to bring pizzas with Oregano to American taste. Pizza parlors were places redolent of cheese, tomato sauce and Oregano in those post-war days. By 1969, the figure of 6,000 percent increase in importation of Oregano as a seasoning, was noted by Frederic Rosengarten, Jr. in his *Book Of Spices.* We watched the interest in the herb on our Laurel Hill Herb Farm seed list in the late 1940's. Until that time Sweet Marjoram or Wild Marjoram, with little flavor, were the only Origanums available by seed. Sorting out the differences between the two herbs and the cultivars of *Origanum vulgare* has been a life-time endeavor. In 1948, we grew four test plantings, of about 1,000 plants total in New Jersey. The Oregano seed came from Mexico, Sicily and Greece.

CULTURE: Seeds were sown in flats filled with shredded sphagnum moss. The wooden flats were covered with glass after the moss was thoroughly soaked from below in a pan of water. They were placed in the dark where the temperature remained between 60° and 65° F. Germination began in 5 days. Growth did not spurt ahead until seedlings were watered with a weak 'tea' of manure water. A month later seedlings were pricked out (transplanted) into potting soil in deeper flats, then moved into 2 inch clay pots because these were the days before plastics. Later we read in Philip Miller's *The Gardener's Dictionary,* 1731, that plants of Marjorams needed transplanting to give sturdy growth. Oregano seedlings are not as weak as those of Sweet Marjoram but transplanting helps them, too. After all danger of frost, and a week's hardening off (putting pots out in full sun for several hours each day and returning them to shade before night) the seedlings were set out in our seed growing rows. It was noticed that the leaves had a darker color on the underside of the leaves from glandular dots of oils and were slightly hairy. The Mexican seed produced plants from 6 to 12 inches in height. They were bushy and full of bloom by August 25th. The Sicilian plants averaged 18 inches in height with less branching; blooming two weeks earlier with flowers only on the top two inches. All had the typical fragrance of Oregano as noted in the bunches of dried herb marked "Product of Greece". The flowers were white, two-lipped with calyces having five points. With the help of taxonomists at the Bailey Hortorium at Cornell University, we learned that one of our Oregano types was *Origanum vulgare cv. 'Heracleoticum'* now classified as *O. heracleoticum..* The bracts (green leaf-like wrappers round the caylx) were shorter than those of Wild Marjoram; only ⅛ inch

Oregano/Origanum vulgare   Oregano/Origanum vulgare

long, green with densely glandular outer surface. Another wonder about it was that this is the Winter Marjoram of the English herbals, cultivated in gardens near London, in 18th century, and brought to market before Sweet Marjoram was ready for picking. Both were "used by the people who make up nosegays," wrote Philip Miller. He mentioned forms of the Winter Marjoram with variegated leaves. In our garden, we have had since those early days, Oregano, *Origanum vulgare cv. 'Viride'* with white flowers, green bracts, and lighter color oval leaves. It and *O. vulgare cv. 'prismaticum'* from Greece, with longer spikelets of blooms and bracts firmly overlapping, have been hardy in Zone 4, with us for many decades. *Origanum virens,* another species called Oregano in Spain, has white flowers, with narrower spikelets. The scent and flavor are excellent but it is not reliably hardy.

USE: To dry Oregano, cut the stems down to the base just as the plants come into flower. There may be a second cutting in late summer as the plants make new spreading growth close to the ground before winter. Stems are slightly woody which makes them easy to gather in small bundles. Turn them, heads down into a brown bag. Tie the bag around the stem ends with a loop of string for hanging. In 2 or 3 weeks, check the progress of drying by rubbing the outside of the bag between your palms. If leaves rattle to the bottom it is time to open it. Take the stems in hand and strip the leaves off onto a cookie sheet. Flower heads may be separated and saved, too. Finish drying in a cool oven, 100° F. Let the herbs come to room temperature before rubbing through a coarse screen for bottling. Whole leaves may be put in a container but sharp bits of stem should be removed first. A wood stove with a rack over it would make a good place to finish off herbs. They could be hung in bundles, as removed from the bag, if the room is not humid, so don't put a kettle on the stove at the same time. The uses of Oregano are so well known now that they hardly need restating. A good recipe from a lady who lived on Crete and used fresh Marjorams in variety is—

MAYGAR MACARONI

Mince 1 large onion and saute in 3 tablespoons butter until golden. Add 1 teaspoon of salt, 1 green pepper cut into 4 pieces and one teaspoon each of chopped fresh Parsley, Dill, Marjoram or Oregano, French Tarragon and Savory. (Only ½ teaspoon of each if the herbs are dried.) Cover and cook slowly for about 10 minutes. Remove and discard the pepper. Sprinkle the sauce with 1 tablespoon flour. Stir in 1 tablespoon tomato paste and 1 cup of sour cream. Meanwhile cook half a pound of macaroni in boiling salted water until just tender. Drain well, put in a heated serving dish and pour the hot sauce over it.

Dorothy Whallon's interest in cooking led her to absorb much of the lore of herbs in the 9 years she lived on Crete. Her husband spoke Greek and read it. From her description of the way *Origanum Dictamus* grew out of limestone ledges, we tried growing it in an old barn foundation wall through one winter. The plant flowered with lovely pink blossoms trailing over the marble. It could stand the drought of summer but on Crete it would make new growth in autumn. When that happened in cold Connecticut, the second year, the plants were too succulent, despite their white woolly hairs, to survive. We did learn a surprising thing from this experiment. 'Dittany of Crete' will root in our hard water from a sprig when placed in a green glass bottle. If it is in a sunny window, small slips, just a couple of inches long, with lower leaves removed will put out masses of short white roots in less than a week, in late summer. Also, we no longer give it a place in the garden, but keep the choice pot plant in an unglazed miniature strawberry jar. It will stand drying out repeatedly on a patio. When it is brought indoors, it is better left without much watering until leaves fatten up towards spring. Then it can take moisture and provide more cuttings.

USE: "There is much controversie among the moderne writers about these two hearbes," wrote John Parkinson, 1629. He listed the Golden-leaved Marjoram, (a variety of *Origanum vulgare)* as a plant to put in the flower garden for its beauty and fragrance. It has been with us since 1969, when a slip was brought from the beautiful Stoke Lacy Herb Farm in Herefordshire, England. From that small bit the plant has been offered by nurseries specializing in herbs in the U. S. It is not the only form Mrs. M. M. M. Hooper has been propagating for 40 years. She has the ones that Parkinson describes as "in summer somewhat wholly yellow, or partly green, green more or less, as nature listeth to play, in winter dark green with some white and green." The one with leaves tipped with gold is most attractive. The golden forms are valuable for dried leaves to add to potpourri. The all-green Oreganos are cut as they come into bloom, hung in brown bags and finished off when convenient, for packing for winter use. There are other genera which are sold as Oregano in this country. They include *Lippia graveolens* from Mexico, *Coleus amboinicus* from Puerto Rico, *Monarda fistulosa cv. menthifolia,* from New Mexico, and *Thymus nummularis* from Spain. All of which proves that Oregano is a special flavor, rather than a single species of plant. Those from sub-tropics and the Southwest are plants for their locales or pot plants in places where *Origanum vulgare* cultivars are hardy. No doubt there are more species in other parts of the world with that imitative taste. See Marjoram, Sweet, for more species of this varied genus.

PARSLEY   ANNUAL OR BIENNIAL

Petroselinum crispum

Umbelliferae, native to the Mediterranean region

HABIT: The best known herb, most often pushed aside when used as a garnish on a dinner plate, is usually grown as an annual. The roots will live over the winter where they have good drainage but the leaves do not produce much a second year. The plant's biennial nature causes it to run to flower and seed early in the following summer. Where snow cover is absent, Parsley may be cut all through the winter months. In New England, we sometimes cover it with salt hay or leaves to keep it from dying back completely in cold weather. Then some green herbage may be found as long as the snow holds off. Curly Parsley has many trade names. It is an attractive edging for herb and pot-herb gardens.

Italian Parsley, with smooth, dissected leaves which resemble celery's is now known as *Petroselinum crispum var. neapolitanum* rather than *P. latifolium.* Quite a bit more to put on a label for growers of bedding flowers and vegetables but the taxonomists are not in touch with them. It has a higher vitamin content than Curly Parsley, which is richer than most herbs in vitamin A and C and iron.

CULTURE: Growing Parsley is not for the impatient. The seeds are slow to germinate when planted directly in the ground. We used to mix seeds of Parsley with those of Radishes. The latter marked the row and were ready to be thinned by the time the Parsley germinated in 3 weeks. Now we don't attempt Radishes because a few are as good as a feast of those. Besides they were said to 'stop a woman's chatter' by the herbalists. So various means to speed up Parsley have been tried. The most recent was placing seeds on wet paper toweling on a plastic meat tray. It was enclosed in a pliofilm bag and put atop the furnace where the temperature was a constant 70° F. Germination was total in 7 days. The sprouted seeds were then placed with tweezers on a small flat of soil substitute. They were lightly covered with the Sow and Grow mix and kept moist in the plastic bag for several days. By the third day, the spear-shaped cotyledons had emerged and the bag was removed. The seedling flat was put on a sand tray by a south window. They gained time in sprouting but did not really put on much growth until the days lengthened a

Parsley /Petroselimum crispum   *Clam Sauce Ingredients*

month later. Soaking the seed before sowing in moist ground in the garden would have much the same effect. If the ground is warm, sprouted seeds can be put out in very shallow drills and kept moist until emergence.

Parsley can be transplanted when small but it gets set back if moved with a full crown of leaves. The One-Step pots are ideal for presprouted seed as they can then be put into the garden without disturbing the roots. Pellet pots are not deep enough for Parsley. Once the root has to curl at the tip, it has a hard time straightening out again. Plants respond to feeding with a dilute liquid fertilizer or weak manure tea at least every two weeks, when grown in pots. The desired 'pot of Parsley' on the kitchen windowsill should be planned and planted ahead. Seedlings started in mid-summer, grown on in pots and returned to the house are more likely to produce greens in winter than older plants dug up just before the ground freezes. Length of day must be considered with herbs indoors unless there is a light garden. The foliage plants that are used for seasoning must have means to carry on photosynthesis. They also need feeding if they are cut frequently. Chervil, with its quick growth and need for less light, many be a better herb for growing in a pot in winter. The flavor is more reminiscent of French Tarragon than of Parsley.

USE: Parsley should be used fresh as often as possible. It also dries well if there is a surplus. Parsley ice cubes are made by packing a 2 cup container with destemmed leaves. Fill the cup with water, about 1½ cups, and place in the blender. Whirl it till you have a green puree. Pour into an empty ice cube tray, replace the divider and freeze in refrigerator or freezer. When hard, remove and put cubes in a plastic bag or freezer container. Label them before storing. Most herbs done this way look alike when frozen.

PARSLEY CLAM SAUCE FOR SPAGHETTI

White Clam Sauce—
    1 pint fresh clams (shucked but not steamed) and juice
        They may be Quahog or cherry stone (hard-shelled clams)
    ½ cup olive oil
    2 cloves Garlic pressed or minced
    ¼ cup white wine
    1 large bunch fresh Parsley chopped
    ¼ cup butter
    freshly ground black pepper, a few twists of the mill

Saute the Garlic in olive oil. When browned lightly add butter, clam broth and wine. Simmer until·liquid is reduced. Add the chopped clams and Parsley. Grind pepper over all. Cook clams 5 minutes until firm but not tough. Have ready one pound cooked linguine pasta. Pour clam sauce over spaghetti and toss. Serve with freshly grated Parmesan cheese.

121

Parsley/Petroselinum crispum

Parsley/Petroselinum crispum

Drying Parsley

This durable herb keeps its vitamin content and color with quick drying at high temperature. It means constant watching, but the leaves taken off the stems may be spread on a cookie sheet and placed in a 400° F. oven. Do not close the door completely so you will be reminded to stir and turn them every five minutes. Italian Parsley will burn quickly if not tended; it dries well but needs more attention. In about 15 minutes the majority of the herbage will be crisp. Take the tray out of the oven and scrunch the leaves through a coarse strainer or with your hands to pick out the still limp bits. Remove those and replace in oven until they, too, will get powdery. Do not pack the verdant greens until they have cooled thoroughly.

A gas oven with a pilot light may be used to dry Parsley prepared the same way but without additional heat. It takes overnight to dry in the 100° F. oven. Do not hang Parsley or Lovage up to dry, in a bag or out. It simply yellows and does not dehydrate when stems are pressed close together.

ICEBERG LAYERED SALAD

Cook and cool 1 cup fresh peas. Fry ½ pound bacon, drain and cool. Chop one small head iceberg lettuce. Place in the bottom of a rectangular pyrex baking pan. Sprinkle peas over lettuce. Chop ½ cup celery and spread over peas. Chop ½ cup onion or Shallot and sprinkle over celery. Distribute chopped Parsley evenly over onion. Grate 1 cup sharp cheddar cheese over all. Dot the top of the salad with mayonnaise, then spread carefully to make a complete covering over all the greens and cheese. Crumble the bacon on for a topping. Place salad in refrigerator over night or for a day ahead. It should be covered with the pyrex top of the baking dish or foil or pliofilm while in the refrigerator, so milk and butter will not take up an allium air.

122

American Pennyroyal/Hedeoma pulgioides

English Pennyroyal in Hanging Basket

PENNYROYAL
Mentha Pulegium
Labiatae, native to England and Europe

PERENNIAL
Zone 5

HABIT: The name and the aroma of Pennyroyal are more familiar than the botanical aspects of the plants. Herb gardens are more likely to have the English Pennyroyal than the native American species. This member of the Mint family which gives us Oil of Pennyroyal from its narrowly ovate, light green leaves of about ½ inch in length and ¼ inch in width, is a creeping plant for most of the season. In late summer it puts up flowering stems with whorls of lavender flowers about 12 inches tall. This is the Pennyroyal used for lawns under trees in England. It has been planted out to spread under trees where grass would not grow in some places in this country, even in upper New York State. Walking on the grass mixed with Pennyroyal is a pungent experience. It would be the ideal ground cover for places like Tanglewood, in Massachusetts where thousands gather to sit on the grass and listen to the Boston Symphony Orchestra in summer. But, even as robust as Pennyroyal is considered in England, it would not stand all the traffic through the summer.

CULTURE: Pennyroyals may be grown from seed which is very fine. It must be planted in a sterile medium, at 55°-72° F. for germination in two weeks. Seedlings will be small and close to the soil even when transplanted before setting out. Plants may be set 6 inches apart in spring to make a dense mat of green. Some people regard the smell as 'peppermint' while others associate it with citronella. There are native Pennyroyals which differ from *M. Pulegium* (which means *fleabane* in Latin, because the herb drives away fleas). American Pennyroyal, *Hedeoma pulegioides,* is an annual which looks like a small-leaved Bush Basil until it produces little blue leaves up the stems. The taste and odor are that of what is called "true Pennyroyal" and the herb grows just as easily from seed. The fine grains can be thrown out on a prepared spot in the garden in late summer, when the seed is ripe, or in early spring. There will be crowds of seedlings which are easy to thin to stand 4 inches apart. In New England, this Pennyroyal is often found among the grasses in meadows, detected more by scent than sight as it is not nearly as attractive a plant as in cultivation. There are two other creeping Pennyroyals, with whorls of mauve or lavender flowers which grow in the Southwest and the Far West. One that is found in Texas is hardier in our sandy soil and cold climate than the English Pennyroyal. Another grows up to 18 inches in northern California, with lavender whorls of flowers, and seems to be very similar to the southwestern form.

USE: Fresh Pennyroyal is a good insect repellent for man or beast. The English one is used for 'puddings' by country people and for flavoring grilled fish in southern Europe. American Pennyroyal or 'mock Pennyroyal' is used in the U. S. for tea to relieve indigestion.

Perilla/Perilla frutescens   *Perilla/Perilla frutescens*

PERILLA   ANNUAL
Perilla frutescens
Labiatae, native to eastern Asia and Japan

HABIT: Perilla has been called 'Beefsteak Plant' in the South, where it is a ready volunteer in gardens. The dark purplish red foliage, with wrinkled leaves, indented sharply on the edges in one form *(var. 'Crispa')* and more bluntly in the flat-leaved types, glows when sunlight shines through it. The square grooved stems are purplish, also. They enable the three foot tall annual to stand erect even when growing in partial shade. Perilla branches out with racemes of pink flowers, which are shorter than the calyces. In late summer the whole inflorescence seems to shine because the sepals have glistening white hairs. The first frost will cause Perilla to drop its leaves, or they will hang like tired flags on the still-stiff stems.

CULTURE: Seed may be started indoors in soil substitute, kept at temperatures 65°-75° F. Simply press the round brown seeds onto the medium without covering them as Perilla needs light to germinate. Seedlings may be potted when they have 4 true leaves, and are easy to transplant at any stage. Perilla self-sows readily in most gardens where volunteers are welcome as foliage plants to fill in where Alliums die down. It is a good plant for light gardens, too, as the purple color contrasts well with green and silver plants. In Japan, where Perilla is known as 'Shisho', the herb is grown in greenhouses in winter. Seed may be broadcast in the herb garden when soil is truly warm.

USE: Dark purple-leaved plants are at a premium in the herb garden for foils in flower arrangements and contrast to the greens and grays in beds. Perilla, with its fruit-scented nature is decorative because of its ruffled foliage, but the smooth-leaved species is attractive, too. The puckered edges of the leaves and crimping along the mid-rib produce the 'crisped' look. It is well to condition the stalks for use in arrangements. They should be placed in warm water for several hours before putting in bouquets.

In Japanese cookery, purple-leaved Perilla is used both as leaves and seeds in making *tempura.* Seeds are salted and served as a savory after dinner. They become the zesty core of certain Japanese candies, while with fish they are eaten raw as an accompaniment to the entree. Pickled plums made in Japan and available in the United States, get their color and piquancy from the leaves and seeds of Perilla. There is a green-leaved Perilla with a lemony aroma, which is used for perfume oil in Russia and is called 'Aoziso' in Japan. It grows easily in this country. For more information on Japanese herbs that grow in the U. S. see the Brooklyn Botanic Gardens *Handbook On Japanese Herbs And Their Uses,* #57, in their *Horticultural Handbooks.*

Pyrethrum/Chrysanthemum coccineum

Pyrethrum/Chrysanthemum coccineum

PYRETHRUM   PERENNIAL
Chrysanthemum coccineum   Zone 4
Compositae, native to South West Asia

HABIT: It is always fun to find herbs in the flower garden. Pyrethrum or Painted Daisy is one that adds delightful color to the herb garden in May and June. This source of the insecticide *pyrethrum* has varied by decades according to where the flowering plants could be grown most profitably. In the early part of the century, *Chrysanthemum coccineum,* formerly called *Pyrethrum roseum* was collected in the wild in the mountains of Persia. Since that time another species *C. cinerarifolium,* growing in Dalmatia and also cultivated in Japan and Kenya, has become the main source of insect powder called pyrethrum. It is less hardy than the ornamental garden variety. The leaves are more silvery and the plant is more difficult to grow in cold climates. Painted Daisy, with its carrot-like foliage and 2½ foot tall, literally 'painted' flowers, in pink, red or shades between the two, has some of the same properties. Mrs. Maude Grieve, in *A Modern Herbal,* suggested testing the strength of the Pyrethrum by placing a little of the powdered dried herbs of flowers under a glass with some flies. If they are not stupefied in one minute, then you may not have the right species.

CULTURE: The plants are grown from seed and may be planted in flats in sterile medium, at 70° F. to germinate in 2 to 3 weeks, or sown in the garden in spring or mid-summer (in the North), for flowering the following year. They need excellent drainage and protection from other plants or weeds. Seedlings are slight and should be spaced a foot apart the following spring. Shade them after transplanting. After blooming, cut flower stalks to the base of the plant to encourage a second blossoming in autumn. The plants may winter-kill if the soil is very heavy or the least bit wet. In their native lands, the Pyrethrum species may develop 80 to 100 flowers on a single plant. As they are mountain natives, the crown of leaves requires a dry surface, sunlight and heat for sufficient growth.

USE: The Painted Daisy is grown for colorful flowers in the garden and in bouquets. It seldom produces enough blooms to tempt the gardener to try drying them to make insecticide. It is interesting to know the special qualities of the herb, but to sacrifice its beauty for pestilence duty is like cutting off your nose to spite your face. If it goes wild in the garden, then it might be worthwhile to dry the flowers, powder them and dust special plants with their product. The leaves have none of the properties attributed to this and the Dalmatian species.

"The double daisy, thrift, the button bachelor Sweet William, sops-in-wine, the rampion; and to these some Lavender they put, with rosemary and bays, Sweet Marjoram, with her like sweet basil for rare smell, with many a flower, whose name were now too long to tell."

Rampion/Campanula Rapunculus

RAMPION   BIENNIAL
Campanula Rapunculus   Zone 4
Campanulaceae, native to Europe

HABIT: It is hard to think of the pretty bluebell flowers of Rampion being sacrificed by eating the leaves as winter salad or the roots as spring parsnip-like vegetable. It is still cultivated in France, Germany and Italy for such purposes. The herb gardener delights in the dainty lavender-blue flowers the second spring which hang from graceful stems rising 18 inches from the bluntly rounded leaves in a basal rosette. Stem leaves are narrower and sometimes absent. Where other flowering Campanulas have somewhat hairy foliage, Rampion's is smooth and rather shiny. It is easy to picture the German bride who looked over the garden wall to covet a salad of Rampion greens when she was pregnant. She sent her husband into the witch's garden to get a handful. They tasted so delicious that the poor man had to risk climbing down again. This time the witch in the fairy tale caught him and demanded that he give her his first-born child in payment for his freedom. The child was Rapunzel, which is the German name for Rampion. Perhaps the tale was fair warning to those who did not grow their own saladings to keep out of other people's gardens! We grow the medieval herb for its mythology as well as its beauty.

CULTURE: Seed of Rampion is fine as dust and should be sown in a flat, soon after it ripens in late summer. No covering of the tiny grains is necessary as they germinate best in full light. Temperatures 65°-72° F. are advised for biennial Campanula species, and work well for this herbal member of the genus. Germination is slow. Self-sown plants may volunteer some distance from the original planting as the seeds are shaken from the capsules or washed away by rains. Plants need only 6 to 8 inches between them as the stalks are so delicate that they help to hold each other up as flowering begins. If Rampion is grown for greens, the plants are not allowed to bloom. Moist sandy soil suits the herb best. The roots were blanched, as for Chicons, in olden days but they are so small as to be less than finger-size so it is not worthwhile.

USE: Rampion is a collector's item among herb growers. Our first plants came from seed shared by a botanical garden in Europe. We cherish every self-sown specimen lest it be the last one grown in our garden. It is easy to forget the biennials in the spring and seeing them in bloom and watching for seed, is often the only way to keep such an oddity with you. We have shared Rampion seedlings with the herb gardener at the Cloisters in New York City in days past. Some were given to a young man who was making a medieval garden within a wattle fence of his own construction in Vermont.

Rocambole/*Allium Scorodoprasum* Rocambole/*Allium Scorodoprasum*

ROCAMBOLE PERENNIAL
Allium Scorodoprasum Zone 3
Amaryllidaceae, native to Europe

HABIT: French or Serpent Garlic produces purple skinned bulblets on the top of the scapes (flowering stems). It does not have clove-like bulbs at the base and it lives over from year to year. The identity of this form of Garlic has been confused since pre-Linnean times. Whatever the taxonomists may determine it to be, the herb gardener finds it interesting and useful. Before the clumps of flat, 18 inch long leaves begin to produce 'flower' stalks, the plant is thick with greens, almost like Garlic Chives. Then from the middle of the clump rise round stems which make a complete circle before they reach their 3 foot height. The scapes unwind and hold their pointed buds high but at an angle that suggests a crane's bill. Finally, in mid-summer, the show ends with the spliting of the skin covering a cluster of popcorn kernel size, pleasantly garlic-tasting bulblets. Following their maturing and turning from violet to grayish, if the season is not wet enough to cause some to green up and sprout, the plant dies down. But it is not through. In early autumn, it sends up narrow flat leaves in a clump again. Sometimes the bulblets are offered as "Garlic seed."

CULTURE: French Garlic is not propagated by divisions of the basal bulb, as with Garlic, though the clumps can be pulled apart in the spring when producing their leaves. It is the little bulbets which make new plants wherever they fall from the matured stems. They may be set out one by one, as for seed, in a furrow and will take two years to reach reproductive capacity. Soaking speeds up sprouting of the kernels which have been allowed to dry for kitchen storage. The plant is very hardy. Some writers believe it is a small form of Elephant Garlic, because of its habit of growth, but there is no divisible bulb at the base. The stems go down to a Leek-like swelling that is the hold-fast in the soil. For this reason, the clump falls apart as it produces scapes a second year. These extra basal leaves can be propped up with twigs until they begin to die back. In deep, rich loam, the roots may be strong enough to support the whole mass of leaves and inflorescence. But the urge to reproduce at the top can't be thwarted.

USE: The gardener would not want to miss the dramatic changes of Rocambole. Its bulbils were introduced to the trade by our importation of them in the 1940's from France. They were welcomed as we never seemed to get an increase when planting Garlic cloves on our New Jersey acres. Apparently, that Allium needs cool conditions for 2 months, even in California, to hasten bulbing. The Rocambole is not fussy, offers dozens of little mini-cloves in one head, and keeps without going soft through the winter in the kitchen. Great for a 'little' Garlic in use.
The little clovelets of Rocambole do not need peeling. They are a bit tricky to cut up - it's better to mash them slightly with the flat side of a knife. Two heads of bulbils will flavor cider or wine vinegar with a rich aroma of Garlic. Just pop them individually down the neck of a quart of either. A pot of Rocambole bulbils starting to sprout makes a delightful hostess gift. Chances are she will not know about its flavor as greens and will be delighted to grow it on till spring in

127

the kitchen window. The rounds of Rocambole are not too attractive en masse as the papery shell which holds them together dries to a rather tarnished color. If you are preparing a dip to take to an impromptu party, you can use them and then take one bunch to demonstrate how the herb is packaged by nature.

HOT CRAB DIP

8 oz. cream cheese
2 Tablespoons sour cream
6½ oz. cooked crabmeat or shrimp
2 Tablespoons mashed Rocambole bulbils
2 Tablespoons grated Horseradish
2 Tablespoons fresh Parsley, chopped
Salt and Pepper

Blend the above and pack into a small baking dish. Heat at 350° F. for 20-25 minutes. Serve warm on crackers.

BLUE CHEESE BALL

8 oz. package of cream cheese
¼ lb. blue cheese crumbled
½ teaspoon dry mustard
Dash Worcestershire sauce
2 Tablespoons fresh Rocambole leaves
2 Tablespoons chopped fresh Thyme

Mix all the above ingredients in a bowl until well blended. Form into a ball and roll in chopped fresh Parsley. The spread freezes and may be rolled in the Parsley on removal from the freezer, for carrying to a picnic.

REGULA, ROQUETTE   ANNUAL
Eruca vesicaria subsp. sativa
Cruciferae, native to the Mediterranean

HABIT: The irregular, wavy edged leaves resemble those of Radish's but are a darker green. If allowed to flower, plants have 4 petaled, white blossoms with dark red lines on them. It is an Italian salad green which has become rather chic in this country partly because it grows quickly but most people don't know how to use it. The plants should not be allowed to bloom. When they do they are up to two feet tall. The key to enjoyment of the herb is rich soil with enough moisture to produce tender leaves which should be eaten in moderation, especially mixed with other lettuces. If the plants grow slowly in hot weather, the flavor is bitter and texture tough. There is a skunky aroma to them but the taste resembles peanuts when put with Italian salad dressing.

CULTURE: Devotees can grow the plants indoors, in a soil substitute kept at 60-70° F. It will succeed in a light garden as the seedlings can stand cooler temperatures once started. Sow outdoors as you would radishes, early in the spring when the soil is thoroughly moist. Cover seed lightly in a shallow drill, not as deep as for radishes. Thinnings may be eaten so there is no need for transplanting. Put the seeds in the drill as evenly spaced as possible and pull the plantlets that crowd others.

USE: The harvest is a one-time thing. Pull and use as often as possible when they are tender but once the flavor gets very strong, replace the row with Dill or Summer Savory. This herb was carried to Europe and Britain by the Romans. It came to this country early enough to be

Sweet Rocket/Hesperis matronalis

Regula/Eruca sativa

naturalized in some places but don't try to pick it in the wild unless you know botany. When Regula, Roquette or Rocket, as it has been named, is grown in poor soil it is not only bad tasting but has somewhat emetic properties.

ROCKET, SWEET   PERENNIAL
Hesperis matronalis   Zone 4
Cruciferae, native to Europe

HABIT: A showy flower with oval, pointed, slightly hairy leaves, Sweet Rocket has naturalized along roadsides as a garden escape in New England. It's bright magenta to mauve, phlox-like flowers, sometimes white also, are welcome in the shady places where it takes up habitation. Plants stand erect at 3 feet but may bloom at half that height. They are easily transplanted at any stage. The name 'Dame's Violet' is more appropriate as the blossoms are sweet-scented at night. They attract moths and butterflies and are welcome where they appear.

CULTURE: Seed may be sown outdoors at any time and needs light and 70° F. temperature to germinate in a flat. Somehow plants in the woods are in bloom before any such weather or warm ground. They keep on flowering off and on for months. A double white form is much sought after in England. It doesn't seem to be in the U. S. Blossoms can be expected the first year from seed. If the spent flowers are cut off there will be less problem of self-sowing. Volunteers are easily moved, though they wilt down at first. Sweet Rocket needs renewing every other year as the plants do not last long. We have pulled up 3 foot tall flowering specimens and pressed them into loose soil on the edge of the woods with no setback in their blossoming.

USE: Despite the similarity of names, Roquette and Sweet Rocket are not interchangeable in use. The first, Italian salad plant that it is, is not grown for blossoms. The second, fragrant flower, scarcely needs planting again once it is started in an herb garden or flower border. But it does not stay in the same spot in the way that phlox does. The 'Mustard Family' heritage of both plants is their only real link. The seeds are numerous and with the perennial Rocket they are needed to maintain its flowering. If you like to try new flavors, put some fresh leaves of Roquette, Regula, or Ruccola, *Eruca sativa,* in a mixed green salad and slather with—

Salad in Bowl   *Rosemary/Rosmarinus officinalis*

LIGHT MAYONNAISE

2 cups cottage cheese
¼ cup yogurt
1 egg
1 to 2 teaspoons light prepared mustard
1 Tablespoon lemon juice
2 Tablespoons salad oil
½ teaspoon salt
¼ teaspoon white pepper
Dash of red pepper sauce

Combine ingredients in food processor or blender and whirl till smooth (beat it to death!). Makes 2¼ cups with about 18 calories per tablespoon. Try just a few young leaves of Regula with lots of lettuce until you judge its strength and taste.

ROSEMARY   PERENNIAL
Rosmarinus officinalis and cultivars   Zone 8
Labiatae, native to the Mediterranean

HABIT: This pungent, evergreen herb has but one species with many cultivars. It has been in gardens so long that natural hybrids have occured to give us forms for many different situations, so it is hard to say what is the typical Rosemary type. Where the ground does not freeze, it may become a shrub 6 feet tall and 3 to 4 feet or more wide. In California, the creeping prostrate Rosemary is a ground cover, used as street planting and wall landscaping. In the North, it is a cherished house plant in winter. The leaves are needle-like with decurved edges and whitish undersides. Stems may be woody, on older plants, or softly light green on cuttings and certain grayer types. No matter what it looks like, Rosemary is known by its piney scent and wonderfully aromatic, almost resinous foliage. To touch it is to become perfumed yourself and to learn its romantic associations is to fall in love with Rosemary. It is a plant with many habits of growth and multiple uses. The blossoms are two-lipped, varying in shades of blue to white, and nestle in the axils of the clustered leaves on older stems. Those of us who must keep the plant in pots in winter may or may not see it bloom. If the greens have to be cut back on coming indoors, the flowering is lost for buds form on last year's growth. Leaves are half to one inch in length, stems variable.

CULTURE: Rosemary may be grown from seed, in fact, some of the softer, grayer forms come mainly from seed. Sow seeds in sterile soil substitute, in a flat, at temperature of 55° at night to 75° in the daytime. Seedlings appear in 15-20 days but then grow very slowly for months. If they can be potted when they are an inch or two in height, put each one in its own smallest size plastic

130

Rosmarinus off./Prostratus　　　　　　　　*Rosmarinus off./"Miss Jessup"*

pot. Peat mixtures are inimicable to Rosemary and Lavender which thrive in alkaline soils. Some sand should be added to the potting soil used for both plants as soon as they are to be potted up. Overwatering is one of the principle causes of losing Rosemary seedlings but slips taken to propagate the herb need to be kept moist. When we saw a blooming specimen of *Rosemarinus officinalis 'Lockwood de Forest'* growing out of a crack in a sandstone wall along a street in Santa Barbara, we could only marvel. There was no visible root run, the sandstone blocks were cemented together but the plant was shiny with its healthy green leaves and deep blue blossoms. A book could be written about the problems and pleasures of growing Rosemary. It is said that where the herb flourishes the woman rules. One author has wondered about that but the other, her daughter, has always had the most beautiful plants of the herb she was named for, in her home and even on her desk in an insurance company office where she first worked after college.

The ambition to have a lot of Rosemary for its many uses in cooking, tea and sweet bags and sachets is best realized by taking cuttings. Plants put on new growth in March indoors and in gardens in California and along its native Mediterranean coast. The name means *'dew of the sea'* from *Ros marinus,* and is accounted for by its proximity to the coast. The smell of Rosemary is said to be noticeable off shore from Spain and Portugal. The gardener tries to simulate the climatic conditions where Rosemary has a gravelly or sandy root run but frequent mists from the sea fogs. Too much wet around the roots will rot it, but even in a pot, it cannot stand to go entirely dry. The foliage is oily and where plants of Rosemary are crowded by other specimens in a light garden or on a windowsill, branches will die back or cause other plants, on which they rest, to do so. Good air circulation is important to the bushy and even spreading Rosemarys. Where it may be left out in winter, the foliage may burn somewhat from wind and sun, towards spring. So a gardener who has cared for a large pot of Rosemary indoors has certain rewards in putting out a beautiful pot of it in the spring. It, too, must be sheltered from winds those first days in the sun in April or May.

KINDS: It might be helpful to make up a buyers' list of types of Rosemary available now in the nurseries in this country and in England. Each cultivar or variety has its own peculiarity in appearance and needs. A California catalog lists nine varieties. They include *Rosmarinus officinalis;* 'Benenden Blue' *(R. off. 'Angustissimus')* originally from a garden called Benenden in England, belonging to Mr. Collingwood Ingram; 'Pink Rosemary' a variety from Majorca; Santa Barbara Rosemary, the hybrid of *R. officinalis 'Prostratus'* which originated in the garden of Lockwood de Forest in Santa Barbara, California; 'Trailing Rosemary', *R. officinalis 'Prostratus'* which is lower and less shiny green than Santa Barbara; 'Tuscan Blue', upright as the typical Rosemary but with light blue flowers on 5 foot tall stems; 'White Rosemary', a softer gray leaf with white flowers and white downy stems; 'Wood Rosemary', a shortened version of Collingwood Ingram's name (it and 'Pine-scented' have the narrow needle-like leaves, with darker blue flowers). The last would have been called *Rosmarinus officinalis 'Angustissimus'* before *Hortus Third.* In California, the above plants might look quite different from the same varieties grown in pots in Ohio or further east in this country. In England, there is a fastigiate form of *R. officinalis,* called 'Miss Jessup', which grows 5 feet tall with rather thick, shiny green leaves, the bottom ones yellowing off towards autumn. Names vary according to sources there. In New Zealand, where Rosemary wreaths are placed on soldiers' graves, on their Memorial Day, there is a deep-blue form called 'Blue Lagoon'. The golden striped Rosemary which Mrs. Cathleen Maxwell discovered in a nursery and introduced to the Mt. Vernon Garden replica at The American Museum in Britain, is in the hands of a few herb specialists in this country. A New Jersey nursery lists it and 19 other forms they have named.

ROOTING CUTTINGS: Most of the unusual Rosemary types are propagated by cuttings. Methods vary according to the individual. An older plant with woody stems may have short pieces which can be pulled off with a 'heel' which some people believe roots more quickly. We think it is the state of the plant and time of year which has a governing effect on rooting. If the plant is more or less dormant and going into a short day period, cuttings take longer to root. As new growth begins toward spring, slips may take hold in 3 to 4 weeks. There are people who find the woody stemmed slips root in water. This has its hazards as the roots must not be allowed to grow more than an inch or two in the liquid medium. If they are longer they will not adapt as well to potting soil. A rigid clear plastic box with a top acts as Wardian case when half filled with equal parts of perlite and peat. Cuttings, which have been stripped of their lower leaves and dusted with hormone powder before inserting in the medium, root faster than in sand or water. If the box develops condensation on the inside of the lid, wipe it often or set the top slightly ajar. The moist air inside it acts as a mini-misting system but droplets should not fall on the foliage. Keep it in light but not direct sunshine. *Laurus nobilis* will root in such a container in 3 months instead of the year or two its cuttings take if in open air. It needs hormone powder of strength for shrubs. Rosemary and Bay are truly evergreen herbs which make good house plants if handled properly. They may be fed with seaweed fertilizer when they are growing strongly and left to themselves when they are resting. Both evergreen herbs make lovely topiary plants. The prostrate Rosemary blooms constantly when potted and trimmed.

LAYERINGS: Rosemary is easily layered when it is growing in the garden. In spring, side branches are pegged down under a mound of earth and will be ready to be cut off when it is time to bring the plant indoors in autumn. Thus the large specimen which has grown rather scraggly at the bottom may be set deeper in the ground than usual and layered while it is outdoors. Philip Miller, writing in 1731, suggested that 3 or 4 foot branches of Rosemary be placed in a deep trench for rooting. He was curator of the Chelsea Physic Garden in London, which was and still is a garden of medicinal and other herbs used for teaching purposes located along the embankment of the River Thames. Elizabeth Blackwell, the lady herbalist, lived on Swan Walk, overlooking the Garden, where she gathered live specimens of herbs to draw for her *A Curious Herbal*, 1737.

Two sources of damage to *Rosmarinus officinalis* are a root rot, possibly from overwatering or wet conditions of the ground and powdery mildew. The latter is new to herb gardeners but seems to be prevalent where begonias and Rosemary are grouped together. A thorough dusting with sulphur powder and good air circulation and sunlight can cure the mildew. Root rot is more difficult and eventually travels throughout the plant. Save all the needles if this happens as they have many uses fresh and dry.

Uses for Rosemary

The fresh or dried herb steeped in boiling water makes marvelous steam to inhale when your head is stuffed with a cold. Drinking the tea with honey clears the nasal passages and lifts the spirits. A strong infusion is a fine hair rinse for brunette or black hair. If you rub the liquid in you may find its true that Rosemary is good for remembrance. The rinse takes away all the smell of permanent wave lotion. One author takes it with her to the hairdresser who begged for a plant. The daughter of the author has naturally curly hair. Dried leaves, even from a plant that has failed, are natural incense to throw on the coals of a wood stove or fireplace. Burning it was an old-timey way to clear the air in a sick-room. The herb is easily dried by hanging a bunch of woody stems in the kitchen or anywhere that it will be enjoyed for its aroma and use.

ROSEMARY RECIPES

Although widely used in Europe to flavor pork and lamb, Rosemary is one of the most under-used herbs in the American kitchen. Possibly this is because its pungency is strong and the flavor can come through too blatantly if too many dried leaf needles are sprinkled freely on bland foods. Breads and pizza take the resinous overtone of Rosemary well.

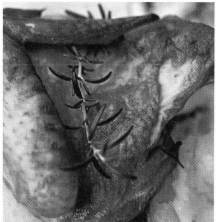

Chicken with Rosemary

Rosemary Pizza

MRS. BATJER'S ROSEMARY BREAD

Have ingredients and bowl at room temperature.

2 cups cottage cheese

2 eggs
2½ envelopes dry yeast

½ cup sugar
1 Tablespoon plus 2
  teaspoons salt

2 Tablespoons crushed
  dried Rosemary
2/3 of a stick of margarine
2 teaspoons soda, stirred
  into ¼ cup water
6-9 cups all purpose flour
1½ cups water (hot)

Put cottage cheese, sugar, eggs, salt in blender. Blend and pour into a *large* bowl. Put hot water into blender container to rinse, and add to ingredients in bowl. Add Rosemary, margarine, yeast, baking soda in water before the flour and beat that in thoroughly. Knead on a board or marble slab for 10 minutes or until dough does not stick to the hands. Let rise until double in bulk. Cut down and shape into 2 large French loaves. Let rise on greased cookie sheet for 30 to 40 minutes. Bake at 350° F. for 20 minutes, reducing heat to 325° and baking another 20 minutes. For a crusty top, brush with cold water at the time heat is set down.

ROSEMARY PIZZA

Use the bread dough with Rosemary in it and roll out for Pizza pan, which has been greased with oil. Sprinkle oil on the rolled dough, spread with tomato sauce, a dusting of sugar and ½ teaspoon dried Rosemary, topping all with grated Italian cheese that melts beautifully. Bake at 400° F. for 20 minutes. Serve hot or cool and freeze for another day. Small pizzas would allow for different toppings with this super dough with cottage cheese and Rosemary. With a bowl of soup, the bread and a salad, you have fed.

CHICKEN WITH WHITE WINE AND ROSEMARY

Put four chicken pieces in a shallow pan - pour over them—
½ cup white wine
¼ cup soy sauce
Sprinkle with 1 teaspoon fresh Rosemary leaves. Baste every 15 minutes, while baking uncovered at 350° F. for one hour. Put a few sprigs whole Rosemary leaves around the platter on which chicken is served.

Rue/Ruta graveolens

Rue/Ruta graveolens

RUE   PERENNIAL
Ruta graveolens   Zone 4
Rutaceae, native to southern Europe

HABIT: First it is the blue-green color of Rue that catches the eye and then it is the curious shape of the leaves that holds it. Rue is a classic herb of literature and romance but not one for holding close or consuming freely. Each plant is a small shrub with yellowish, woody stems which stand upright and are clothed with patterned flat leaves whose terminal leaflet is unusally club shaped. The flowers are yellow with scoop-ended petals surrounding a prominent ovary with central pistil. Maurice Maeterlinck noted that the anthers ranged round it bent with their weight of pollen to dust it on the female part of the flower in a numerical sequence. Rue is a study but in hot weather should be held at arm's length. The oil of the foliage brushing against the skin and subjected to sunlight can cause a severe rash or dermatitis. This was known to the ancients who advised spreading olive oil on hands and arms before handling the plant. Reaction to Rue is not as likely when the plants are young but increases in intensity as they come into bloom. The upright habit makes Rue of service as a low hedge, growing not more than 2-3 feet in height. Its pungency is medicinal and its insect or disease enemies few. Bunches of Rue were used in times of plague to ward off germs which were then unrecognized. A leaf is put in the Italian liqueur *grappa.*

CULTURE: This perennial is grown from seed sown in a sandy medium and held at 60° to 70° F. for 10-14 days in a flat. Outdoor sowing is possible but the little plants are too frail for placing in competition with other herbs. When Rue grows up to full height for flowering it can take care of itself if spaced a foot apart. It is a native of the Mediterranean shores so requires sharp drainage and soil that is not rich. In moist garden loam it is apt to winter kill in the North. Also where it is overshadowed by trees or shrubs it grows weakly. Plants may need pruning back to new growth in the spring but do not cut the main stems straight across until new shoots are breaking. Then do it selectively. The seed heads are four-channeled and interesting in dried arrangements, sometimes gilded for wreath decorations. But again, handle them with care and wash hands after doing so instead of chancing the phototropic reaction on delicate skin. A non-flowering form 'Blue Beauty' is very decorative.

USE: Rue's romantic association with wedding ceremonies in Lithuania gives no hint of possible dermatitis. It was the traditional herb of brides there and as the weddings were mostly held in winter, perhaps rashes did not occur. There is a narrow-leaved Rue, *Ruta chalepensis,* sometimes sold as *Ruta graveolens* seed. It is beautiful to look at but has a stronger aroma and can cause dermatitis. It is not hardy as it comes from Crete and southern Greece. Seed capsules are pointed, not indented at the top and leaves have no club-shaped tips.

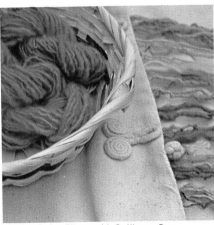

Dying Fibers with Safflower Dye   *Safflower/Carthamus tinctorius*

SAFFLOWER   ANNUAL
Carthamus tinctorius
Compositae, native to Eurasia

HABIT: 'False Saffron' is another name for the thistle-like annual which may be used in place of the delicate *Crocus sativus* which is the source of true Saffron powder. The stigma or female part of the flower of Saffron is the source of flavoring from the small bulb. It is the petals of bright orange Safflower that are dried for similar use and for herb dyes. Plants grow to three feet tall with somewhat prickly leaves of shiny green and heads with spiny bracts around the flower petals. Plants stand straight with branching stems topped by flower and seed heads. The seeds themselves resemble white teeth and are the source of Safflower oil. The oil is better known than the plant today. Safflower was grown in Egypt at the time of the Pharaohs and is now a major crop in this country for seed which is pressed for Safflower oil.

CULTURE: Seeds are sown in the garden in ½ inch deep drills and covered with soil to a depth of twice the size of the seed. If the spacing is even, there will be little need for thinning. Plants should stand 8-10 inches apart. Seed may be started indoors at 65°-70° in peat pots or One Step growing devices to set out when all danger of frost is past. Safflower does not transplant readily unless potted first. Germination takes 10 days to 2 weeks when the ground is warm. The herb grows well in poor dry soil which makes it a viable crop for arid lands in the West. Considering that the oil was first used for adding to paint to hasten drying, it is interesting to see that it is now coming into its own as a clear, low cholestrol cooking and salad oil. *The Herb Grower Magazine* carried an article on the progress of the herb from an experimental planting at Beltsville in the 1920's to its much larger cultivation in Montana and the Great Northern Plains in 1947, in Volume II, 1948.

USE: For the home gardener, Safflower offers orange petals to dry for coloring and flavoring food. Its ancient reputation as a natural dye for silk was tested by one author in 1965. Dried orange flower petals of *Carthamus tinctorius* were infused in boiling water and allowed to cool overnight. A mordant of household pickling alum and cream of tartar was mixed in 4 gallons of soft water. A pure silk banker's coat was washed in mild soap and rinsed. It was then immersed in the mordant bath and heated to 150° F. Following this it was stirred and allowed to soak till the next day. Vinegar was added to the dye solution and the pure silk garment was stirred carefully at 130° F. After coloring and rinsing the jacket took on a subtle gold color and has remained color-fast for 15 years. Directions were taken from the Brooklyn Botanic Garden's *Handbook #46, Dye Plants And Dyeing.* The petals of Safflower dry easily after washing, patting dry and placing on brown paper in a ventilated place out of the sun. It takes several teaspoonfuls to color rice while cooking or it may be steeped in soup stock and strained out before serving.

Sage/Salvia officinalis   Sage/Salvia officinalis

SAGES, HERB   ANNUAL, BIENNIAL AND PERENNIAL
Salvia officinalis   Zones 4 & 5
Labiatae, native to southern Europe

HABIT: Garden Sage becomes quite woody after its first year. The stemmed leaves are persistent, oblong or pointed, with a gray color produced by tiny hairs on the much veined surface, giving it a pebbly effect. They may be 2 inches long and ¾ of an inch broad, or narrower, with finely toothed margins. The plant attains 2½ feet in height when in flower. The loose spikes of two-lipped blossoms 1/2-1/3 inch long are so arranged that a bee landing on the lower lip will trip the anthers with its head to assure pollen being carried to the next blossom. The culinary Sage may have blue, white or pink flowers in May. First year plants grown from seed may carry some inflorescences at the end of summer if they have not been cut for drying.

Three colored leaf forms are grown in herb gardens. They are variants of the species and may be used as culinary seasonings also. The best known has been called "Red Sage" in England, but it is not the annual flower, Scarlet Salvia, nor is it really red in color. *Salvia officinalis "Purpurascens"* has soft purplish leaves which do not suggest the 'Red' in its familiar name. It is said to have been favored over plain Garden Sage for making Sage tea. The form 'Tricolor' has been propagated from it because some of the foliage is streaked with white, purple and pink. When grown on its own, the variegated shoot is a weaker plant with narrower leaves often centered with green. A golden and green form, 'Icterina' has yellow-edged leaves. It too is delicate, not wintering well in the North. If left to tough it out for one winter, the plant may go all green and never recover the variegation. As Gerard would say, nature has had fun with these plants. They are nice for warm climate accent use.

CULTURE: Cooking Sage, called "Garden Sage", is easy to grow from seed. The seeds are round and brown, big enough to sow in a shallow drill in early spring. If started 6-8 weeks before last frost, indoors, germination will occur in 2 to 3 weeks if the medium is kept at 60°-70° F. Plants should be set out, (after hardening off by setting transplanted seedlings in the sun a few hours each day,) 18 to 24 inches apart. Sage grows as wide as it does tall. There is a cultivated broad-leaf Sage, with rounded tips to the foliage, which spreads out to 3 feet. It is one that commercial drying companies prefer for its abundance of herbage. A narrow-leaf form, much pointed at the tips, stays scarcely more than 18 inches tall but grows outwards, too. It is used where a little Sage-flavor is desired.

The cultivars or fancy colored Sages are quite tender perennials. They need protection from wind in winter and perfect drainage. They will die back in Zone 4 but usually make it in Zone 5 and south. We take cuttings from the plants to put in a mixture of equal parts peat and perlite in colorful plastic bowls which once held margarine. They make delightful gifts or windowsill plants in the house. When spring comes each one is rooted and may be put in the garden after frost. Watering is minimal, just enough once or twice a week to keep the medium slightly moist. The cuttings, which root before spring, are pinched back but left right in the container.

Fresh Sage Stuffing Ingredients

USE: Fresh Sage has a much nicer flavor than the dried herb. It is chopped fine and put with creamed cheese beaten up with a little cream or cottage cheese to spread on sandwiches or crackers. Try it before adding much to any dish; there are some who do not like the strong pervasiveness of Sage. It is a flavor you can't subtract but it has more uses than just in turkey dressing. Try using it with squash and eggplant or in—

FRESH SAGE CHICKEN STUFFING

Cube one loaf of slightly stale bread (not rock hard)
Add ½ cup chopped onion
Add ½ cup chopped celery
Mix in 4 Tablespoons fresh chopped Sage
 or 2 Tablespoons dried Sage
Add 4 Tablespoons chopped Parsley
Mix gently with hands and stuff and truss bird.

Sage is easily dried by hanging a loose handful tied together in a bunch, and is pleasant to have in the kitchen when drying. It can be placed in the brown paper bag if you need quantity beyond that strung up for its ambience. The herb needs finishing off to crispness if it is to be powdered before packing. It is surprising how the leaves turn into a fluffy mass when ground in a mortar with a pestle or just rubbed through a coarse strainer. Be sure to pick out bits of stems before placing the herb in jars or in food. Herb teas take on authority when a leaf or two of Sage is added to the Mint, Lemon Balm or Bee Balm leaves. It gives a darker color also.

There is an old saying, "Why should a man die, whilst Sage grows in his garden?" The very name means to be safe or unharmed. The herbalists suggested that Rue should be planted among Sage to keep away noxious toads. Our toads are friendly creatures who eat slugs, but Sage and Rue do grow well together.

Clary Sage/Salvia viridis

Clary Sage/Salvia Sclarea

SAGE, ANNUAL CLARY AND BIENNIAL CLARY
Salvia viridis
Labiatae

HABIT: The pretty annual Sage with gray leaves and pink, white or purple flowers that appear in the axils of the leaves, used to be called *Salvia horminum*. It has curious colored bracts above the blossoms, at the top of the 18 to 24 inch stalks. Though the foliage is similar to that of Garden Sage it has none of the strong scent. It is valuable for drying for arrangements because the showy top leaves or bracts are veined with pink or purple and last long after the blossoms fall. It was once considered a medicinal herb because the seed had the same gelatinous quality as that of the larger biennial Clary Sage.

True Clary Sage cannot be mistaken for the annual when it comes into flower. The seedling leaves look similar but the inflorescence of the biennial is of such an odor that it is unforgettable. It does not throw its scent, but just brush against it and you will match the Italian name for it that means 'smells like sweat'. It is a great plant for dry soils and stunning effects when in bloom. The seeds are mucilaginous when moistened and were used to clear specks from the eye, hence the name Clary or clear-eye. This is not a thing to try.

CULTURE: Sow seed of Annual Clary in early spring indoors. It will germinate quickly at 55°-65° F. in sterile soil substitute. Seedlings are easily transplanted into small pots or flats and may be set out, after danger of frost, to stand 12 inches apart. Once placed in the garden and allowed to flower and seed, *S. viridis* may volunteer in subsequent years. It is a great filler for tall perennials which become rather bare of leaves as they bloom. Purple Coneflower looks nice with a facing of Pink Sundae Annual Clary or a group of Monarchs (mixed colors). It blooms and keeps its bracts which are more colorful than the blossoms.

Biennial or Clary Sage, may be started from seed in the same way. It, too, will self-sow and seedlings may be picked up and placed where desired in early spring. Allow 2 feet between plants. Leaves are 3 to 4 inches wide and somewhat heart-shaped with scalloped edges. The inflorescence may bring total height of the plant to 4 to 5 feet. Blue and white or all white widelipped flowers attract humming birds in mid-summer. As they form in the open calyces, the green seeds are the delight of goldfinches. Clary Sage is an old favorite for sandy, dry soil. Seeds may be planted in the ground in summer for blooming the next year.

USE: Annual Clary has no flavor or scent but rates high in looks. Biennial or Clary Sage does have a certain piquancy to the leaves which can be dipped in batter and deep-fried as Clary fritters. The oil of the flowering plant is a fixative in the perfume industry, to tone down artificial scents.

Pineapple Sage PotPourri

Sage/Salvia elegans

SAGE, PINEAPPLE   PERENNIAL
Salvia elegans   Zone 8
Labiatae, native to Mexico

HABIT: A fruit-scented, dark-green, pointed-leaved Sage that is a great favorite for indoor and garden growing. The stems are fuzzy when young but harden to woody in late summer before the plants produce stunning narrow, tubular red blooms. These may continue on plants brought indoors if they have not become too large for repotting. The foliage is pretty and pleasantly scented. The blossoms come singly at the ends of stems and attract attention always. Small plants made from cuttings rooted in water may bloom as the days shorten. In the North, we seldom see the flowering of Pineapple Sage in the garden because it does not begin until frost catches up with the plant. By then it may be three feet tall with many branches.

CULTURE: Pineapple Sage is grown from cuttings that root in water or in sand and peat. The herb is one of the most satisfactory for the window garden because it can flower even with reduced day length. Every leaf is useful. If cuttings need pinching back once they have rooted, save the leaflets for topping a fruit cup. When whole stems need pruning, let the fragrant branches form the basis of a bouquet. Once you obtain a plant of the obliging herb, you have material from which to take slips, dry foliage for tea and potpourri, and, in warmer climes, enjoy the flowers far into the winter.

USE: The abundance of foliage that Pineapple Sage produces in one summer lends itself to many uses. The leaves gathered from plants that must be cut back to bring indoors may be dried for potpourri. That is a mixture of herb foliage and dried flowers with the addition of essential oils and a fixative such as Orris, made from the dried root of old-fashioned Bearded Iris.

Pineapple Sage PotPourri Base
(Courtesy of Patricia Reppert)

Mix equal parts of dried Pineapple Sage leaves and Lavender blossoms, Rosemary, Lemon Balm and Rose Geranium leaves, all of which have been dried first. To a quart of dried herbage, add ¼ cup Orris root granules, ¼ cup Patchouli leaves and some dried Pineapple Sage blossoms, Pot Marigold petals and other everlasting flowers for color. Mix the above in a wooden bowl and put into a closed pottery, glass or tin container. Let it meld for several weeks before opening to see if a few drops of Lavender oil, or Rosemary oil are needed for strengthening. When the mixture has been stirred every few weeks and allowed to blend, put a small amount in an open bowl and stir it to see if the scent pleases you. Orange peel and dried Lemon peel may be added for zest and sprinkling of powdered Cinnamon, Cloves and Allspice. Potpourri and herb tea are principal uses of dried Pineapple Sage leaves. The fresh go in iced tea and fruit cup. Cream cheese with minced Pineapple Sage is a nice tea sandwich filling.

Santolina virens | Santolina Species/Santolina Chamaecyparissus

SANTOLINA SPECIES   **PERENNIAL**
Santolina Chamaecyparissus   Zone 6
Compositae, native to southern Europe, Mediterranean

HABIT: The beautiful Santolinas are considered sub-shrubs but they never get taller than 2 to 2½ feet in height. The foliage is distinctive, with curiously crimped gray leaflets on either side of a woolly white stem. The whole effect of Gray Santolina, called 'Lavender Cotton' in the U. S. and 'Cotton Lavender' in Great Britain, is that of a mound of gray coral. It is soft to the touch and delightfully aromatic. It is that which must have given the idea of calling it both lavender and cotton. The flowers are yellow buttons on leafless, unbranching stems which top the plant by several inches. They dry beautifully but the leaflets shrink. In sandy soil, such as at Cape Cod, Santolinas can grow out to 4 to 5 feet in diameter over a period of years. Where it is subject to snow cover, it will die back to the root almost every winter. The evergreen herb adds scent to potpourri if the whole branch is spread out on a screen for drying. The name 'Santolina' is said to have come from the high regard in which the herb was held by the Spanish Padres who brought it to this country at the mission stations in California. It was likened to the saints for its great durability in dry, warm soils.

CULTURE: In the South, Santolina is grown from seed, planted in a medium at temperatures of 65-70° F. Germination may take 15 to 20 days. In the North the plants are layered in autumn, by heaping soil over the woody stems of side branches and pinning them down. A good lot of tips of branches must be allowed to stay free of the earthing, so that the plants to be cut off in the spring from the main clump have had their heads in the air. It is slow-growing but worth accomodating. Santolinas like a more acid soil than that suitable for Lavenders and must have good drainage. They will sometimes turn black in summer in humid, hot weather. There is no help for it but to take cuttings which take a long time to root in a mixture of peat and sand. The other species, *S. virens,* with its green, narrower leaves, stands the winter in the North better than the gray woolly one. *Santolina neapolitana* has more feathery foliage in both silver gray and lighter green. It's flowers have slightly raised florets in the center of the buttons which are more lemon-yellow than either *S. Chamaecyparissus* or *S. virens.* Pruning in early spring helps to keep Santolinas from falling apart in the middle of the clump.

USE: The herb gardener uses Santolinas for borders and dividers in knot gardens if it does well in the particular situation, which should be hot and dry but with a deep root run to provide moisture. Huge ones grew between boulders at The Brooklyn Botanic Garden, holding a steep slope above the knot garden. One way to keep the plants trim is to cut lots of foliage, about 4 inches in length, to use as a natural ruffle around small nosegays called Tussie-mussies. They enable one rose and circle of small flowers of Lavender, Thyme and scented Geranium to carry a message of love, admiration or good wishes, in the language of herbs.

Winter Savory/Satureja montana

Summer Savory/Satureja hortensis

SAVORY, SUMMER	ANNUAL

Satureja hortensis

SAVORY, WINTER	PERENNIAL

Satureja montana Zone 5
Labiatae, native to Europe

HABIT: These herbs, for which an English dish is named, have much the same taste but quite different habits. The hardy annual, Summer Savory, may be sown in the garden as soon as the ground can be worked. Some of the best plants come from seed that has self-sown out of those gone to seed the previous year. They transplant easily, so seedlings may be started in a flat, indoors in a soil substitute kept at 68° F. at night and 86° F. by day, in a sunny window. Don't sow seeds as early as you would other herbs because they germinate in a week and should be set out when only 6 inches high, spaced 12 inches apart. Leaves of Summer Savory are narrow and darker green than those of Winter Savory. Its stems are reddish and later become slightly woody when the plants produce leafy tops bearing pinkish flowers in the axils of the leaves. Winter Savory grows slowly, is almost evergreen, and the mature leaves are pointed and rather spreading. White flowers dot the tops in short spikes in late summer. The annual is the choice for culinary use either fresh or dried but the perennial is there, offering a few sprigs whenever needed all summer and most of the winter.

CULTURE: Winter Savory makes very nice plants when started from seed in a soil substitute 6 to 8 weeks before planting out time. The seedlings are smaller than those of Summer Savory, as are mature plants. In height, Summer Savory grows to 18 inches, Winter to not more than 12. Keep seeding medium 60°-70° F. for germination in two to three weeks. It is advised to let light reach the seeds in a flat, so do not cover, merely press the seeds down into the medium. The plants require well-drained soil which need not be as rich as that for quick-growing Summer Savory. They should not be cut back heavily as winter comes, so the annual is the better cropping plant. Winter Savory and Thymes need much the same situation of full sun and a moist root-run between rocks but dry soil around the crowns to prevent rot. Pruning of dry tops should be done in spring, not in the fall.

Summer Savory becomes top heavy as it produces many short branches full of aromatic leaves. Some sort of bracing, such as hilling up the slim stems, or strings tied along either side to posts at the ends of the row, keeps the herb up off the ground during heavy rain. Last year we put a tent of 1 inch mesh chicken wire, folded so that it was less than a foot high, over the row of Summer Savory. The wire was intended to keep rabbits and deer from nibbling the plants. It worked for that purpose and for another. The leafy tops of the Summer Savory grew up through the wire mesh. They were cut three times in one season as after each trimming of the top 4 inches, a new set of leaves developed. There was no self-sowing this spring as we had not let the herb flower

Broccoli Casserole with Savory

and go to seed. But in another spot in the herb garden, there were volunteers enough to make several rows of Summer Savory transplants between bean plantings.

USE: Both Savories flavor beans so satisfactorily that it is no wonder the Germans named it 'Bohnenkraut' or bean herb. Anyone who doesn't care for the flavor of Sage should try Savory in place of it in poultry dressing. Summer Savory is not as strongly flavored as Winter Savory but it offers more material for drying without woody stems that must be picked out before packaging.

SCREEN DRYING

Cut the tops of Summer Savory into a box or basket. Wash them carefully in cool water if they are mud-splashed. If they do not have any gritty feeling and are well away from animal visitations, the leafy sprigs may not need washing. Spread them evenly on a wire or nylon mesh, elevated slightly to let air pass under as well as over the tray or frame. Stir the leaves daily to turn both sides up for even evaporation. When they have begun to curl and feel quite dry to the touch, take the time to finish them off with some heat, not over 100° F. If there is any moisture left in dried herbs that are packaged, the product will be musty in a short time. Look for misting in a glass jar or feel the lid of a metal one after a day or two of storing. Rewarming may be possible if the leaves are merely limp but not moldy. After warming in a cool oven be sure the herb itself, whether rubbed to a powder or left as whole leaf, is not warm when packaged.

BROCCOLI CASSEROLE WITH SAVORY

1½ lbs. broccoli, cut up
1 Tablespoon all-purpose flour
¼ cup chicken stock
½ cup dairy sour cream
¼ cup grated carrot
3 Tablespoons chopped Chives
¼ teaspoon salt
⅛ teaspoon pepper
¾ cup stale bread cubes
1 Tablespoon fresh Summer Savory, chopped
2 Tablespoons butter

Cut up broccoli. Blend chicken stock, flour and sour cream, grated carrot and chopped Chives. Add broccoli pieces and pour into the bottom of a two quart casserole. Mix bread cubes with Savory, salt and pepper. Cover broccoli with them and dot with butter. Bake at 350° F. for 30 minutes. Serves 6.

Sesame /Sesamum indicum

Herb Popovers - see page 171

SESAME   ANNUAL

Sesamum indicum
Pedaliaceae, native to the Tropics

HABIT: The magic phrase "Open Sesame" refers to the way in which the 3 foot tall annual sheds its seeds by popping open its channeled capsules when they are ripe. The plants have pointed leaves on a single stalk which stands straight and grows rapidly in warm weather. Bells of white flowers appear between the floral leaves making a showy plant in late summer. If soil is not sufficiently moist and seedlings are crowded, they may rush to bloom at half the normal height and produce little in the way of flowers and seed pods. Sesame is now an economic crop in the United States. Sesame seed oil, called "tahini", used to be the only way it was known when imported from the Middle East. That product is thick and rather gummy and is used in salad dressings and Arabian dishes. The clear oil is now an ingredient in the manufacture of margarine. It is expressed from the seeds of Sesame which may be creamy white, red, brown or black according to the variety of the herb. They are called "Bene" down South.

CULTURE: Sesame is not seen in herb gardens in the North but in Texas and other southwestern states it is a tremendous crop and a handsome plant. There it is sown in fields but it may be started indoors in temperatures of 68°-86° F. for a headstart to planting in the garden after the soil is warm. Use a One-step peat pot or individual planting device for the seeds which are large enough to set in the medium, one or two to a container. Germination is very rapid at the above temperature and growth should not be set back by allowing the medium to dry out. Sesame has a longish tap root which does not transplant well, so seeds sown in the garden should be thinned instead of reset. Plants need 12 inches between them for optimum growth. Full sun and good loam are essential for development of the flowers and square seed pods. In field growing, the stalks stand close to each other and are harvested as soon as upper pods are green, so that the lower ones, which ripen first, do not shatter the seed on the ground. The gardener can do the same thing by cutting the stalks and putting them upside down in a brown bag. As the seeds complete drying they will fall out.

USE: Sesame seeds have little flavor until toasted or included in baked goods or candy. "Bene" is the name for them when made into a carmelized sugar confection. If put with pie crust dough, in the amount of a cup of Sesame seeds and a cup of grated cheddar cheese, with a sprinkling of Cayenne pepper and water to mix, they make a delightful biscuit when rolled ½ inch thick and baked at 400° F. until done but not really browned. The seeds are nutritious and add crunchiness to cookies.

143

SESAME SEED COOKIES

½ cup butter or margarine
1/3 cup Sesame seeds
Melt together over medium heat until seeds and butter are brown.
COOKIE DOUGH
½ cup butter or margarine
1 cup granulated sugar
Blend above together till smooth and add:
1 beaten egg
1 teaspoon Vanilla
Beat in dry ingredients:
1 cup all-purpose flour sifted with
1 teaspoon baking powder
¼ teaspoon salt

Mix completely then add 3 Tablespoons of browned butter and Sesame seed. Save the rest for icing. Drop teaspoonfuls of the dough on greased cookie sheet and bake at 350° F. for 10 minutes till outside edges of cookies are lightly brown. Remove cookies from sheet while still warm. When they have cooled, ice with Sesame Frosting made by putting 1½ cup powdered sugar, 1 teaspoon Vanilla and 2 Tablespoons milk or cream into the remaining Sesame Butter. This is a crisp butter cookie with Sesame frosting.

SHALLOT
Allium ascalonicum
Amaryllidaceae, native to the Middle East

HABIT: The botanical name of *Allium ascalonicum* has been changed to that of the plain Onion, *Allium Cepa, Aggregatum Group.* This denotes the fact that the bulb is made up of several, clove-like clusters, which in the case of Shallot are brown-skinned. It doesn't settle the matter of name because Scallions are called "Shallots" in Louisiana markets. The French name is Echalote and it is they who have made them famous by calling for the multiple bublets in recipes. The flavor is sweeter than that of any scallions or small onions and the separating cloves are convenient for a small savor of Allium in a dish. Shallots do not seem to cause as much distress to delicate stomachs as other members of its family, when used raw or cooked. There is a faint suggestion of apple-plus onion in its taste. There are gray skinned or white skinned Shallots in France where regional differences dispute what is the 'real Shallot'. The one available to us most often is the small, brown-skinned variety.

CULTURE: It is said that Shallots grown from seed will run to seed. The bulblets are divided easily to plant in rich soil, early in the spring. They are not buried, but set so that the top third of the clove is above ground. Sometimes the green shoots sprout in storage which shows it's time to pot them for windowsill greens. The tubular top leaves are flavorful, too. Shallots are frost hardy and will remain in the ground without rotting over winter if they have good drainage. Autumn planting can be done in the South for early summer harvest. The foliage begins to yellow when the bulbs have formed their aggregations. They are lifted and dried in the sun before storing in an open mesh bag or berry basket. Shallots do not go soft as quickly as Garlic cloves do in storage. They are more likely to sprout if kept where they get light. The cloves of Shallot are less expensive when bought for planting than when picked up in the grocery store. It is really worthwhile to grow them because they bring a premium price in markets.

USE: If you have Shallots, you may find that you won't use onions as often. The flavor is appealing and the handling much less odoriferous in peeling and chopping. Shallots are virtually without tears, that is unless you can't find or grow them. Try them in a dish from their native land—

Shallot/Allium ascalonicum

Garden Sorrel/Rumex species

ARABIC MINT, SHALLOT AND PARSLEY SALAD

1 cup fine bulgor wheat
½ cup finely chopped Spearmint
1½ cup finely chopped Parsley
½ cup finely chopped Shallots
¾ cup chopped tomatoes (optional)
¾ cup salad oil
½ cup lemon juice
Salt and Pepper
Soften wheat by soaking 1 hour in water, drain and press out water. Mix with other ingredients, let stand a few hours in refrigerator before serving on lettuce.

SORREL, GARDEN   PERENNIAL
Rumex species   Zone 4
Polygonaceae, native to Europe

HABIT: As with Shallots, there is a difference of opinion as to what is the true French Sorrel. *Rumex Acestosa* is described as 'green to 18 inches in height with edible leaves'. The plants in our garden fit that role until late summer when they produce 3 to 4 foot tall flowering stems with dock-like seeds. However, Sorrel is grown for its leaves rather than its inflorescence. The foliage is produced in a thick clump of pointed leaves with light green mid-rib. Seeds are flat and brown following brownish blooms that resemble those of the little weedy wild Sorrel. The shamrock-like yellow flowered 'wood Sorrel' which springs up in cultivated areas in hot summers, is what we knew as children as 'sour-grass'. Garden Sorrel has the same acid but intriguing taste and is milder than any of the wild species which can be too rich in oxalates for frequent use.

CULTURE: Sow seed of Garden Sorrel as early in the spring as possible. Furrows can be made in ordinary rich moist soil, 1 inch deep and plants should be thinned to stand 1 foot apart. The plants need watering in dry weather or the greens become tough. They are very hardy and produce more than can be eaten. Therefore, leaves and flowering stems should be cut back as hot weather sends them into early seed production. The roots will send up new shoots which will be better for greens than the heavy growth that may have become slug infested. Plants should be replaced with new seedlings every three or four years as they take a lot out of the soil and sometimes rot at the root if left in the same bed. The wild species move above by seeding but the Garden Sorrel is thwarted by use so deserves a new place in the sun that often.

145

French Sorrel Soup

USE: The acidity of Sorrel leaves will turn metal knives black when used to chop them. Sorrel should not be cooked long or in an iron pan. Only the young leaves are used raw and a stainless steel knife is used. Sorrel Soup, a great spring tonic in France, is one of the most delightful ways to know Sorrel. The British make a sauce of the leaves, by pureeing them in melted butter and adding flour for thickening and a little chicken stock. It goes well with pork, fish or omelet. In the last it would be folded in when turning the egg mixture in the pan.

FRENCH SORREL SOUP

2 handfuls of Sorrel leaves	2 Shallots, minced
4 Tablespoons butter	2 cups chicken stock
3 Tablespoons flour	2 egg yolks
2 Tablespoons fresh Lovage	1 cup cream
Salt and Pepper	4 Tablespoons fresh Chervil

Remove midribs of Sorrel leaves by folding them and tearing from the top down. Chop fine and cook in butter with minced Shallots. Sorrel will become a sad green color and puree itself in a few minutes. Blend in flour, chopped herbs, salt, pepper and stock. Pour ½ cup into beaten egg yolks in a bowl. Return to pan, add cream and heat thoroughly but slowly. The soup may be put in blender to chop herbs and prevent lumps, as a time and work saver. It's good hot or cold.

Southernwood/Artemisia Abrotanum   *Camphor Southernwood/Artemisia Abrotanum*

SOUTHERNWOOD   PERENNIAL
Artemisia Abrotanum   Zone 4
Compositae, native to Europe

HABIT: The woody stemmed, green Artemisia called "Southernwood" is almost evergreen. Its finely divided leaves have a lemony scent. The herb seldom blooms but is hardy and long-lived. It has been called 'Old Man' for this reason and 'Lad's Love' for its supposed romance-inducing effects. There are two other forms, with similar thread-like leaflets on woody stems. One is Camphor Southernwood with looser, more spreading habit and low-lying stems that root down where they touch the earth. The other has been variously known as "Tree Southernwood" and "Tangerine Southernwood" for its 6 foot tall stems and fruit-scented leaves. Unlike the Camphor one, it has no means of propagation beside cuttings. The herb with the camphor-scented foliage does bloom with panicles of greenish flowers at 2 to 2½ feet; plain Southernwood, sometimes called "Lemon Southernwood", may reach 3 to 4 feet.

CULTURE: It would be possible to grow Southernwood from seed if it flowered and set viable seeds. The only regularly flowering form is the one with Camphor aroma. It does its own rooting where branches touch the ground and then grow upward. Tree-like Southernwood roots easily from cuttings taken as it produces new leaves in the spring. In the North, the foliage becomes rather limp and finally has to be pruned away in March or April. This helps to keep the sub-shrub trim for another season. If it is not cut back, there are branches that stand straight up and others make tufts of foliage at lower reaches. Several year old clumps may be divided in the fall.

USE: The Southernwood of the herb garden has a long history of household uses. It was one of the 'strewing herbs' spread on dirt or wooden floors to sweeten the air and discourage insects. The leaves were put into a cream to promote the growth of a young man's beard, hence the name 'Lad's Love'. Sort of a 'pre-shave' ointment. Gerard suggested that this same concoction would prevent baldness.
The leaves dry easily on the stems which may be hung up in the kitchen or put in a brown bag. A few of the desiccated leaflets, put on the coals of the fire will make a nice incense if you have burned something in cooking on a wood stove or over a log fire. Camphor Southernwood is dried to make moth bags to hang in the closet. There are a number of herbs which take the place of the unpleasant smelling naptha balls. Wormwood, Southernwoods and Rue, to name just a few, were used for preventing moths 'and beetles in the large clothes presses that preceded closets.

Tansy /Tanacetum vulgare   *Tansy /Tanacetum vulgare*

TANSY   PERENNIAL
Tanacetum vulgare   Zone 4
Compositae, native to Europe and Asia

HABIT: Tansy is listed in Thomas Tusser's *Strewing Herbs Of All Sorts,* part of his work on good husbandry, dated 1557. The tall, dark green perennial with pungent fern-like leaves and yellow button flowers, is said to keep ants away, even today. The plants spread by creeping root stock and self-seeding. The 4 foot tall heads of small tubular flowers, packed together in a tightly compressed rayless, flat, slightly concave button are hung up to dry when they are most colorful in late summer. The aromatic leaves, which make a thick clump before the flower stems develop, may be cut repeatedly for doorstep strewing to keep ants from entering or dried on the stems as the flower heads are hung upside down.

The Curly Tansy, *Tanacetum vulgare var. crispum,* is the choice for herb garden ornament. It does not spread as rapidly as common Tansy and the leaves are cut and curled making more showy foliage of brighter green. Some forms of the *var. crispum* flower, others do not, but neither self-sows as does the plain herb. Either one grows only 2½ feet tall at most.

CULTURE: Tansy is easily grown from seed planted outdoors in spring or fall. It is almost a weed around the site of country homes and can quickly become one in a vegetable garden. The idea of using it to deter deer or act as a catch plant for insects in such a planting does not reckon with its invasive nature. It borders our gra/el driveway and is kept in place by the mower which trims the grass in front of its stand. The spreading roots and profligate seed dispersal will make a little Tansy into a broad patch very quickly. The Curly type is not as difficult to root out if it spreads too rapidly but should not be combined with other plants in beds or borders. Tall Tansy should stand alone and Curly may be allowed to creep about where it can't encroach on less sturdy herbs.

USE: The idea of Tansy tea is discouraged by the ruling that the dried herb may not be sold by herbal shops. It could be made so strong as to be quite toxic. In Elizabethan England 'Tansies' were puddings or cakes flavored with the green herb. The custom of eating them at the end of Lent might have originated with the longing for bitter herbs to offset too much fish during Lent. William Coles wrote, in 1656, that the herb counteracts the ill-effects of "the moist and cold constitution winter has made on people . . .". Dried Tansy foliage keeps moths out of woolens and insects from attics and basements. Ants may walk over the plants in the garden, but when the fresh foliage is cut and laid where they enter or take up trails indoors, it does turn them away. As one old lady said, "It doesn't kill the ants, but it makes them nervous." Fresh Tansy leaves give a pleasant green color to wool dyed with them.

Russian Tarragon/Artemisia Dracunculus

French Tarragon/Artemisia Dracunculus

TARRAGON, FRENCH

Artemisia Dracunculus var. sativa

Compositae, native to Europe and southern Asia

PERENNIAL
Zone 4

HABIT: No one knows when it happened, but somewhere a plant of Tarragon which did not flower, or rather did not set seed was discovered and propagated by cuttings. It is called "French" because the cuisine of France made good use of the plant, calling it "Estragon". The Anise-flavored shiny leaves are narrow and rounded at the tips early in the spring when the plant, which dies down in winter, begins to grow again. As the growth becomes more upright on branching stems which harden to green wood, the new leaflets are pointed. The whole plant does not exceed 3 feet in height, even if it produces some infloresences bearing panicles of small greenish white flowers. Despite many reports of flowering and seeding we have not had proof that this popular clone with the tangy taste can be grown from seed. Its roots are thickly entangled and sometimes die out in the center after having exhausted the soil where it grows. Tarragon is one of the most difficult herbs to grow where there is no winter cold for its dormancy. There is a Tarragon, attributed to Russia or Siberia, which does set seed and may be grown from it. Unfortunately, the name *Artemisia Redowski* which distinguished it from French Tarragon has been dropped in *Hortus Third.* It is simply called *Artemisia Dracunculus.* It is offered as Tarragon without a modifier in the name in some places. The plants grow to five feet tall, with spreading root stock, paler leaves without the glossy surface, and very little flavor in the foliage. To the nurseryman Tarragon is a problem. If he cannot get divisions of the clone that is French Tarragon, should he eschew growing the herb Tarragon altogether? If he does, seed of it will soon be dropped from catalogs. When that happens there will be no way to compare the two varieties and an educational process will be lost. The important thing for the gardener to know is that French Tarragon is *A. Dracunculus var. sativa,* with a distinct over-tone of Anise in its taste and a peculiar slightly numbing effect when it is chewed. This is why ancient physicians had patients nibble some "French" type Tarragon before taking bitter medicine.

CULTURE: French Tarragon is propagated by divisions of the root. A second-year plant may be lifted early in the spring, when new leaves begin to appear but before they are more than four inches high. The mass of roots may be carefully shaken of soil and gently worked apart. Each section that comes away with a stump of last year's stem, will make a new plant if reset immediately. That is why the herb should not be cut back late in the season. The woody stems are good markers of the extent of its growth and help to keep the plant from making soft new growth in a warm spell. Cuttings may be taken in mid-summer, as the branching shoots begin to firm up. They take 2 months to root in a soil substitute and need to be carried through the first winter in a coldframe or greenhouse. One possible reason for the great dirth of French Tarragon is that the demand is exceeding supply and cuttings which have not had a chance to form winter-hardy roots are being sold. This idea should not lead anyone to dig up French Tarragon to bring it indoors for the winter. The herb is hardy if it has good drainage. It cannot stand 'wet feet' or

Tarragon Vinegar   Tarragon and Mushroom Quiche

soil that is soggy in winter. The Siberian Tarragon will never turn into flavorful French Tarragon, no matter how hard you hope. It may have given rise to the culinary herb but the miracle has not been repeated in our 40 years' experience. Still we grow the taller, paler green, non-shiny flavorless plant for demonstrating the difference. It comes easily from seed planted in a flat at 60-70° temperature, with sprouting taking about 3 weeks. Seedlings should be set out 2 feet apart. They will stay small the first summer but next season look for flowering and spreading roots.

USE: Tarragon is used with chicken and fish most frequently but it also goes well with beef stroganoff and other meats. The vinegar is better known than the herb. *Tarragon Vinegar* is easy to make. Take a clean quart bottle with enameled top. Fill it loosely with leaves of French Tarragon. Then pour over white or wine vinegar to cover and fill the bottle. Let the leaves steep in the acid medium for 2 or 3 months. They can be left longer but they become pale and a mass of herbage in the bottle is not as attractive as one floating sprig freshly put in when the vinegar is decanted. The vinegar is called for in Tartar Sauce and some mustard mixes or marinades and bastes. The herb itself has authority and is seldom combined with other herbs of equal strength but it does a lot for vegetables such as spinach, and mushroom dishes.

BLUEFISH SPECIAL WITH TARRAGON

1 filet of blue fish (as fresh as possible)
Put ¼ cup butter in frypan, add 1 Tablespoon oil
Heat the butter till bubbling, then press in 2 cloves Garlic. Brown Garlic and add filet of fish. Saute and turn so skin side is on the bottom. Add ½ cup white wine; reduce heat and simmer. Cover and cook 10 minutes. Sprinkle fish with 2 Tablespoons fresh Tarragon, (½ Tablespoon dried). Cut up ¼ pound fresh mushrooms and put in the pan around the fish cooking them till wine is reduced to ¼ cup. Remove fish to warm platter. Put ½ cup mayonnaise in pan with wine and mushrooms. Add ½ teaspoon ground black pepper and 5 drops Tobasco sauce. Stir till hot and pour over fish. Serve at once.

TARRAGON AND MUSHROOM QUICHE

One unbaked pie shell
1½ cup light cream
3 eggs
1 cup cut up mushrooms
3 sprigs French Tarragon chopped

Beat cream and eggs, add mushrooms and Tarragon and stir. Pour into unbaked pie shell. Put into 400° F. oven for 10 minutes. Turn oven to 350° F. for 30 minutes additional. This is a salt-free recipe but salt and pepper may be added if desired. Allow baked Quiche to cool until set. Serve for luncheon or small slices as hors d'oevre.

Thymes/Thymus species   *Thymes/Thymus species*

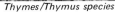

THYMES   PERENNIAL
Thymus species   Zone 4
Labiatae, native to the Mediterranean

HABIT: Common Thyme, *T. vulgaris,* is a shrubby, evergreen perennial, 8 to 12 inches in height with opposite leaves on the short stems which are woody at the base. The two-lipped flowers are light pink to white in interrupted whorls on the upright stems. It is the culinary Thyme of choice for drying. The varied forms are edible also. In fact, any of the genus *Thymus* may be used in cooking, but it is easier to cut the shrubby forms for gathering in any quantity. The one called "Broadleaf English", is darker green with wider ovate to elliptic leaves, is not generally available as seed. It was what the herbalists called "Hard Time" and it is hard to find today in the U. S. Narrowleaf French Thyme has decurved, grayish leaves. It is the one which is offered as Common Thyme or Winter Thyme seed. The flavor is bright and the plant makes a good border where the soil is well-drained. The attractive silver-edged and golden-edged varieties are known as 'Argenteus' and 'Aureus' respectively. They have the typical Thyme flavor but there are two others with the same markings on the leaves with distinctly lemon scent and taste. They are listed as a separate species, *Thymus x citriodorus* in the Cornell University Information Bulletin 123, *Gardening With Herbs,* by Harriet B. Flannery and Robert G. Mower. The leaves are wider than those of the typical *T. vulgaris,* or seem so because of their colored leaf margins. Either one may go entirely green in certain soils unless lifted and divided often. The variegated forms are not quite as hardy as the Common Thyme.

CULTURE: The upright *Thymus vulgaris* may be grown from seed sown in a flat that is kept at a temperature of 55° F. for germination in three weeks to a month. Seedlings are small with reddish color under the pointed leaves. They will make nice plants about 8 inches tall the first season and flower the following summer. Thymes need good drainage. The roots go quite deep but the crowns should not be crowded by other plants (set them 12 inches apart after hardening off) or mired in mud. Layering is a good method of propagation of the species and its variants but be sure that the side branches covered with soil have their tips turned upwards, not pressed into the earth. The silver and golden edged types divide easily if the whole plant is lifted and a cluster of stems is pulled away with root attached. This should be done early in the spring so that the plantlets can resume growth. To move Thymes in autumn is to invite winter-kill.

151

Thymus/"Annie Hall"

Thymus/serpyllum Coccineus

THYMES, CREEPING PERENNIAL
Thymus praecox ssp. articus Zone 4
Labiatae, native to Europe

HABIT: The low-growing, ground cover Thymes grow flat until their trusses of bright, small flowers rise to 4 inches in height. One very small, round leaf, light green creeper, variety *"Albus"* has snow-white flowers which seem to appear on the green foliage without any stems of their own. It is perfect for the interstices of flagstone paving (in the sun in the North, in shade in the South). The name used to be *Thymus serpyllum,* meaning 'creeping' but that has been changed to *'praecox'* translating to 'very early'. This does not cover all species as the time of flowering varies from 'Annie Hall' in May to 'Woolly Thyme' somewhat later and on through the summer. In this subspecies there are several colors of red-flowering Thymes, *'Coccineus'* with crimson tufts of bloom and *'Splendens'* with reddish purple. It seems strange to buy plants in flower but with the creeping Thymes it may be the way to get the one shade you want. The whole species was known as "Mother-of-Thyme" to distinguish it from the upright garden varieties. The wild Thyme which grows along road banks in the lower Berkshire Hills is said to have escaped from the cultivated acres of the herb grown by the Shakers, the first packagers of garden seeds. We have found it on the banks of the Housatonic River, no doubt brought down by flood waters from Massachusetts.

The creeping Thymes are fine for banks, rock gardens and raised beds in herb gardens. They can be trodden on if they grow in full sun and have room to move to fresh soil after two years in the same spot. There is a delightful lemon-scented variety with lightish green leaves; one with smaller darker green leaves with touches of gold on them, is also pleasantly citrus in perfume and flavor. Fortunately, Miss Flannery, who did her Masters' thesis on "Ornamental Herbs", is now making the genus Thymus the subject of her PhD work. She grew the herbs and photographed them for the Cornell Bulletin and is doing her research at the same university.

CULTURE: When seed is available, creeping Thymes may be sown in the garden or started in flats in soil substitute with a thin layer of coarse sand at the top. They take the same 55° F. temperature as Common Thyme and plants grow slowly at first. The dream of a Thyme lawn or a bank covered with Mother-of-Thyme takes years to realize. The first order of business is weeding out all other plants so that the divisions or seedlings of Thyme have a chance to spread. It is a time-consuming and patience-trying process. Where the summers are very hot, Thymes need shade. In cooler sections, they may need protection in winter to save the evergreen tops from drying winds and ice. Evergreen boughs, pine needles, or other light material will do as a mulch after the ground freezes. Salt marsh hay, (wiry grass harvested along the seacoast in the East) is fine where available. The salt in the hay does not damage plants, it does not rot easily so it can be used over and over if it is raked off in the spring, dried and stored in plastic bags. Maple leaves and other material that mat down should not be used for winter cover. Well-rotted compost that has been screened is a good protection and restorative of the soil for Thymes.

Thyme and Rice Pilaff   *Woolly Thyme/Thymus articus*

USE: The upright Thymes are used fresh and dry for flavoring clam chowder, adding to soups, stews and sauces, a few leaves at a time. It is one of the strongest of seasoning plants meant to be used with a light hand. The lemon-scented varieties may be added to potpourri, when dried, and make a nice tea if not steeped too long. Thymol is the medicinal extract of the herb. It has been used in patent medicines, particularly, cough syrups, and still is considered a valuable antiseptic today. Caraway Thyme, *Thymus Herba-barona,* is a low-growing species which has delightful association with old England as it was considered the only seasoning to enhance a huge roast beef, called a 'baron'. Alas, we don't have large beef dinners any longer, but Caraway Thyme is something to enjoy when mixed with bread crumbs used in meat loaf. The flowers are rose purple and plants have rather narrow leaves of medium green with a pleasant aroma. It is a bit taller than most of the creeping Thymes, reaching 5 inches in bloom.

THYME AND RICE PILAFF

1 cup long grain white rice
2 Tablespoons cooking oil
2 cups chicken stock
3 Tablespoons fresh Thyme

Saute uncooked rice in oil over medium heat until lightly brown. Stir continuously being careful it does not burn. Add chicken stock and Thyme. Cover pan and simmer for 15-20 minutes (or as long as rice takes to become fluffy after absorbing all the stock). Stir rice with a wooden fork and serve hot. Serves 4.

Valerian/*Valeriana officinalis*

Valerian/*Valeriana officinalis*

VALERIAN   PERENNIAL
Valeriana officinalis   Zone 4
Valerianaceae, native to Great Britain, Europe and Asia

HABIT: The true Valerian is a good example of the confusion caused by common names of plants. Because it has heads of small white to lavender flowers with the fragrance of Heliotrope, it has often been mistaken for that Peruvian plant of the Borage family. Calling this tall hardy perennial, "Garden Heliotrope" brings to mind the clusters of sweet-scented purple blossoms surrounded by broad, dark-green leaves of tender perennial, *Heliotropium arborescens,* or "Cherry Pie" in Victorian days. It also suggests that the bedding plant will live over winter in the North, as the true Valerian does. The 'officinalis' in its botanical name means that it was used medicinally and sold in the shops of the druggists and apothecaries. The flowers are decorative, reaching 4 to 5 feet tall in moist soil. Leaves make a basal clump of divided leaflets in 7 to 10 pairs either side of the stem. The flowering stems shoot up in May and last for many weeks. The habit of spreading roots is one drawback to the plant in small garden beds and its attraction to cats is another. But as with Catnip, the felines may not know it's there unless the roots are disturbed. They have none of the sweet scent of the flowers. In fact, the plant has been called "Valerian Phu", in one species. But it is the root which formed the medicinal basis for the use of the plant. It is calming to women, exciting to cats and made into an infusion for hysterics.

CULTURE: Valerian has small seeds which are wafted about in the breeze by their pappus or fluffy hairs which act as tiny parachutes. Seeds may be sown in a flat, with the medium kept at 60°-70° F. Germination will take up to 3 weeks. Plants self-sow in the garden, as well as spreading by roots, Valerian is usually obtained as a division. It is tolerant of shade, making a bright spot of light flowers and fragrance in the back of the garden. Seldom needs staking but it is subject to aphids as the flowers go to seed. They had best be cut off anyway, so spraying can be avoided. The botanical name Valerian comes from the Latin meaning "to be strong". This may refer to its endurance in the garden under adverse conditions, or the smell of the roots.

USE: In the Middle Ages the root was used as a spice, even as perfume. This may have been another species as it's hard to picture such a use if you smell the root. A lady gardener at the Queen's Garden of herbs at Kew was told by an American woman that if she had taken some Valerian before the opening day she wouldn't have been nervous. She did add that "you might lose your husband but you would steady your nerves". When no one was looking a few days after the Queen presided at the opening of the Garden, the gardener dug a plant of Valerian and sniffed the roots. She decided to keep her husband and forget about her nerves, she told us.

Watercress/Nasturtium officinale　　　　　　*Watercress/Nasturtium officinale*

WATERCRESS　　　　　　　　　　　　　　　　**BIENNIAL**
Nasturtium officinale　　　　　　　　　　　　　　　Zone 4
Cruciferae, native to Europe

HABIT: The delicious plant we have growing in the overflow stream from our spring house, which is the source of sparkling water that stays 45° F. even in winter, is the true Nasturtium, botanically. Watercress is cultivated in England where the waters are supplied with natural limestone. We have two seasons of picking the biennial plant. It makes a flat rosette of leaves just above the surface of the water with long roots fastened in mud along the edge of the stream. In autumn the seedlings from summer's white flowers, with their typical four petals, begin to grow up from round green seedling leaves. With some protection over the Watercress bed, we can pick leaves most of the winter. Those plants bloom as soon as the weather is warm and their seedlings provide the next crop. As the flowers form, the leaves become smaller and the taste gets bitter.

CULTURE: Watercress is easy to grow from seed sown in pots indoors, with medium kept at 55° F. Germination will occur in a week if the seed is not covered and is kept thoroughly moist. Plants may be set out where there is a slow but changing source of fresh water or kept moist during the spring with hose water in a shady corner of the herb garden. In commercial production the herb is grown in tanks with a base of soil in the bottom and water just enough to float the crowns. Again, an alkaline solution is necessary as is sunlight for continuous production. We have given roots of Watercress to many people who have wood ponds but unless there is moving water and sunlight they do not persist past the first crop. The plants grow wild in meadows in limestone areas but should not be gathered for eating if animals are grazing. Watercress can take up pollution from water and parasites from animals. It is easy to grow your own if you have a pure source of water.

USE: Watercress is usually mixed with salad greens, put in sandwiches and used as a garnish. We have an abundance in season and can cook it like spinach, for a beautiful, spicy green vegetable. There is a similar piquancy about Garden Cress, *Lepidium sativum,* one of the earliest greens to plant indoors or out. Seeds germinate in a week when sown in the garden. They should be eaten before the flowers run up to a foot or more. In the window garden, they can be sprouted on paper towels and used as soon as the true green leaves develop. Sometimes the seeds of white Mustard and Cress are mixed for winter cropping, one germinating just as the other is cut off. The Mustard is used in sandwiches in Britain and as a plate garnish. Cress may be replanted in the fall, as it, like Watercress is a cool weather crop. It needs no watery situation but gets bitter when old.

Egyptian Tree Onion/Allium caeruleum

Welsh Onion/Allium fistulosum

WELSH ONION
Allium fistulosum
Amaryllidaceae, native to the Far East

PERENNIAL
Zone 4

HABIT: It is curious that plants which come from China and Japan, are sometimes called Welsh. Seems that "Welsh" meant something "foreign" in plant names. The distinguishing feature of *Allium fistulosum* is its hollow leaves, some half an inch thick, and the fact that it does not have a bulbous base. It does flower, in June, with a fat, leek-like head, without the pointed cap or bract at the peak of the bud. The plant does not grown more than 2 feet tall and is almost evergreen, even in northern gardens. There are new leaves coming at its base which can be cut to use like Chives. Another is the round-leaved, hollow stemmed Egyptian Tree Onion, *Allium viviparum (properly, A. caeruleum var. bulbilliferum).* It develops onion-like green-skinned bulbs at the top of hollow stems, about 2 to 3 feet tall. Where members of the *Allium Cepa* group have flattened leaves, these two have hollow, round ones. The 'Top Onion' has a way of moving from one spot to another as the heavy bulbs cause the stems to fall over. They put out roots immediately they touch the ground or even while still in the air. The combination of flowers, bulbs and roots are found on the top of some of the plants in mid-summer. They are very hardy and can become too numerous, whereas the Welsh Onions do not move around, just thicken their leafy clumps.

CULTURE: Welsh Onion forms seeds the second year of growth. Plants may be divided by splitting off pieces with a few roots at the base if seed is not available. When it is, sow it in a sterile medium at 70-75° F. as for onion or leeks. The fresh seed will germinate in 10 days to two weeks. Seed may be sown in the fall, even where the ground freezes all winter. The young shoots will not appear until early in the spring if seed is planted just before the ground freezes. As with all onions, and members of the Allium genus, both non-bulbous types prefer rich soil but will carry on without it to give perennial onion greens spring, summer and most of the winter. They will tolerate some shade, as well.

USE: When onions are expensive and out of season in the spring, the 'top onion' and 'Welsh Onion' prove their worth. They are ready in the garden from earliest spring to snow cover in the North and grow year round in the South.

Potato Salad with Perennial Onion

POTATO SALAD WITH PERENNIAL ONION

6 medium size potatoes

2 carrots

½ cup chopped top or Welsh Onion greens

½ cup white wine

⅛ cup Tarragon or wine vinegar

1 small green pepper

3 stalks celery

¼ cup chopped Lovage stems (small ones)

½ cup oil (salad)

Peel potatoes for cooking quickly and cut into bite-size pieces. Boil until tender (20 minutes). Chop pepper, carrot, celery. Add to potatoes and pour white wine over mixture. Add Lovage and Top Onion or Welsh Onion stem rings. Beat oil and vinegar together and pour over all. Toss gently until mixed. Salt and pepper may be added to taste.

WOODRUFF, SWEET
Galium odoratum
Rubiaceae, native to Germany and Europe

PERENNIAL
Zone 3

HABIT: One of the loveliest ground covers for partial shade is Sweet Woodruff. It has whorls of pointed leaves on jointed stems which do not exceed 6 inches in height even when covered with starry white flowers. The margins of the leaves have many rigid hairs which give them the saw-tooth feeling of the Bedstraw family to which it belongs. The fuzzy round seeds are few for all the blooms a patch of Sweet Woodruff produces in May. They are usually carried away by ants before the gardener takes note of quarter inch green balls. The herb is known as "Waldmeister" in Germany where it grows wild in the Black Forest. The fragrance is that of new mown hay, as the herb wilts and dries.

CULTURE: If there is no ideal woodland site for the herb, a heavy mulch of well-rotted leaf mold or some woods' soil should be incorporated into the bed. Sweet Woodruff can be grown from seed if the fresh fruits are available. It is slow to germinate and needs 55° F. temperature. Seed sown in a flat with covering of fine gravel should be left outdoors to freeze and thaw if germination is not evident. It may come up the following year. Gardeners who want to make May Wine (Mai Wein) which is flavored with Sweet Woodruff leaves find it easier to buy a few

Sweet Woodruff/Galium odoratum

Making May Wine

clumps in the spring and set them out. The herb makes the most growth by surface runners in the fall, so should be top dressed with fresh soil or nourishing compost then. Lifting and dividing them in the fall is likely to cause winter kill. Sweet Woodruff makes a nice indoor plant in the light garden or just as a dish garden all to itself. Propagation is more often accomplished by taking parts of a clump and potting them than by individual cuttings. The plant will grow in full sun but leaves become yellow green and flowering is less. It needs drainage but plenty of humus in the soil. Sweet Woodruff is easily grown in the North but may need coddling in the South.

USE: Sweet Woodruff was more appreciated in olden days than it is now. The lovely clover-aroma increases with drying. Crisp, pointed leaves dry more easily than any other herb because they hold the foliage up when it is spread out on a screen. Keep it out of bright light to retain the dark green color and store in glass jars when most pungent and really free of moisture. Don't finish it off in an oven, simply air-dry, because the volatile oils will be driven off by any artificial heat. Gerard advocated that it be "made up into garlands or bundles", to cool the air and make a room smell fresh which it does today as it did in 1597.

MAY WINE

May Wine is usually Rhine wine in which fresh Woodruff leaves have been steeped. The commercial product may have some dried herb in the bottle or may be made with essential oil of the plant. It is easy to make at home by taking a jug of white wine and pouring it over a quart jar stuffed with fresh Woodruff. It may be decanted in a few weeks or left to steep until ready to use in punch or for a spring tonic. The herb contains coumarin and therefore is somewhat medicinal.

WORMWOOD   PERENNIAL
Artemisia Absinthium   Zone 4
Compositae, native to Europe

HABIT: When you see a clump of silvery, much-cut leaves of Wormwood it is hard to realize that by end of summer it will be sending up 4 foot tall, graceful panicles of small yellow, rayless flowers almost hidden in silky hairs. The leaves are alternate, 2-to-3-parted into oblong segments. The lower ones are about 12 inches long, the upper ones almost without stems but all have a silvery look because of many hairs. The plant actually looks better as a basal clump than when it is in bloom because the tufts of blossoms soon turn brownish after they flower in mid-summer. It's just as well to cut them back then and enjoy new growth on the fountain-like clump.

CULTURE: Wormwood is grown from seed started in a flat in soil-substitute, at 60-70° F. without covering. It needs light to germinate. Seedlings can be expected in a week to ten days. They will be small but may be transplanted to potting soil in another flat for hardening off before planting out. Set plants 18 inches apart, in full sun. Wormwood thrives in soil with some clay in it and prefers dry weather to wet. The whole Artemisia genus makes its own place in the garden by exuding a substance in the soil that keeps down other plants, weeds and flavored herbs, too. So the whole clan needs space but Wormwood is not one that spreads by stolons. It remains in a clump but self-sows in some soils if flowers are left on till autumn. The plant has a bitter taste but rather a nice aroma, reminiscent of chrysanthemums.

USE: *Artemisia Absinthium* gave its name to an aperitif, Absinthe, which is so powerful in its effect on the brain, if imbibed frequently, that its manufacture is banned in France. But it is a main ingredient in Vermouth, along with several other Wormwood species, such as Roman Wormwood, *A. pontica*. It has lacy foliage that does not exceed 2 feet, but roots spread excessively unless curbed by spading out excess plants in the spring. Bitter Wormwoods are not much used in cooking in this country except as flavoring for Vermouth. The herbage is dried for use in moth preventive sachets or bags to hang in closets. It is not good for wreath-making because most of the leaves shrink when the inflorescense is cut and hung up to dry. Individual leaves do not grow in tufts as on the more broad-leaved or thick foliaged types. Mugwort, *Artemisia vulgaris,* should be mentioned here as something to avoid placing in the garden because of its extremely weedy nature. It has leaves of green, with somewhat the same pattern as Wormwood, but they are silvery underneath. Stems are woody and only the variety *lactiflora* which produces showy panicles of sweet-scented white flowers, 4-5 feet tall on hardy perennial plants, should be considered for a border or background in the herb garden. It does not spread.

SWEET WORMWOOD   ANNUAL
Artemisia annua
Compositae, native to China

HABIT: The tall, Christmas tree form of Sweet Wormwood and its ready self-sowing makes it hard to believe that it is a Wormwood at all. The filmy green foliage is truly sweet-scented. In some old-fashioned gardens it is called "myrrh". The branching habit is perfectly symmetrical, coming to a peak from three foot width at the bottom to pointed top when the plant is in bloom at 6 feet or more in height. Though we offered seed of it in the 1940's when it was known as "Chinese Fragrant Fern", it was not popular until herb gardeners took up wreath making. The branches are supple and easily bent for the purpose when green before and during flowering. After the yellow blossoms fade, the stems turn woody and the plant takes on a reddish-brown shade. Winds and rains do not blight its beauty through autumn and winter. It was a pleasant surprise to notice the fragrance of one brown, mini-Christmas tree of Sweet Wormwood while shoveling snow on a winter morning.

159

Achillea species/"Rose Beauty"   *Yarrow/Achillea species*

CULTURE: Sweet Wormwood is grown from seed sown in soil substitute and kept at 72° F. for rapid germination. Seedlings look like green moss when first sprouted. They are easily moved about when four true leaves develop and may be potted or pricked out in a flat until all danger of frost is past. Plants that have gone to seed in the garden will lay down an astonishing number of volunteer seedlings in loose soil; most have to be weeded out as mature plants need 2 to 3 feet between them. The hardy annual is always welcomed by those who smell its fragrance but warning should be given to anyone who doesn't like to weed or thin an abundant crop. If you don't have it, you may want to seed it outdoors.

USE: Besides wreath material, the aromatic plant offers a delicate form of leaf for making pressed flower and leaf arrangements on cards or for framing. It is delightful to work with for any craft making. One lady, who makes hand-dipped candles, finds the leaves of Sweet Wormwood perfume the wax beautifully. In China, the plant has become something of a wonder of herbal medicine. It has properties similar to those of quinine and is used in treating malaria, according to Paul Rogers, who visited medicinal gardens in the Republic of China, recently. Sweet Wormwood is rather a garden Cinderella. Those of us who have weeded it out for many years have discovered it is a popular plant for potpourri bulk and many craft projects.

YARROW   PERENNIAL
Achillea species   Zone 2
Compositae, native to Europe and Asia

HABIT: 'Milfoil' is said to be the herbalists' name for common Yarrow, because the leaves are cut into innumerable parts. It is known to herb gardeners as the 'wild' or white-flowered Yarrow and more likely to be found along the roadsides than in our gardens. The leaves may be hairy with a gray look or bright green as in the *Achillea Millefolium, var. 'Rosea'.* That one is the variety called 'Red Beauty', or 'Cerise Queen' or 'Rose Beauty'. It causes exclamations of delight from all who see its bright colors against the glossy green foliage. Its only draw-back to the flower arranger is that the color fades to gray when it dries. Otherwise it is a pleasant plant, though spreading as a clump; the flowers develop in mid-summer. As there is no species *Officinalis* in the genus, we can assume that all of the Yarrows have much the same medicinal properties. Certainly all of them are showy, with stems, from 6 inches up to 4 feet tall bearing flat, 2 to 6 inch wide clusters of small flowers that last a long time in blossom. If cut back there may be sparse second flowering. The fern-leaf Yarrows are more stiffly erect and seldom wander out of their original clump, as do the *A. Millefolium* types. *Achillea filipendulina*, 'Coronation Gold', has rigid stems three feet tall, with green leaves which are toothed on the edges. The flowers are the largest in convex umbels of gold, needing no staking. The same species in variety 'Moonshine' is shorter with silvery gray fronded foliage, not over 2 feet in bloom, but constantly flowering without fading. Foliage and flowers cut well and the hardy plant makes a wonderful subject for the herb garden as well as the perennial border. *A. Ptarmica* (meaning sneeze-producing) has glossy green foliage, on 2 foot

Achillea decolorans/"Mace"

stems, topped by white rayed flowers in heads resembling pearl buttons. The toothed, linear leaves on not very strong stems need support of twigs or brush when the plant begins to bloom. It is an old-fashioned favorite for its fragrance, though sniffing can lead to sneezing.

CULTURE: There is scarcely another genus that lends itself to all of the uses of Achillea, has such beautiful species, varieties and is hardy as far north in the U. S. and Canada. It may be grown from seed sown outdoors in spring and summer or started in flats indoors, at temperature in the medium of 78°-80° F. Fine seed should be pressed down merely on the medium and allowed light to promote germination. It may take 2 weeks to produce seedlings but they will be blooming plants in 4-5 months. After that, propagation is by divisions of the roots in early spring. The fern-leaf types do not creep about the garden so need care in lifting to take off-shoots from the base in early spring. 'The Pearl' is a form with double flowers which increases the intensity of the truly opaque white.

In addition to being very hardy, the Achilleas do not require rich soil; indeed the gray-leaved forms actually suffer from too rich loam. All types should be set 12 to 18 inches apart for reason of air circulation, so that foliage is not kept wet for long periods by crowding. The creeping root stocks should be lifted every three years and reset; that is *A. Millefolium* types. *A. tomentosa,* or Woolly Yarrow, is thought a good rock garden plant, as it blooms with showy heads up to 12 inches above its silvery carpet of foliage. They are yellow in small convex clusters. Zones 3-9 are the limits of this species which is recommended as a ground cover for light sandy soil. It needs full sun as do most of the others, though *A. filipendulina* will tolerate partial shade.

USE: Aside from their horticultural value, the Achilleas have a long medicinal and legendary history. The yellow species may be hung upside down to dry for winter arrangements. The blossoms should be fully out before picking as the color effect is somewhat diluted if the whole inflorescence is not at its peak. Individual segments of these heads are used to decorate wreaths made of Artemisias or Ambrosia. Too bad the cerise and red forms of the flowers fade to dull gray on drying. But golden shades in abundance are found among the other species and pearly white of the Sneezewort. It is aromatic in foliage as are all the others. There is one all green, glossy foliage plant whose leaves have toothed edges, that is called "Mace" in England. It has more cream-colored flowers than to those of "The Pearl". Mace has been lately introduced into this country. We have had it in our garden for some years, kindness of Britain's leading authority on herb gardening, Mrs. M. M. M. Hooper of Stoke Lacy Herb Gardens, in Herefordshire; she has placed some plants with our daughter-in-law, (who is her daughter), in her garden on the Thames River, near New London, Connecticut. It seems to be perfectly hardy in northwestern Connecticut, in two locations at our daughter's home (on a hilltop near Litchfield) and in the Falls Village valley. "Mace", *Achillea decolorans,* has to be grown from divisions. The leaves have been used as flavoring in soup and salads. It is also cultivated in New Zealand and from Gilian Painter of Auckland we have the following Folk Charm that applies to this Achillea;

> "I will pick the smooth Yarrow that my figure may be more elegant, that my lips may be warmer, that my voice may be more cheerful, may my voice be like a sunbeam, may my lips be like the juice of the strawberries . . ." *The Herb Garden Displayed*

161

CHAPTER III
GARDEN STYLE AND DESIGN

HERB GARDEN STYLE AND DESIGN

The style and placement of an herb garden is dictated by the people who will enjoy and use plants. This means that the style of the herb garden should reflect the life style of the gardener. For example, a rural farmhouse would be likely to have an informal kitchen garden; on the other hand, a country estate might have symmetrical, formal garden with fancy walks and fountains.

You may decide that one particular place would be perfect for an herb garden. Perhaps the view from the living room's bay window is dull and would be enhanced by a colorful garden of herbs. The plants are selected by listing those things that will grow best in the conditions given by that particular space. A need for bloom, to add color, will require a list of plants that have showy blossoms and interesting foliage. After choosing the spot for the garden, you should record how much sun shines directly on the garden, the type of soil currently in that location, and the impression to be conveyed by looking at the garden. Will you be looking down upon it or up towards its slope?

Another way of find a location for a garden is to review the yard to find the most favorable place for all the desired herbs. For a culinary garden this will mean the sunniest, most sheltered location available. It will also keep the garden away from tall trees, damp low spots and northern exposure. Herbs need conditions very similar to vegetables therefore, it is common to place them together. However, perennial herbs should be grouped at one end so they don't become uprooted when spring cultivation of the vegetable garden occurs. Annual herbs may be planted with the perennial herbs or set out in the area of the vegetables or 'pot-herbs'.

ANOTHER FACTOR OF DESIGN

Time is another factor that will govern the design of the garden. How much time will be spent on maintenance and replanting? For people with little time to devote to it, a small planting near a commonly used entrance is best. As household members come and go during daily activities, the garden is viewed and enjoyed often. This constant contact is an important part of finding time to garden. One that is hidden away from view will be forgotten unless you go there frequently specifically to work with the plants.

There are some people who find that a short, intensive gardening period is most successful. This could be an early spring garden of bulbs and early flowering herbs. Sweet Woodruff lives happily in the shade of deciduous trees. Early spring before the trees leaf out is sunny enough for Forget-me-nots and Sweet Cicely. Later in the season when the trees have their leaves, the plants will make a lush green texture of foliage. Woodruff spreads to make a ground cover. Once established it is an easy plant to maintain. This herb, which defies clipping and exact edging, is best used informally.

FORMAL DESIGNS

For the gardener with abundant time or help, designs are limitless, even the formal knot garden with its clipped plants woven into patterns is possible. When space is at a premium, this style of completely controlled plants gives dramatic results. The garden that depends on symmetrical placement of plants will need more new material each year than one with random spacing. Weeds are more noticeable in a formal garden than in the informal one. However, if someone is inexperienced in recognizing herb plants at all stages of growth, a regular or even spacing of plants facilitates identification when weeding or cultivating.

An herb garden to be viewed from afar will need large masses of plants. Gray foliage plants are a favorite because they are set off by the contrast in color from the surrounding grassy lawn. Dark leaved plants such as Perilla, Purple Basil and Orach may be used to add variety to a bed of gray or green herbs. Tall plants with large leaves and flowers show off better than delicate tiny plants.

"I never had any other Desire so strong, and so like covetousness, that I might be Master at last of a small House and large Garden, with very moderate conveniences joined to them, and dedicate the remainer of my Life, to the Culture of them, and study of Nature." A. Cowley, 1666

FLOWERS PLAY A PART

Flowers, too, play a part in garden style. A formal one is enhanced by the use of many herbs with bright flowers. However, as the flowers fade they must be picked off to keep it at the peak of condition, and to prevent scattering of seeds which will make more young plants to weed out. The symmetrical formal garden has no space for impromptu additions, the result of self-sowing. If continuous blossom is desired, blooming dates of perennial plants must be noted to assure color for the entire gardening season. In some cases, annual bedding plants are used in borders or strategic locations to add color to the herb garden.

MAKING THE LAYOUT

When you have chosen a definite location and style of garden, the actual design may be worked out on paper. It is helpful to use graph paper. Drawing things to scale is easy. Allow one or two squares of the paper per square foot of garden space. When laying out the garden, mark the corners or edges of the proposed plan with a stone or stick stuck in the ground. Then measure and write down the dimensions. After measuring the size, lay out the outline on graph paper. If it is to be bordered by a building, trees, rocks, fences or walls, be sure to note those things on the plan. Mark the compass points, north, south, east and west on the paper.

ACCESS PATHS

The gardener must be able to reach each part of the garden for ease of maintenance. If the area is more than four feet wide, pathways or stepping stones provide a place to stand or rest a basket while weeding or harvesting the plants. The pathways through the garden allow easy access for the gardener and visitor and are an invitation for people and plants to find themselves together. For the most pleasant experience while walking in the garden, it is important to make the paths wide enough to be comfortable; two people should be able to walk side by side and talk in the garden. Sharing your garden is a pleasure. Even if there is a good view of it from a window, visitors will enjoy your garden more if they can touch and smell the plants at first hand.

PLANT SELECTION

After the garden is outlined and the pathways drawn in, it is time to list the plants that will be used. On the graph paper write the name of the plant and the height to which it will eventually grow. If foliage color, blossom time, and flower color interest the designer, those facts may be noted, too. However, the most important factor is the visibility of the individual plants when they are at their peak of growth. Since most will start to grow at the beginning of the growing season and continue until the close of the season, it is usually a good idea to place the tall plants to the back or side of the garden and the smaller, shorter plants in the foreground. There are other ways to organize the plants, also. In the herb garden, use is often a factor. The culinary herbs can be grouped together, as well as the tea herbs, and medicinal plants in areas specifically designated for that use. This grouping is helpful for public gardens where visitors come to see plants with which they are not familiar.

When the list of plants is complete, their names are then written on the graph paper. The larger and taller plants should be given more space on paper as they will take up more space in the garden. Once the outlines of the beds and the pathways are established, the materials for actual construction must be decided upon. The overall effect of the garden will be dictated by the style. This style is punctuated by the look of the paths contrasting with the plants in the beds. Factors governing the materials used to edge the beds and create the paths are availability, cost and maintenance.

POSSIBLE PATHS

The most common material used in the traditional gardens with large paths is grass. It is inexpensive and, aside from mowing and edging, easy to maintain. If the garden area is currently lawn, then the grass in the bed area may be dug out, and new earth added to bring the soil back up to the grade, then the plants arranged in the garden area. Periodically the garden beds will need to be re-edged to keep the grass from encroaching on the herbs. This may be slowed by the

use of an edging material on the boundary of the garden; some common materials used for edging are bricks, boards, patio blocks, plastic or metal rolled border. To be most effective the edging material should extend down into the ground far enough to stop the root spread and high enough above the ground to curb the grass from over-topping it. When grass near a garden is mowed, the clippings should not be allowed to blow into the plants. This can be prevented by using a grass-catcher, cut close to the garden with the grass chute pointed away from it. If there is a grass-restricting edge on the border of the garden the mower may not be able to do a complete job of trimming. This can be a separate chore requiring extra time.

BRICKS IN SAND

Bricks for paths require a well-prepared foundation of sand. They must be carefully laid in an even manner to insure a stable, level walking surface and prevent heaving. The sand will also drain off the rain and prevent formation of puddles in the path. Standing water is bad for plants and inconvenient for the gardener. If the bricks are old, some will start to deteriorate and must be replaced annually. If broken bricks are taken up, the vacant spot may be filled with soil and a creeping Thyme plant put in to fill the void. Some gardeners plant creeping plants along the edges of the pathways (so they will grow where people walk) and the passerby may enjoy the scent.

Brick paths need occasional weeding, even if a ground cover is used between them. Grass seed and other weed seeds are tracked in on the shoes of garden visitors. There are chemical weed preventatives that can be used to minimize this chore of keeping the paths clear.

GRAVEL WALKS

Gravel paths do not require preparation. The bare dirt is simply covered with "pea stone" or crushed stone to a depth of about an inch. If the gravel is deeper it slides underfoot and makes walking difficult. Gravel walkways benefit from an edging, as do the grass paths. Boards or brick lined up and troweled into the soil help keep the gravel in the paths and out of the garden beds. Gravel, too, needs weeding occasionally. This is a difficult job since the roots tend to go deeper into the soil and are more tightly trodden down in the path than in the looser loam of cultivated beds. Tools such as a hoe tend to dig the gravel into the soil while removing the weeds. A Dutch type hoe with a rounded top to the flat blade scrapes gravel paths without making dents in them.

Paving stones, such as flat field stones, make a long-lasting informal path. If you have an old stone wall or an abundance of rocks adaptable to such use on your land the material may be free except for the labor of moving and setting the stones. Working with stones is hard work; however, the results are a permanent addition to the garden. Broad, flat stones make a handsome path that will require very little weeding or other maintenance. They are easy to walk on and the plants like the warmth given off by the stones after the sun has set.

Herb	A/B/P	Height Inches	Time of Bloom	Color of Bloom	Foliage Color	Foliage Scent
Aloe	P	36		Yellow	Green	Little
Allium	P	24	Spring	Various	Green	Onion
Ambrosia	A	24	Late Summer	Yellowish	Lt. Green	Aromatic
Angelica	B	60	Early Summer	Greenish	Green	Aromatic
Anise	A	18	Mid Summer	White	Green	Aromatic
Anise-Hyssop	P	36	Late Summer	Purple	Dk. Green	Pungent
Anthemis	P	30	Early Summer	Dk. Yellow	Gray	Sweet
Artemisia	P	36	Late Summer	Yellowish	Silver	Pungent
Balm, Lemon	P	24	Early Summer	White	Green	Fragrant
Basil, Bush	A	18	Summer	White	Green	Aromatic
Basil, Camphor	A	36	Summer	White	Gray	Pungent
Basil, Opal	A	18	Mid Summer	Pink	Purple	Aromatic
Basil, Lemon	A	18	Mid Summer	White	Green	Aromatic
Basil, Sacred	A	24	Late Summer	Pink	Green	Pungent
Basil, Sweet	A	24	Mid Summer	White	Green	Aromatic
Bee Balm	P	48	Mid Summer	Red/Pink/White	Green	Aromatic
Betony	P	30	Summer	Pink	Green	Little
Betony, Woolly	P	18	Mid Summer	Pink	Silver	Mild
Borage	A	30	Mid Summer	Blue	Green	Mild
Burnet, Salad	P	18	Late Spring	Red	Green	Mild
Butterfly Weed	P	36	Mid Summer	Orange	Green	Mild
Calendula	A	12	All Summer	Orange	Green	Mild
Caraway	B	24	Early Summer	White	Green	Aromatic
Castor Bean	A	60	Late Summer	Yellowish	Bronze	Little
Catmint	P	12	Early Summer	Blue	Green	Aromatic
Catnip	P	36	Summer	White	Gray/Green	Pungent
Chamomile	A	24	Early Summer	White/Yellow	Green	Aromatic
Chamomile	P	12	All Summer	White/Yellow	Green	Aromatic
Chicory	P	36	All Summer	Blue	Green	Little
Chervil	A	24	Early Summer	White	Green	Aromatic
Chives	P	24	Late Spring	Pink/Lavender	Green	Onion
Chives, Garlic	P	30	Late Summer	White	Green	Onion
Cicely, Sweet	P	36	Late Spring	White	Green	Aromatic
Comfrey	P	36	Late Spring	Pink/Blue	Green	Little
Coriander	A	18	Mid Summer	Pinkish	Green	Pungent
Costmary	P	48	Late Summer	Yellow	Green	Aromatic
Cress, Garden	A	12	Mid Summer	White	Green	Little
Cumin	A	12	Late Summer	Pinkish	Green	Aromatic
Curry Plant	P	24	Late Summer	Yellow	Silver	Aromatic
Dill	A	48	Mid Summer	Yellow	Green	Aromatic
Dittany	P	12	Late Summer	Pinkish	Gray	Aromatic
Epazote	A	18	Summer	Greenish	Green	Pungent
Fennel, Florence	A	48	Summer	Yellow	Green	Aromatic
Fennel, Bronze	P	36	Summer	Yellow	Bronze	Aromatic
Fennel, Sweet	P	48	Summer	Yellow	Green	Aromatic
Fenugreek	A	12	Summer	White	Green	Aromatic
Feverfew	B	36	Early Summer	White	Green	Pungent
Germander	P	24	Mid Summer	Pink	Dk. Green	Little
Good King Henry	P	18	All Summer	Yellowish	Green	Little
Honeywort	B	24	Summer	Yellow	Spotted	Little
Horehound White	P	18	Mid Summer	White	Green/Gray	Mild
Horehound Silver	P	18	Mid Summer	White	Silver	Mild
Hyssop	P	24	Early Summer	White/Pink/Blue	Green	Pungent
Job's Tears	A	24	All Summer	Yellow	Green	Little
Lamium	P	12	All Season	Pink/White	Silver	Little
Lady's Mantle	P	18	Early Summer	Gold	Gray/Green	Little
Lavender, English	P	24	Mid Summer	Lavender	Gray	Aromatic
Lavender, French	P	24	Mid Summer	Lavender	Gray	Aromatic

167

Herb	A/B/P	Height Inches	Time of Bloom	Color of Bloom	Foliage Color	Foliage Scent
Lemon Balm	P	30	Summer	White	Green	Lemony
Lemon Verbena	P	48	Mid Summer	Lavender	Green	Aromatic
Lovage	P	60	Early Summer	Yellow	Green	Aromatic
Love-in-a-Mist	A	24	Mid Summer	Blue	Green	Little
Marigold	A	18	All Summer	Yellow	Green	Pungent
Marjoram, Pot	P	24	Summer	White	Green	Aromatic
Marjoram, Sweet	P	12	All Summer	White	Green	Aromatic
Marjoram, Wild	P	36	Early Summer	Pink	Green	Mild
Mint, Apple	P	48	Mid Summer	Lavender	Gray/Green	Aromatic
Mint, Eau de Cologne	P	24	Mid Summer	Purple	Purplish	Aromatic
Mint, Peppermint	P	36	Mid Summer	Purple	Dk. Green	Aromatic
Mint, Pineapple	P	24	Mid Summer	Purple	Variegated	Aromatic
Money Plant	B	24	Early Summer	Magenta	Green	Little
Nasturtium	A	12	All Summer	Yellow/Orange	Green	Mild
Orach, Purple	A	60	Summer	Purple	Red	Little
Oregano	P	24	Mid Summer	White	Green	Aromatic
Parsley, Curly	B	24	Mid Summer	Yellow	Green	Mild
Parsley, Plain	B	24	Mid Summer	Yellow	Green	Mild
Pennyroyal, American	A	12	Mid Summer	Blue	Green	Pungent
Pennyroyal, English	P	18	Mid Summer	Lavender	Green	Pungent
Perilla	A	36	Late Summer	Pink	Red	Mild
Pyrethrum	P	30	Early Summer	Pink/White	Green	Mild
Rampion	B	24	Early Summer	Blue	Green	Little
Roquette	A	18	Summer	White	Green	Pungent
Rocket, Sweet	P	36	All Summer	Pinkish	Green	Little
Rosemary	P	12-72	Spring	Blue	Green	Aromatic
Rue	P	24	Late Summer	Yellow	Gray	Pungent
Safflower	A	36	Late Summer	Orange	Green	Little
Sage	P	24	Early Summer	Purple	Gray	Aromatic
Sage, Clary	B	60	Late Summer	Blue	Gray	Pungent
Sage, Pineapple	P	48	Late Summer	Red	Green	Aromatic
Santolina, Gray	P	24	Early Summer	Yellow	Gray	Aromatic
Santolina, Green	P	24	Early Summer	Yellow	Green	Aromatic
Savory, Summer	A	18	Summer	Pink	Green	Aromatic
Savory, Winter	P	12	Mid Summer	White	Green	Aromatic
Sesame	A	36	Summer	White	Green	Little
Shallots		18	Infrequent	White	Green	Onion
Sorrel	P	36	Late Spring	Brown	Green	Little
Southernwood	P	30	Late Summer	Yellowish	Gray	Aromatic
Tansy	P	48	Late Summer	Yellow	Green	Pungent
Tarragon, French	P	24	Unlikely	Unlikely	Green	Aromatic
Tarragon, Russian	P	48	Summer	Yellowish	Green	Mild
Thyme, Common	P	12	Early Summer	Lavender	Various	Aromatic
Thyme, Caraway	P	6	Mid Summer	Pink	Green	Aromatic
Thyme, Lemon	P	6	Mid Summer	Lavender	Green/Gold	Aromatic
Thyme, Wild	P	6	Mid Summer	Rosy	Green	Aromatic
Valerian	P	48	Early Summer	Pinkish	Green	Little
Watercress	B	12	Spring	White	Green	Mild
Welsh Onion	P	18	Summer	White	Green	Onion
Woodruff, Sweet	P	8	Early Spring	White	Green	Mild
Wormwood	P	36	Late Summer	Yellowish	Silver	Pungent
Wormwood, Sweet	A	60	Late Summer	Yellowish	Green	Fragrant
Yarrow	P	4-48	All Summer	Various	Various	Fragrant

HERB GROWER'S CHART OF USES

Herb	Dry Arrangement	Indoor Culture	Insect Deterrent	Kitchen Garden	Pot-Pourri	Tea	Propagation Method	Tussie-Mussie Symbolism	Vinegar
Basil	Seed Pod	Tender Annual	Flies	Full Sun	Clove Scent	Leaves	Seed	Hate-Love	Leaves
Bay	Leaves	Tender Perennial		Light Shade		Leaves	Cutting	Victory-Reward	
Catnip	Seed Heads	Hardy Perennial	Ants	Full Sun		Leaves	Seed		
Chives	Blossoms	Hardy Perennial	Aphids	Full Sun			Pl. Div., Seed		Bloom
Dill	Seed Head	Annual		Full Sun		Seed	Seed		
Fennel		Perennial		Full Sun		Seed	Seed	Praise	Seed Head
Lavender	Bloom	Hardy Perennial	Moths	Full Sun	Sweet Scent		Cutting	Acknowledgement	
Lemon Balm		Hardy Perennial	Aphids	Full Sun	Lemon Scent	Leaves	Plant Division	Sociability-Sympathy	
Lemon Verbena		Tender Perennial		Full Sun	Lemon Scent	Leaves	Cutting	Delicacy of Feeling	
Mints	Bloom	Hardy Perennial	Snakes	Sun or Shade	Minty Scent	Leaves	Plant Division	Virtue-Wisdom	
Rosemary		Tender Perennial		Full Sun	Pungent Scent	Leaves	Cutting	Remembrance-Wedding	Leaves
Rue	Seed Pod	Hardy Perennial	Flies	Full Sun			Seed	Disdain-Grace	
Sage	Seed Head	Hardy Perennial		Full Sun		Leaves	Seed or Cutting	Esteem-Long Life	
Scented Geraniums		Tender Perennial		Full Sun	Sweet Fruity	Leaves	Cutting	Happiness	
Sweet Marjoram		Tender Perennial		Full Sun	Pungent Scent	Leaves	Seed		
Tansy	Bloom		Ants				Plant Division	Hostility	
French Tarragon				Full Sun			Plant Division	Activity-Bravery	Leaves
Thymes				Full Sun		Leaves	Plant Division	Activity-Bravery	Leaves
Wormwood	Bloom Stalks		Many Pests				Plant Division	Absence-Displeasure	
Yarrow	Bloom			Full Sun		Leaves	Plant Division	Cure for Headache	

CHAPTER IV
COOKING ADVICE

HOW TO START COOKING WITH HERBS

A neighbor once commented, when offered a clump of chives, "No, thank you, my husband doesn't like strong flavored food." Later her ten year old daughter was overheard to say, "I like my mother's spaghetti sauce. She always puts in hot sausage, peppers and mushrooms." This misinterpretation of herb cooking happens frequently.

For those cooks who have just started the exciting exploration into the flavors of herbs, there are a few guide lines. First, use recipes. Choose a dish that includes ingredients that you like and with which you are familiar. As an example, a family who loves pasta, garlic and cheese may find a recipe of "Pesto" (Basil sauce) a great introduction to fresh Basil.

Secondly, ask about food you like that you don't cook yourself. If you have tasted a new dish at a restaurant note the name of the dish and look up in the library a recipe for that dish and then make it at home. If you are at a friend's home for dinner don't hesitate to get a recipe for the food you enjoyed. Most cooks are proud to share their successes.

Next, try introducing a new taste as a side dish or an optional sampling. Cream cheese combined with a newly used herb could be offered with crackers and other old favorite snacks. This way each person can judge the new flavor for himself. It is better to serve your traditional favorites in the same way and leave new tastes for new recipes.

BRANCHING OUT INTO NEW TASTES

When the cook is familiar with the world of herb flavors, the personal favorites will become evident. Then the meals served from that kitchen will be distinctive with an individual style.

Herb Butter with chopped fresh herbs or dried herbs will be a quick flavoring for reheating a loaf of bread. Any vegetable that is steamed, sauteed or boiled will have a few leaves from that list of favorite herb flavors put in with it. Special combinations of herbs will become everyday tools to be used against the boredom of chopped beef or other budget stretchers. This knowledge is the magic that transforms sliced meat sandwiches and canned soup into "Oh, can I have seconds!"

Some examples of using herbs creatively could be made from bland foods. Cottage cheese or cream cheese can have two tablespoons of fresh herb chopped into an eight ounce container. If dried herb is used, one tablespoon will do. A recipe of popovers or baking biscuits will be ever the better when a tablespoon of fresh Rosemary or one teaspoon of dried Rosemary is added to the batter.

Any food that uses mayonaise can have Dill, Tarragon, Basil or a variety of other herbs added either to the mayonaise which is stored in the refrigerator for handy use, or sprinkled on top of the mayonaise after the dish is assembled.

Sunday brunch with herb omelet is a chef's delight. Here, chopped fresh herbs, Parsley, Thyme, Chervil, Basil, Chives should be handy in containers at the stove. Beat gently the eggs with a bit of cream. Be certain the omelet pan is hot. Then put a pat of butter quickly in the pan, swirling it around to coat the surface. While the butter is bubbling, but before it browns, add a ladle of beaten egg. Allow it to cook until the edge is easy to lift away from the pan. The center of the egg should be set but still moist. Sprinkle the fresh herbs over the egg and fold in the two sides carefully. This should make an envelope to hold the herbs. Serve the omelet immediately with a pinch more of fresh chopped green herbs on top for color and taste.

CHART OF COMMON CULINARY HERBS

	Breads	Butters	Cheeses	Eggs	Fish	Fruit	Jelly	Meat	Salad	Sauces	Teas	Vegetables	Vinegars
Angelica	X					X	X				X		
Basil	X	X	X	X				X	X	X		X	X
Burnet			X	X					X			X	X
Caraway	X		X					X				X	
Chervil	X	X	X	X	X			X	X	X		X	
Chives	X	X	X	X	X			X	X	X		X	
Cicely	X	X	X	X	X	X	X	X	X	X	X	X	X
Dill	X	X	X	X	X			X	X	X		X	X
Fennel								X		X		X	
Lovage			X						X	X		X	X
Marjoram	X	X	X	X				X	X	X		X	
Mint	X	X				X	X	X	X	X	X	X	
Oregano	X	X	X	X				X	X	X		X	
Parsley	X	X	X	X	X				X	X		X	
Rocambole	X	X	X	X	X			X	X	X	X	X	
Rosemary	X	X	X	X	X		X	X		X	X	X	X
Sage	X	X	X	X				X		X			
Savory	X	X	X	X	X			X	X	X		X	
Sesame	X	X	X	X		X		X	X	X	X	X	
Tarragon	X	X	X	X	X			X	X	X		X	X
Thyme	X	X	X	X	X			X	X	X		X	X

WHAT PART OF THE HERB PLANT TO USE IN COOKING

	LEAVES	STEMS	FLOWERS	ROOT	SEEDS
ANGELICA	YES	YES			YES
ANISE	YES				YES
BASIL	YES	YES			
BAY	YES				
BORAGE	YES		YES		
BURNET	YES				
CARAWAY	YES				YES
CHERVIL	YES	YES			
CHIVES	YES	YES	YES		
CICELY	YES				YES
CORIANDER	YES	YES			YES
DILL	YES	YES	YES		YES
FENNEL	YES	YES	YES		YES
LOVAGE	YES	YES			YES
MARJORAM	YES	YES	YES		
MINT	YES				
OREGANO	YES				
PARSLEY	YES	YES			
ROCAMBOLE	YES		YES		YES
ROSEMARY	YES				
SAGE	YES		YES		
SAVORY	YES		YES		
SESAME					YES
SHALLOTS	YES	YES		YES	
SORREL	YES				
TARRAGON	YES				
THYME	YES				

SALAD BAR WITH HERBS

The ever popular salad bar can be more exciting with the addition of herbs. Small bowls of fresh chopped green herbs give a wide choice of flavors adding interest to the lettuce, carrots, celery, radishes, etc. The most well known salad herbs are, Dill, Parsley, Chives, Tarragon and Basil. But the true green salad adventurer will want to include, Salad Burnet, Chervil, Lovage, Marjoram, Sesame Seeds, Sorrel, Borage, Nasturtium, Purple Basil, Garlic Chives, Rocambole and Costmary. That makes a list of sixteen different flavors (the green and purple Basil taste the same). Of course, if the cook is creating one large bowl of salad any of those herbs may be included. If green herbs are out of season dried herbs are the logical substitution. They are best included in the salad dressing, the oil and vinegar liberated the oils from the dried leaves. One tablespoon of dried herbs to two cups of dressing is a good guideline. If you are using a combination of herbs the total quantity of herbs should equal about one tablespoon. When choosing fresh herbs three times that amount, or three tablespoons of herb leaves to two cups of dressing should be used. However, if you put out small bowls of chopped fresh herbs for people to sprinkle over their salad you will find that they really do enjoy a liberal taste of fresh tangy herbs.

USING FRESH HERBS

A recipe that lists quantities of herb in dried form can be transformed by using fresh growing herbs right from the garden. The amount of herb has only to be doubled or tripled to give the same strength of herb flavor.

The reason for increasing the quantity is confusing to some cooks, however, it is necessary. When herbs are used in cooking it is the essential oil, contained in the cells in the leaves, that provided the taste. This oil is what is smelled when an herb is rubbed or touched. The smell is the taste. In drying herbs the moisture is removed from the plant leaves and the oil remains. A large part of any living plant is moisture. With this moisture gone the leaves take up much less space. A small bottle of dried herb actually represents a large quantity of fresh leaves.

There are recipes in which only fresh herbs will do. Dried Sorrel will not provide the tangy flavor essential in creating "Sorrel Soup". The delicate cucumbery flavor of Salad Burnet is lost in drying. Therefore, they are herbs to be used fresh from the garden. Sour cream with Salad Burnet could be a dressing for sliced cucumbers or a garnish for baked potatoes.

Fortunately, for the gardener there are no herbs that need to be dried before they are useable. The perfection of flavor is always in the fresh and growing herb. Herbs are stored, dried or frozen, for those times of the year when fresh material is not available. Another reason to store herbs is to make use of an abundance that will pass with the season.

SUBSTITUTION OF ONE HERB FOR ANOTHER IN A RECIPE

If a recipe lists an herb, the cook does not have, a substitution may be made. A consideration,decision of which herb to use "instead", is the strength of the herb. Mild herbs are Chervil, Burnet, Parsley or Borage. Some stronger herbs would be Rosemary, Sage, Tarragon and Thyme. If the recipe asks for less than a teaspoon of dried herb it is probably a strong herb. One strong flavored herb may be used in place of another. If a mild herb is used instead of a strongly flavored one, the amount of mild herb should be increased. Conversely, if a strong herb is used in place of a mild one it would be advisable to reduce the amount.

Another reason for making a substitution is personal preference. Some people dislike certain herb flavors. If a cook does not like the taste of Dill on fish, Tarragon, Rosemary or Chervil may be a better choice. In a recipe that uses a cup or more of one herb, changing that herb will make an entirely different dish.

LIST OF 27 HERBS FOR SUBSTITUTION IN RECIPES

You Can Substitue	Thyme	Tarragon	Sorrel	Shallots	Sesame Seed	Savory	Sage	Rosemary	Racambole	Parsley	Oregano	Mint	Marjoram	Lovage	Fennel Seed	Dill	Coriander Seed	Cicely	Chives	Chervil	Caraway Seed	Burnet	Borage	Bay	Basil	Anise Seed	Angelica	**Recipie Calls For**
Angelica					X							X						X										Angelica
Anise Seed					X										X		X											Anise Seed
Basil	X	X				X		X					X	X		X												Basil
Bay								X																				Bay
Borage																												Borage
Burnet																							X					Burnet
Caraway Seed																												Caraway Seed
Chervil		X	X							X			X					X					X					Chervil
Chives				X					X																			Chives
Cicely		X	X											X												X	X	Cicely
Coriander Seed																												Coriander Seed
Dill	X					X														X					X			Dill
Fennel Seed																												Fennel Seed
Lovage																												Lovage
Marjoram	X					X		X			X			X		X									X			Marjoram
Mint																										X	X	Mint
Oregano	X					X							X	X		X									X			Oregano
Parsley														X									X		X			Parsley
Rocambole				X																								Rocambole
Rosemary	X					X													X					X				Rosemary
Sage																												Sage
Savory	X	X					X	X			X					X									X			Savory
Sesame Seed																				X								Sesame Seed
Shallots									X										X									Shallots
Sorrel																		X										Sorrel
Tarragon			X			X	X	X										X										Tarragon
Thyme						X	X	X			X					X												Thyme

CHART OF HERBS FOR COOKING WITH VEGETABLES

Herb	Zucchini Squash	Winter Squash	Turnips	Tomatoes	Spinach	Potatoes	Peppers	Peas	Onions	Mushrooms	Lettuce	Endive	Eggplant	Corn	Carrots	Cabbage	Beets	Beans	Asparagus	Artichokes
Basil	X	X		X	X	X	X	X	X	X	X		X		X	X		X	X	X
Burnet											X									
Caraway Seed	X		X				X									X				
Chervil	X	X	X	X	X	X	X	X	X	X	X		X			X	X	X		
Chives	X	X	X	X	X	X	X	X	X	X	X	X	X	X	X	X	X	X	X	X
Cicely		X	X	X																
Dill	X			X	X	X	X	X	X	X	X	X	X		X	X	X			
Lovage	X			X	X	X					X				X					
Marjoram	X	X		X	X	X	X	X	X	X	X		X		X	X	X	X		
Mint	X	X	X	X		X	X	X	X				X		X	X	X	X		
Oregano	X	X		X	X	X	X	X	X	X	X		X		X	X	X	X		
Parsley	X	X	X	X	X	X	X	X	X	X	X	X	X	X	X	X	X	X	X	X
Rocambole	X	X	X	X	X	X	X	X	X	X	X		X			X		X	X	
Rosemary		X		X		X	X	X	X	X			X	X						
Sage									X											
Savory	X	X		X	X	X		X	X	X			X		X	X	X	X		
Tarragon	X			X	X	X	X	X	X	X	X									X
Thyme	X	X	X	X	X	X	X	X	X	X		X	X		X	X	X	X		

WHAT METHOD TO USE TO PRESERVE HERBS FOR COOKING

Herb	Candy	Dry	Freeze	Seeds	Salt	Vinegar	Oil
ANGELICA	Stems						
ANISE			Leaves	Seeds			
BASIL		Leaves					
BAY		Leaves	Leaves				
BORAGE	Flower						
BURNET						Leaves	
CARAWAY				Seeds			
CHERVIL		Leaves	Leaves		Leaves		
CHIVES			Leaves			Blossom	Leaves
CICELY				Seeds			
CORIANDER				Seeds			
DILL		Leaves	Leaves	Seeds	Leaves	Leaves	Leaves
FENNEL		Leaves	Leaves	Seeds			
LOVAGE	Root	Leaves	Stems	Seeds			
MARJORAM		Leaves	Leaves		Leaves	Leaves	Leaves
MINT	Leaves	Leaves	Leaves		Leaves	Leaves	
OREGANO		Leaves	Leaves		Leaves	Leaves	
PARSLEY		Leaves	Leaves			Leaves	
ROCAMBOLE		Leaves	Leaves	Seeds	Leaves	Leaves / Seeds	
ROSEMARY		Leaves	Leaves		Leaves	Leaves	Leaves
SAGE		Leaves	Leaves		Leaves	Leaves	
SAVORY		Leaves	Leaves		Leaves	Leaves	
SESAME				Seeds			Seeds
SHALLOTS		Bulb				Leaves	Bulb
SORREL			Leaves		Leaves	Leaves	
TARRAGON		Leaves	Leaves		Leaves	Leaves	
THYME		Leaves	Leaves		Leaves	Leaves	Leaves

THE IMPORTANCE OF HERBS

DRUG INDUSTRY

BREWING & DISTILLING

COSMETICS

GARGLES

EXTRACTS

TINCTURES

TOBACCO INDUSTRY

BOTANY

GARDENING

LINNAEUS
1730

FARMING

SURGERY

COOK BOOKS

BAUHIN
1623

LOTIONS

POWDERS

SOAPS

PERFUMES

MEDICINE

FLOWERS

HUSBANDRY

CONDIMENTS

BARBERS

REA
BLAKE
MEAGER
SCOT
GOOGE
TAVERNER
PLAT
AUSTEN
EVELYN

HYLL
MASCALL
SURFLET
MARKHAM
GARDINER
LAWSON
PARKINSON

HOUSEHOLD RECEIPT BOOKS

INSECTICIDES

TUSSER

HANNAH GLASSE
E. SMITH
ELIZABETH RAFFALD
TOILET OF FLORA
REFRIGERATION

OLD GARDENING BOOKS

1500 - 1700

LADY SEDLY
MARY DOGGETT
SUSANNA AVERY
MARY CHOLMELEY

HOUSEHOLD
MEDICINE

CANNING

PRESERVING

HILL 1755
BLACKWELL 1737
BLAIR 1723
J. MILLER 1722
TOURNEFORT 1716
SALMON 1710
PECHEY 1694
WESTMACOTT 1694
COLES 1656
CULPEPER 1652

STILL ROOM BOOKS

SNUFF

PARKINSON 1640
GERARDE 1597
BULLEIN 1562
FRAMPTON 1577
WM. TURNER 1568
MAPLET 1567
GRETE HERBAL 1526
ASKHAM 1550
BANCKE 1525

CHEMISTRY

THE PRINTED HERBALS

PRINTING 1440

DE PROPRIETATIBUS RERUM
1280 -

ALBERTUS MAGNUS
1256 -

LEECH BOOK OF BALD
1000 A. D.

THE MONKS

LELAMOURE
1373

MACER
900 A.D.

GALEN
150 A.D.

SAXON
TRANSLATIONS

APULEIUS
500 A. D.

DIOSCORIDES

FIRST CENTURY

A. D.
B. C.

HERBS

SCHOOLS OF
HERBALISTS

ARISTOTLE

PLATO

300
TO
400
B. C.

THEOPHRASTUS

HIPPOCRATES

HERBALS

EGYPTIAN
3000 B. C.

ASSYRIAN
600 - 700 B. C.

CHALDEAN
5000 B. C.

CHING-NONG
3000 B. C.

SPEAKING OF HERBS

A young woman visiting our garden remarked that, "Herbs speak to me, I don't tell my family about it as it's such a personal thing." She had several children with her and we understood what she meant. It is easy to lose yourself in working among fragrant plants. The ancient conviction that they are 'cheering of the spirit' or as would be said today, 'good therapy' is a true experience. The poets, Shakespeare, historians and even religious of every era have written and spoken of herbs. Gardeners and cooks have their own terms for them. A few explanations might be helpful as the language can sound a bit odd to those who are not familiar with herb gardening and do not know how to use them in cooking. From the French cuisine we have—*Bouquet garni* meaning 'herb bouquet' made of sprigs of fresh herbs tied in a small bunch before immersing them in soup or stew. They may be left in during the cooking process or removed as soon as the desired flavor strength is reached. Only the aroma and taste of herbs then appear in the finished dish. A Bay leaf, Thyme and Parsley or Chervil are traditional in the 'herb bouquet', but other combinations may be used to enhance different foods. To make an herb bouquet with dried herbs, tie a teaspoonful of each of the herbs in a cheese cloth or muslin bag before steeping them in the liquid.

Court Bouillon is a fish stock made by adding an herb bouquet and a dash of French Tarragon vinegar to the water in which fish is poached. The resulting savory stock may be used in making the sauce to serve with the fish.

Fines Herbes means herbs that have a fine flavor, usually chopped fine, also, to be added to the food. The blend includes Chervil and Chives with a touch of Tarragon, Thyme, Sweet Basil or Sweet Marjoram. The minced herbs are put in during the last few minutes of cooking or sprinkled on an omelet prior to folding. Thus the scattered greens serve as a garnish and seasoning for the finished product. Dried herbs in a mixture of similar seasonings are often referred to by this name.

Herb butter is made by creaming butter or butter substitute with chopped fresh herbs or fine quality green dried herbs. The latter may be steeped in a small amount of hot water first and drained before blending them with the spreads. This brings out the flavor. Let the mixture stand for several hours at room temperature. Herb butter is sometimes made by wrapping a stick of butter or oleo with strong-scented leaves of herbs such as Rose Geranium to impart the flavor without the actual blending. It takes longer for the flavor to penetrate this way. The seasoned butter makes a good spread on sandwiches and canapes. It is also nice on hot vegetables or fish.

Marinade is a sauce of wine or wine vinegar, herbs, salt and pepper in which meat, poultry or fish are placed before cooking. They are kept in a covered container, in the refrigerator, for several hours. Turn over each piece so it gets its bath or marinade for tenderizing and flavoring. When tomatoes are added the taste resembles barbecue sauce, which may be made at home most reasonably. The same liquid may be used for basting during cooking. If salt is left out of the marinade it can take the place of soy sauce which must be avoided in salt-free diets.

Ravigote is a mixture of herbs with chopped Shallots. Usually Tarragon, Chives and Parsley are combined with wine vinegar in making it. The variations are infinite and sometimes the herbs are worked into butter for spreading on fish or poultry before broiling.

Tisane, The French word for a tea made of a single herb. Dried Flowers of Chamomile; Lemon Verbena leaves (also called Verveine) Catnip or Linden (known as Tilleul in France), are used in making a light colored tea taken as a digestive drink. Catnip and Linden are said to promote restful sleep. To make any herb tea very strong may produce the exact opposite from the desired effect. Not only will the taste be bitter but the action may be harmful.

Other Terms With Medicinal Associations

Decoction means boiling the herb for 10 minutes or pouring boiling water over it and allowing it to stand for 30 minutes. This is most suitable for external use, such as in a Chamomile or Rosemary rinse or a Lemon Balm or Wormwood rub for a sprain or bruise. Self-diagnosis of internal problems in most unwise. Herbs have valuable properties but there are dangers in using them without medical supervision.

Extract requires either water or alcohol to draw out oils as in perfumery. It is a concentration of liquid requiring special equipment.

Infusion is an extract made by steeping the herb in water. The strength of the potion, if it is to be imbibed, should be on the weak side. Herb teas are infusions but some of the mixtures being packaged contain a curious mixture which may have contrary effect. Sun steeping is done by placing cold water over herbs in a glass container and placing it on a sunny windowsill or in the sun outdoors in summer to obtain a pleasant, lightly flavored cold beverage of Mint or other culinary herb.

Liqueurs are made by infusing herbs in brandy or other alcoholic media which are suitable for internal use.

Tinctures are concentrated active principles prepared by extraction in alcohol. The authors do not suggest that gardeners or amateurs use any of the herbs described medicinally. "The Art of Simpling" whereby individual herbs are used medicinally requires years of knowledge of the plants, their history and powers. A *'simple'* meant a single herb used for medicine as opposed to a prescription of several. As Kipling said of Our Fathers of Old, who believed that "Anything green that grew out of the mould was an excellent herb . . . half of their remedies cured you dead." The idea today that all that grows is 'natural', therefore safe, can be dangerous.

Every gardener wishes to save some of the bounty of summer. We do so by drying flowers, freezing and canning vegetables, and putting herbs in vinegar. There is a way to preserve the fragrances of Roses, Sweet Herbs and flowers. It is called *Potpourri*. The name means 'rotten pot' but the result of making either dry potpourri or moist potpourri is a sweet jar. It can be opened to release the aromas of a garden of herbs. When the lid is replaced the perfumes remain richly mingled for years. In our home there are several of the potpourri jars which were filled by the late Rosetta E. Clarkson over 40 years ago. One or two came to her with contents in them which makes the potpourri over 50 to 60 years old.

TO MAKE POTPOURRI

The mysterious way in which natural scents of leaves, flowers, roots and spices blend together are best explained by a chemist. We asked George C. Gross, a retired chemical engineer, if he could outline the process without going into all the technical language of perfumery. He has experimented with moist potpourri which consists of partially dried herb and flower materials mixed with special salts. The glass jars of differently accented mixtures he gave us 12 years ago remain true to their predominant aroma. The moist mixture is never pretty because rose petals darken and green dried herbs blacken. But it can be revived in scent by adding alcohol.

The Dry Method

Dry potpourri is something to look at. In a glass jar, the carefully dried scented Rose petals, flowers of Marigolds, Buttercups, and Calendula petals for yellow tints, green Lemon Verbena leaves, blue Larkspur, and purple Pansies can be arranged to make a picture through the glass. The same dry potpourri may serve as stuffing for sachets or small sleep pillows delicately scented. The uses are legion and recipes abound. But before you start on the process here are some basics—

Base - Rose petals and Lavender flowers are the backbone of most mixes. Rose Geranium leaves can replace part of the Roses. Sandalwood (sometimes spelled santal) is another, though cedar wood can replace it. The woods should be coarsely ground.

Fixatives - Gum benzoin or storax (styax) and coarse Orris root is the traditional mixture. Calamus (Sweet Flag) root and Vetiver give a drier odor, not as sweet as Orris. (Any old-fashioned Iris rhizomes can be dug, washed, split and dried to make Orris at home. If the pieces are ground before drying the process is swifter. Place the material on newspaper or brown paper and keep near a source of gentle heat until the ground Orris will roll freely or chips snap sharply. The scent is not evident till it dries and increases over a period of a year or two. Store in a dark, glass container).

Dr. Gross is pragmatic about the matter of substitutes. He notes that Vanillin or Vanilla beans can be used for a sweet effect. Animal fixatives such as musk, ambergris, castoreum or civet are very expensive and rather difficult for the beginner to use.

Quantity - Normal use is about 1 tablespoon of the vegetable fixative per quart of base (dried materials from the herb garden). Vanilla is used in small amounts.

Spice - The usual mixture is equal parts of Cinnamon, Cloves, Nutmeg and Allspice. A less usual mixture but quite effective is equal parts of Anise, Cardamon and Coriander. The spice and seed mixtures must be finely ground. They are used at the rate of about 1 tablespoon per quart of base.

Top Notes - These are generally floral oils such as Rose, Orange blossom (Neroli), Jasmine, Tuberose and the like. Synthetic oils are less expensive and more readily available. They work well. Citrus oil, Orange, Lemon, Bergamot, Tangerine and perhaps Lime (this must be used with great care) and all other oils are used only as 3 to 5 drops per quart of dried material, not more than 5% by weight.

Modifiers - These are mainly coumarin containing materials, Tonka beans, Sweet Woodruff and Sweet Clover (Mellilot). Vanilla beans ground may be substituted with vanilla extract. Most imitation extracts contain about 1% vanillin equivalent. Use only a few drops per quart of base.

Additions - Many aromatic items can be added to give color, texture or modification of odor. These items should be coarsely broken or crushed. Marjoram, Mints, Rosemary, Basil are very good. Thyme is not much used but Lemon Balm or Lemon Verbena is quite good. Citrus peels, freed of white pith and dried, will add the citrus note as well as texture and color. Dried flowers, even those in old dried arrangements, provide bits of color in addition to the pink of Rose and Lavender of that herb. Corn flowers, Yarrow, Statice and Strawflowers keep their brightness.

Rose Jars - Potpourri makers cherish the true Rose jars with double lids which were popular in Victorian times. They resemble ginger jars but have a top lid to lift off to let the aroma waft out of an inner lid with holes in it. Or the inner lid with small knob for lifting may be taken out and the outer one with slits in it replaced for the time you want to freshen a room with scent of potpourri. So far the lovely china containers especially used for this purpose have not been copied as have ginger jars. The latter work well for holding the perfumed mixture in strength for years. The petal and leaf drying can go on all summer. The blending with other ingredients is done any time and it mellows with storing.

WHAT IS A TUSSIE-MUSSIE?

A little bouquet or nosegay in which herbs and flowers do the speaking has been known since the 17th century as a "Tussie-Mussie". It was John Parkinson, author of the first flower garden book and a large herbal called "Theatrum Botanicum" who so named it. A great upsurge in interest in herbs has contributed to delight in putting together a few flowers of significance and sentiment surrounded by some scented foliage to make a poesy.

The word 'posy' or 'poesy' dates back to the 16th century. It was considered a short motto, or line of verse, in 1569. A Tussie-Mussie is a poesy in that each flower or sprig of Rosemary, Sage or Thyme represents a thought or message. There are many books called "The Language of Flowers" from which the unspoken words of such a nosegay have been taken. One time we made a survey of over a dozen such volumes trying to find agreement on even one herb, such as Basil which can represent love or hate, depending in which country it is known that way. Through the centuries the associations of words to plants have changed somewhat. Pity the tongue-tied suitor who pleads his case with Borage (courage) in a circle of Ambrosia's fragrant foliage (love returned) if he should happen to see a bright orange Butterfly Weed bloom and insert it. The last means 'let me go'.

How to Make a Tussie-Mussie

Making Tussie-Mussies for different occasions is great fun and always a talking point for the recipient. We have used one to greet foreign students who do not speak English, to wish God-speed to a ninety year old lady as she left Connecticut for California (she reported it lasted a week, still fresh after a stopover in Colorado) to make a Baby Blessing Bouquet for a newborn or wish an easy delivery at a pre-birth shower. Studying up on the language suggests all sorts of ideas for combining Pansies (for thoughts), Cowslips (winning grace), Heliotrope (intoxicated with pleasure) which would be hard to express at a first meeting.

The little nosegays, to be held in hand, are often composed of a single rose or rosebud, surrounded by blue flowers of Love-in-a-mist, with pink flowers of Lemon Thyme around them, sprigs of Rosemary, leaves of Lemon Verbena, tips of Mint, especially Pineapple Mint with its variegated foliage. All are then circled with softly fuzzy, scented Geranium foliage or wonderfully aromatic gray and green Santolina sprigs. The making, by simply tying a string round the bunch close to the top and trimming the stems, or slipping a small elastic up under the blooms and foliage to hold them together, is as rewarding as the giving. It is a most pleasing thing to hold the mingled aromas in your hand. Each one will be different and lovely with color, scent and meaning. It is perfect bouquet for a hospital patient, if put in a small paper cup with a bit of water in it. The nurses bless them because they require no fixing and the patient has a story to tell that has nothing to do with an operation.

HERBS IN HOT AND COLD DISHES

The oils in herb leaves give their scent and, therefore, their flavor to food. The transfer and amalgamation of the flavor is effected by heat. The more heat used in preparing a recipe the faster the oils are dispersed. A soup on simmer will take thirty minutes to acquire the flavor. After that time the oils vaporize with the steam and are gradually lost. Long cooking recipes should have herbs added last. One exception to the rule is Bay leaf which takes longer to impart its subtle flavor to a dish. It is normally added at the beginning of the cooking and left in until serving time. Use whole Bay leaf, to be removed at the end of cooking, or finely chopped pieces. Avoid a size that could catch in a diner's throat. Bay leaf does not break down with cooking or combining with liquids.

Sauteed or fried foods are cooked for a short time at high temperatures. This m ins the herbs should be quickly cooked as well. For example, a fillet of fish rolled in bread crumbs, after dipping in egg, would have fresh or crumbled dried herbs added to the crumbs. It would be cooked for about fifteen minutes in a frying pan with butter and or oil. Or the herbs could be soaked in the beaten egg for 15 minutes before the fish is dipped in it and rolled in the crumbs. Either way the herbs are not going to be cooked so long that the flavor takes on a bitter essence.

Cold prepared foods take longer to combine with herb flavors. Cheese, sour cream and butter all are enhanced by the addition of herbs. They take a few hours or overnight to reach their taste perfection, as the transfer is slower than with hot foods. The acid content of a mixed salad dressing or sauce containing vinegar or lemon juice speeds up transfer of flavor. French dressing made with oil and vinegar would develop its herb nuances in fifteen minutes and be ready for serving or using as a marinade.

HOW LONG DO DRY HERBS KEEP?

Cooks frequently receive a gift of a full herb and spice rack. After a year or more they take out a bottle of an unused herb and wonder if it is "good". The best way to determine the strength remaining in the dried leaves, is to open the bottle and smell it. If there is no scent, try stirring the leaves or crushing them in your fingers. There should be a distinct herb aroma. If there is not, the herb may have lost its oil content. In some cases, through improper drying, it may never have been present. A herb with no scent has little or no flavor.

KEEPING HERBS IN THEIR PLACE

A spice rack is a nice idea but clear jars let through light and therefore may bleach out the color of the leaves. This affects the flavor. The most robust dried herbs are distinctly green or close to the color they were in the garden. A tin with a tight fitting lid is ideal, or a tinted glass jar with stopper would be good, as well. If you are given a spice rack, you might want to pack the pretty jars with fine labels with your own dried herbs. If the ones in it have been on a store shelf for some time, as a gift item, they may have very little resemblance to home-grown herbs.

Keep a spice rack away from the heat of the stove or kitchen light. The warmth may liberate the flavor, but you'd rather have it in cooking than in storage. It is beneficial to give them no more than room temperatures; less if possible. Direct sunlight not only removes the color but also heats up the containers. The windowsill is a poor place to store jars of herbs, however decorative they may be.

HERB TEAS AND OTHER BEVERAGES

Leaves, stems, flowers, seeds and even roots of plants have been combined with hot water to make tea. Culinary herbs may be used alone or in combination to make a refreshing beverage. The guide for how concentrated the particular tea is a very personal choice.

For beginning experiments it would be advisable to make weaker concoctions, one half to one full teaspoon of herb infused for 5 minutes in 8 ounces of freshly boiled water. Most leaf teas are not simmered over continuous heat but rather have the boiling water poured over the leaves in a teapot. Increasing either the amount of herb or time the tea is brewed will make tea stronger.

Herb tea can be either delicious or vicious depending on the drinker's taste or the maker's haste. There is no predicting the former but there is every control over the latter. Teas should not be dumped into the tea pot without careful judgement. A tea too strong is a witch's brew, only salvaged by dilution with hot water and then only if the concoction has not become too bitter with standing. Use glass or china tea pots for herb tea. Metals may change the flavor even if stainless steel is used. Honey or sugar may be added but again the taste will be different. Milk is seldom a good modifier, unless a drink of it flavored with Anise seed at bedtime. It is wise to grow your own herbs for tea rather than buy mixes already packaged. Not only does it save money (you pay for pictures on the package) but the combinations may not suit your system. They are made up to color the brew as well as flavor it.

COOL HERB FLAVORS

Cold drinks may be flavored with herbs. The leaves, and if fresh, the stems, may be added to a container of liquid 12 to 24 hours before serving. Mint is always a favorite with cold tea, lemonade or orange juice but have you ever tried Angelica syrup to color and point up lemon or lime ade? Tomato juice with Basil, Marjoram, Lovage, Chives, Burnet or Borage transforms a standard into "the unusually delicious".

The proportions of herb to liquid is the same for cold drinks as for hot teas; a teaspoon of herb to an 8 ounce cup. As with hot tea, the herb is usually strained out before serving. However, for cold drinks, it is attractive to add a sprig of the fresh herb for a garnish. Here are a few cool, herb drink recipes—

GINGER ALE CUP

Crush two sprigs of Mint, put into a pitcher with some crushed ice, then add the juice of half a lemon. Add a pint of ginger ale and the rest of the lemon thinly sliced. Stir, and serve at once.

ENGLISH CIDER BOWL

Mix together a pint of cold tea (made from green tea) remembering the English pint is 20 ounces, a quarter pound of sugar (4 ounces in American measuring cup), a quart of sweet cider, and a pint of ginger ale. Decorate with two slices of cucumber (or sprigs of Borage flowers), three sprays of Lemon Thyme (Golden-edged Lemon is prettiest) and one Sage leaf. Use one of the variegated types of *Salvia officinalis*, such as the purple-leaved, tricolor or golden. Ice and serve in a punch bowl. It is more decorative to put your Sage and Thyme in a mold with clear water to make an ice cake with intriguing appearance. It can be done in the freezer or refrigerator in a ring mold or freezer container.

ROSE MINT CUP

Crush twelve sprays of Mint slightly and put them into a jug with a pint of cracked ice. Then mix a half cupful of grenadine, three teaspoons rose extract, and a quart of white grape juice. Combine all with one pint of water, and put on ice. Before serving, add one pint ginger ale. Orange Mint or Ginger Mint may be used for this to give a slight citrus tang. Grenadine syrup is non-alcoholic but is unspecified as to the actual ingredients. Stobart states that it is made with Pomegranate juice, which would account for some of the pink color. Rose Geranium leaves steeped in a little water could replace rose extract.

When serving cold drinks, or even hot ones, to a crowd, do not put them in plastic foam type cups if there is any lemon or other acid in the beverage. The acidity causes the cups to disintegrate which can mean chemicals moving in the drink.

HERB JELLIES

Herb vinegars are one of the most popular forms of herb products to be offered at a church bazaar or small shop near a home herb garden. They look pretty and are easily offered for sniffing without disturbing the packaging. It's best to have one or two bottles set aside just for the purpose. Herb jellies go even faster at a benefit sale because everyone knows how to use jelly. You eat it on toast or fill thimble cookies with it or make a jelly roll. But the piquant herb jellies are also served with meat and poultry because they are not super sweet.

Rose Geranium jelly is where it all started. A leaf of the old-fashioned scented Pelargonium was placed in the bottom of the glass when pouring crabapple or plain apple jelly. Imaginative herb gardeners have gone on to make up scintillating combinations of herb plus pectin and sugar, sometimes with a bit of herb vinegar, too. Pectin requires more sugar than natural fruit juices. It is a sure thing for success but the apple juice base is easy to work with if you have a candy thermometer.

Mint Jelly

To 1 cup clean fresh Mint leaves and stems put in a pan and bruised, add 4 cups of apple juice which has been put through a jelly bag. Bring slowly to a boil. Strain out the herb and return juice to the large kettle. Add ¾ cup of sugar for each cup of apple (Mint) juice. Stir while returning to a boil to dissolve sugar completely. Let bubble hard until a drip from a wooden stirring spoon forms a sheet. Better still, keep watch on a candy thermometer until it reaches 220° F. degrees. When ready to turn off, add a few drops of vegetable coloring to obtain the shade of green you wish. Skim and pour into hot, sterilized jars. Let the jelly cool before pouring on paraffin. Like sugar, the 'waxy' sealer has gone up in price greatly. If you wish you can place foil or plastic over the still hot jelly jar to form a seal.

Other Herb Flavors

If you wish to follow the directions on commercial pectin jar or package, you can still play variations on a theme. Rosetta Clarkson, author of *Herbs, Their Culture And Uses*, worked out these combinations which have inspired many others—

Summer Savory - 2 Tablespoon Summer Savory leaves, ½ cup water, 1 cup grapefruit juice, 3½ cups sugar to ½ bottle of pectin

Thyme, plain or Lemon Thyme (to serve with meat or chicken) 2 Tablespoons Thyme leaves, ½ cup water, 1 cup grape juice, 3½ cups sugar, to ½ bottle pectin

Sage - 2 Tablespoons Sage leaves, ½ cup water, 1 cup apple cider, 3½ cups sugar, to ½ bottle of pectin.

The fresh herbs are heated to scalding with the liquid and removed before sugar and pectin are added. Herb jellies need some extra color, which you could supply with natural fruit or vegetable juices or Pot Marigold petals but probably will drop from a package of vegetable coloring.

Garden Designs

every man may invent others farre differing from these, or any other can be set forth. Let every man therefore, if hee like of these, take what may please his mind, or out of these or his owne conceit, frame any other to his fancy, or cause others to be done as he liketh best, observing this decorum, that according to his ground he do cast out his knots, with convenient roome for allies and walkes; for the fairer and larger your allies and walkes be, the more grace your Garden shall have, the lesse harme the herbes and flowers shall receive, by passing by them that grow next unto the allies sides, and the better shall your Weeders cleanse both the beds and the allies."

Simple herb garden forms from THE ENGLISH GARDENER *1688*

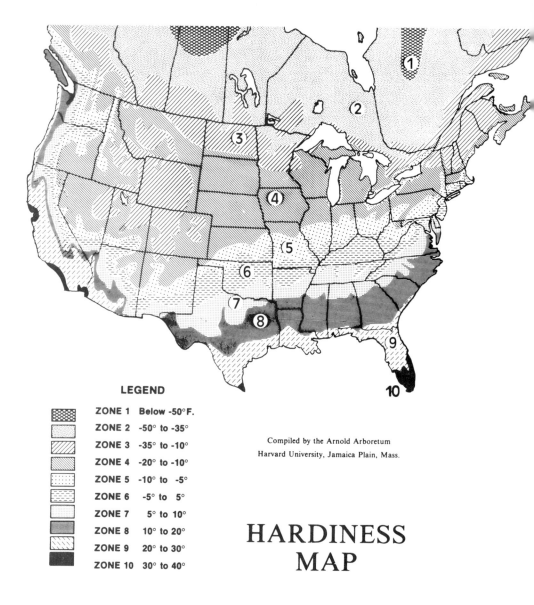

LEGEND

	ZONE 1	Below -50°F.
	ZONE 2	-50° to -35°
	ZONE 3	-35° to -10°
	ZONE 4	-20° to -10°
	ZONE 5	-10° to -5°
	ZONE 6	-5° to 5°
	ZONE 7	5° to 10°
	ZONE 8	10° to 20°
	ZONE 9	20° to 30°
	ZONE 10	30° to 40°

Compiled by the Arnold Arboretum
Harvard University, Jamaica Plain, Mass.

HARDINESS
MAP

The above hardiness map was developed by the Arnold Arboretum, Harvard University, Jamaica Plain, Mass., and is reproduced through their courtesy. The hardiness zones 1-10 are based on the average annual minimum temperatures for each zone and divide the United States and Canada into areas where specific plants perform best as to winter hardiness. Many factors, such as altitude, degree of exposure to wind, modifying effect of bodies of water, soil types and the like can create variations of as much as two zones within a geographical area, but adhering to your specific zone will generally give you the best results. Often, however, inhabitants of the southernmost portion of one zone can safely use plants for the next, more northerly zone.

Herbs described in this book are listed here both by common and botanical names. Numbers indicate pages where they are mentioned, those in bold face show pages where major description and uses may be found.

Historically, herbs have been used for various medicinal purposes, and the author discusses such uses.
However, neither author nor Park Seed Co., as the publisher of this book makes any recommendation that
herbs be used for medicinal purposes.

"I can conceive that there is no body that understands my well meaning endeavors, that will think that the remainder of such Plants, which are not expressed in this work have not come within my cognizance, and therefore I shall not need to make any apology, or laying down of my reasons for the omission of them; yet, if there be any inclined to suppose so, let them know that I willfully passed over some of them and there some which time (a thing I have much wanted ever since I undertook this business) would not permit me to insert. And let them know also, that the present design was not an universall "History of Plants" for how voluminous must we needs have been, but only those which are most useful".

William Coles
Adam in Eden, 1657